Georgetown Journal
of International Affairs

WINTER/SPRING 2015, VOLUME XVI, NUMBER I

international community must also rethink its strategy for supporting African allies confronted with terrorism by focusing on terrorism's root causes, rather than solely military "train and equip" programs.

Politics&Diplomacy

Culture&Society

A Look Back

Georgetown Journal

of International Affairs

WINTER/ SPRING 2015, VOLUME XVI, NUMBER 1

EDITORS-IN-CHIEF ANNA NEWBY, GEORGIA PELLETIER

EXECUTIVE DIRECTOR LUCAS CHAN

MANAGING EDITOR ANGELA RIBAUDO

EDITORIAL STAFF

FORUM EDITORS ESTHER SOHN, RACHEL GREENE, CYNTHIA SOLIMAN, JACOB GLADYSZ
EDITORIAL ASSISTANTS JUAN ASCENCIO, ANDRES BRILLEMBOURG, JACK MILLER

POLITICS & DIPLOMACY EDITOR AZHAR UNWALA, MARTIN SEITZ
EDITORIAL ASSISTANTS AHMET CASKURLU, MICHAEL MCGRATH

CONFLICT & SECURITY EDITOR MATTHEW GREGORY
EDITORIAL ASSISTANTS MATHISON CLORE, LAWSON FERGUSON

CULTURE & SOCIETY EDITOR ASHA THANKI
EDITORIAL ASSISTANT EDWARD MOLÉ

LAW & ETHICS EDITOR CHIEN-YU LIU
EDITORIAL ASSISTANT HARSH THAKKER

BUSINESS & ECONOMICS EDITOR DAVID ATTIA
EDITORIAL ASSISTANT MARGARET SCHAACK

SCIENCE & TECHNOLOGY EDITOR SHABAB HUSSAIN
EDITORIAL ASSISTANT CLAIRE ZENG, OLIVIA BISEL

BOOKS EDITORIAL ASISTANT REBECCA HELLER

A LOOK BACK EDITOR BARRY MCCARRON

COPY-EDITORS SARAH HANNIGAN, SUSANNA RADEMACHER, MADELINE SPOSATO

DESIGN STAFF

DESIGN DIRECTOR YULI LIN

DESIGN ASSOCIATE RAINIER GO, JACQUELINE KIMMELL

EXECUTIVE STAFF

CHIEF OPERATING OFFICER VICTORIA MORONEY

CHIEF FINANCIAL OFFICER JEFF SHAY

DIRECTOR OF EXTERNAL RELATIONS ZHENNING DONG

DIRECTOR OF PROGRAMMING&OUTREACH JISOO KIM

DIRECTORS OF ADVANCEMENT BESSIE ZAVIDOW

DIRECTOR OF SALES&CIRCULATION CAROL YUAN

DIRECTOR OF COMMUNICATIONS ISHA GULATI

DIRECTOR OF SOCIAL MEDIA KELLY LUI

DIRECTOR OF STRATEGY ELIZABETH WALSH

DIRECTOR OF ADVERTISING PRASHANT SHARMA

ONLINE STAFF

EXCUTIVE EDITORS MARIAM SAOMA, IAN PHILBRICK

MANAGING EDITORS REBECCA KUANG

SECTION EDITORS ZACHARY BURDETTE, NICK SARDI, ALEXANDER TEAGUE, MIKE FOX,

EDITORIAL ASSISTANTS KENNETH LEE, CORSO ROSATI, SYDNEY JEAN GOTTFRIED, JACOB HABERMAN, JOYCE YEO, WOO JUNG KO, AONGHUS COCHLAIN, JENNA SMITH, MICHAEL DENG, THERESA CHEN, GRACE JIANG

ONLINE CONTRIBUTING EDITORS BLAKE ATHERTON, MIKE SLIWINSKI, MICHELLE HILL

ADVISORY BOARD DAVID ABSHIRE, SUSAN BENNETT, H.R.H. FELIPE DE BORBÓN, CARA DIMASSA, ROBERT L. GALLUCCI, MICHAEL MAZARR, JENNIFER WARD, FAREED ZAKARIA

SFS DEAN'S OFFICE ADVISORS ALLYSON GOODWIN, JENNIFER LONG

UNIVERSITY COUNCIL JEFFREY ANDERSON (CHAIR), ANTHONY CLARK AREND, MARC BUSCH, MATTHEW CARNES, VICTOR CHA, RAJ DESAI, CHARLES DOLGAS, JOHN ESPOSITO, MARK GIORDANO, MITCH KANEDA, CHRISTINE KIM, CHARLES KING, MARK LAGON, ERIC LANGENBACHER, JOANNA LEWIS, CATHERINE LOTRIONTE, KATHERINE MARSHALL, SUSAN MARTIN, KATHLEEN MCNAMARA, JOHN MCNEIL, JAMES MILLWARD, DANIEL NEXON, DAVID PAINTER, STEVEN RADELET, GEORGE SHAMBAUGH, ELIZABETH STANLEY, SCOTT TAYLOR, CHARLES WEISS, JENNIFER WINDSOR

Notice to Contributors

Articles submitted to the *Georgetown Journal of International Affairs* must be original, must not draw substantially from articles previously published by the author, and must not be simultaneously submitted to any other publication. Articles should be around 3,000 words in length. Manuscripts must be typewritten and double-spaced in Microsoft™ Word® format, with margins of at least one inch. Authors should follow the *Chicago Manual of Style, 15th ed.* Articles may be submitted by e-mail (gjia@georgetown.edu). Full names of authors, a two-sentence biography, and contact information including addresses with zip codes, telephone numbers, facsimile numbers, and e-mail addresses must accompany each submission. The *Georgetown Journal of International Affairs* will consider all manuscripts submitted, but assumes no obligation regarding publication. All material submitted is returnable at the discretion of the *Georgetown Journal of International Affairs*.

The *Georgetown Journal of International Affairs* (ISSN 1526-0054; ISBN 978-1-62616-225-9) is published twice yearly by Georgetown University Press for the Edmund A. Walsh School of Foreign Service, Georgetown University. Subscription rates for individuals: $29 for one year, $55 for two years, or $76 for three years. Subscription rates for institutions: $70 for one year or $132 for two years. Shipping and handling charges are not included.

Editorial and Advertising Office
Georgetown Journal of International Affairs
Edmund A. Walsh School of Foreign Service
Georgetown University
301 Intercultural Center
3700 O Street, NW
Washington, DC 20057
gjia@georgetown.edu

Publisher
Georgetown University Press
3240 Prospect Street, NW
Suite 250
Washington, DC 20007
gupress@georgetown.edu

Subscriptions
Georgetown Journal of International Affairs
Subscriptions
c/o Johns Hopkins University Press
Journals Publishing Division
P.O. Box 19966
Baltimore, MD 21211-0966
Phone: 1-800-548-1784 or 410-516-6987
Fax: 410-516-3866
http://journal.georgetown.edu

Backlist, Single-Copy, and Bulk Sales
Georgetown University Press
c/o Hopkins Fulfillment Service
P.O. Box 50370
Baltimore, MD 21211-4370
Phone: 1-800-537-5487 or
410-516-6965
Fax: 410-516-6998
www.press.georgetown.edu

In an era of globalized economies, broad access to information, and unprecedented mobility, it seems that even the world's most remote communities could find access to the resources necessary for survival and prosperity. If we can deliver our products, technologies, and cultures to the ends of the earth, why can we not relieve the global poor of their famine? On the eve of the 70th anniversary of the founding of the United Nations—as well as the 50th anniversary of Lyndon Johnson's declaration of a War on Poverty and the 10th anniversary of the Clinton Global Initiative—now is an important time to think about inequality in all its facets.

Global trends suggest that worldwide economic inequality is on the rise. As United Nations Development Programme Administrator Helen Clark writes in this issue, "the richest 8 percent of the world's population earns half of the world's total income." Meanwhile, women and girls around the world still face obstacles, with social norms sometimes entrenching existing inequalities. Rural communities and native peoples are all too often underserved by their government. In spite of remarkable improvements in technology and education, access to the capital and tools that empower individuals, businesses, and communities is unreliable for many, and almost nonexistent for some. Debates on the value of development financing, meanwhile, remain unresolved.

Faced with these realities, international institutions, governments, and nongovernmental organizations have redoubled their efforts to ensure that rising tides really do lift all boats. With all of these challenges in mind, Issue 16.1 of the *Georgetown Journal of International Affairs* focuses on the topic of Inequality from a range of perspectives. Inequality manifests itself economically and politically, in legal terms and geographic ones, along gender lines, and in a myriad of other ways. In some cases, discrimination is deliberate, harsh, and obvious. But perhaps more commonly, it is unintended and its exact impacts are harder to identify. This issue's Forum considers the multitude of ways in which people around the globe struggle with structural violence, uneven application of the law, struggles for scarce resources, and other challenges. And it also poses possible ways forward.

Additional contributions to this publication include articles about the role of religion in post-Arab Spring constitutions, the motivations behind Chinese multinational companies, the effects of climate change on cultures, the use of social media by terrorists, and public opinion in Ukraine. The issue also features interviews with Tom Malinowski on struggles for democracy around the world, Gerry Adams on the lessons of the Irish peace process, and Lester Brown on food prices and political instability. The diversity of these topics demonstrates the *Journal*'s continued commitment to pursuing the myriad facets and disciplines that comprise global politics.

In concluding this edition, we are extremely grateful to both our contributors and our dedicated staff members for their work on this issue. We would also like to thank Allyson Goodwin and Dean Jennifer Long for their tireless support. As always, we hope you enjoy this latest issue of the *Georgetown Journal of International Affairs*.

ANNA NEWBY   GEORGIA PELLETIER

Forum

GEORGETOWN JOURNAL OF INTERNATIONAL AFFAIRS

Inequality

Addressing inequality is central to human and sustainable development.

As the world gears up to embark on a new development agenda, it has committed to eradicating poverty. Given the progress in reducing poverty since the 1990s, this now means addressing the hardest-to-reach groups and preventing people from falling back into poverty when they experience setbacks. The imperative of leaving no one behind, now and in the future, requires inequality to be addressed.

Much attention has been paid to high and often increasing levels of *income* inequality and, consequently, to the need for more inclusive economic growth that expands the incomes of those at the bottom of the income distribution. This is critically important. More than 70 percent of the population in developing countries lives in societies that are more unequal than they were two decades ago. The richest 8 percent of the world's population earns half of the world's total income, leaving the remaining 92 percent of people to share the other half.

In tackling inequality, it is important to look beyond its income dimension and also address inequalities in areas such as health, education, and political empowerment. In addition, people's capacities to adapt to changing contexts—which are often characterized by economic, political, and environmental volatility—are critical concerns. Inequalities in income and wealth are compounded by these other inequalities that limit people's choices and freedoms. Biased institutions, legal systems, and social norms can entrench inequalities that disadvantaged groups already face, particularly the poor, women, rural populations, indigenous communities, and other groups. Addressing broader inequalities has both intrinsic value and important practical benefits; high inequality, after all, is detrimental to economic growth and poverty reduction. High levels of inequality undermine social cohesion, increase political and social tension, and can result in instability and conflict.

Despite significant progress in closing gender gaps in education and health, women continue to be disproportionately represented in vulnerable employment positions and continue to earn significantly less than men. They also remain underrepresented among political decision makers worldwide.

Indigenous communities face barriers in many countries. For example, lack of formal state recognition of traditional tenure systems leaves them vulnerable to the expropriation of their land and to involuntary resettlement with serious implications for their way of life.

Environmental degradation, including climate change, also exacerbates inequalities. Many of the world's poor live in coastal zones susceptible to storms and rising sea levels, on farm lands that are increasingly vulnerable to drought, or on hillsides prone to landslides. They rely more on the goods and services provided by nature for their income, livelihoods, food, water, and fuel. This leaves them highly exposed to the effects of ecosystem degradation. Women are particularly vulnerable, since they are often responsible for routine household chores according to traditional divisions of labor. The erosion of ecosystems and lack of modern services may mean that they have to travel further to collect water, firewood, and food. Depending on increasingly unpredictable natural resources for survival is often intensified by a lack of the assets, safety nets, and developmental support necessary to ensure resilience in the face of shocks. When coping mechanisms rely on the more intensive use of already-depleted resources—such as cutting deeper into forests or overfishing—ecosystems degrade further, contributing to vulnerability, poverty, and inequalities.

Meanwhile, patterns of growth that have resulted in high income inequalities and growing vulnerability also make it harder to reverse environmental degradation. When the benefits of growth go to a select few, the structure of power reinforces exclusive and unsustainable growth. High degrees of inequality stand in the way of mobilizing the social cohesion and collective action needed for the equitable and sustainable management of resources.

Without doubt, significant progress has been made at the global level on achieving the Millennium Development Goals. But unfinished business remains, since many people have still yet to see much improvement in their lives. The Sustainable Development Goals, which will feature in the post-2015 development agenda, must commit to inclusive, equitable, and sustainable development. The goal is to rethink development and to pursue innovative solutions to complex and interrelated challenges. In this issue of the *Georgetown Journal of International Affairs,* a wide array of scholars focuses on the role inequality plays in impeding human development and on how it might be tackled more effectively.

Helen Clark IS THE ADMINISTRATOR OF THE UNITED NATIONS DEVELOPMENT PROGRAMME (UNDP) AND IS THE FIRST WOMAN TO LEAD THE ORGANIZATION. SHE WAS ALSO THE 37TH PRIME MINISTER OF NEW ZEALAND.

Urban Transformation, Inequality, and the Future of Indian Cities

Seth Schindler

Seth Schindler is a Lecturer in Human Geography in the Department of Geography at the University of Sheffield.

Most visitors to India are struck by the pace and scope of urban transformation. Ambitious infrastructure projects are ubiquitous and private real estate developments proliferate across urban landscapes. This stands in stark contrast with extreme inequality, another striking feature of Indian cities. The affluence that has come to characterize Indian cities in the past decade has a mirror image that is equally evident. Informal housing settlements sit uneasily alongside exclusive gated communities, and most urban residents work in low-skilled, informal-sector occupations. While portrayals of extreme poverty amid affluence risk veering into the cliché, it is worth reflecting on what is new about India's contemporary urban landscape. In this article I argue that a "new" urban poor has emerged in India, and it has been produced by the same factors that have given rise to the so-called "new" middle class. The future of Indian cities will be determined by localized struggles and negotiations among these and other groups, over access to space, resources, and services such as water, electricity, and waste management.

In the 1930s, an English journalist reportedly asked Mahatma Gandhi what he thought about Western civilization, and his response was: "I think it would be a good idea."

The veracity of this exchange is open to question, but Gandhi's sentiment is not. He considered modern industry a symbol of colonial oppression, and he advocated a decentralized system of governance whose basic building block was the village. After Gandhi's assassination in 1948, the task of forging a nation after centuries of British colonial rule fell squarely on the shoulders

remedy for economic stagnation was to transform peasants into a working class and forge a connection between labor and capital. The idea was to generate a virtuous cycle of industrialization, growth, and development by relocating agricultural laborers to cities where they could work in factories. Overall, however, the pace of industrialization was sluggish. Governmental authorities

In spite of rapid urban transformation, the **cleavage between capital and labor** has never been so deeply etched into the social and physical fabric of the Indian city.

of Jawaharlal Nehru. Unlike Gandhi, Nehru was convinced that India's destiny lay down a path of industrialization that was well-worn by European predecessors, and under his leadership India embarked on a decades-long project of state-led development.

The city occupied a contradictory position in relation to the young Indian nation. While cities were showpieces in the Nehruvian "vision of nationalist modernism," the village was fondly remembered as "a serene, pastoral paradise" in contrast to the hustle and bustle of cities.[1] In popular culture, cities were commonly associated with vice and squalor, and urban planners developed an aesthetic that was designed to "recuperate key features of an older imagined village milieu."[2] Ultimately, cities in independent India failed to live up to the hopes and expectations of a generation. First and foremost, they did not deliver the economic growth that planners had expected. According to orthodox economic planning, the

charged with managing the economy struggled to discipline industrialists, while their control over organized labor was equally tenuous.[3] Ultimately, this model of state-led development failed to catalyze the industrialization and economic growth that planners had hoped for and development economists had predicted.

In order to stave off a looming economic crisis, economic reforms picked up pace in the early 1990s.[4] This led to dramatic transformation of Indian cities as increasingly advanced sectors of the Indian economy experienced impressive growth.[5] Restrictions on foreign investment in real estate were relaxed, and gated communities for the growing middle class proliferated.[6] Policy makers identified dilapidated infrastructure as a barrier to further growth, and public-private partnerships channeled investment into urban infrastructure.[7] Finally, many people were driven to cities over the course of the past two decades because of a prolonged crisis in agriculture, evidenced by a shocking rise in suicides of indebted farmers.[8] In summary, many Indian cities have been transformed by public and private investment in infrastructure and real estate, while their populations have steadily increased as a result of rural-to-urban migration.

Today, Indian cities occupy a very different position in the nation's imagination than they did in the years after independence. Romantic portrayals of village life have given way to disdain for all things rural, and there is "a generation of peasants whose principal motivation seems to be to stop being peasants" and migrate to urban areas.[9] Meanwhile, the rural elite employ a range of strategies to gain a foothold in cities.[10] The wistful objective of recreating a village utopia in the city has given way to a consensus among a range of interest groups—including policymakers at multiple layers of government, the middle class, and private-sector elites—that Indian cities should become "world class." The pursuit of a vision of "world class" cities preoccupies many municipal governments, and to this end a complex set of zoning laws has been replaced by a governance regime based on aestheticism.[11] In short, buildings and communities that are inconsistent with the "world-class" aesthetic can be classified as "informal" and demolished, while buildings that conform to these subjective aesthetic standards are recognized as lawful by municipal authorities.[12] The "world-class" city vision has ushered in a sustained period of dizzying urban transformation. Metropolitan areas across India are veritable construction sites, as expensive real estate projects and business parks are being built and networked by elevated highways and metro systems.

In spite of rapid urban transformation, the cleavage between capital and labor has never been so deeply etched into the social and physical fabric of the Indian city. Economic growth has failed to translate into increased formal-sector employment, and as a result many urban residents cannot sell their labor for a wage in the formal economy.[13] These people typically earn meager livelihoods in the so-called informal economy.[14] These occupations include street hawking, food vending, waste collecting, cycle rickshaw pulling, and domestic service.[15] Delhi's economy is now predominantly informal, and it is increasingly geared toward tertiary activities.[16] Until the 1970s, anyone not employed by a formal enterprise or the public sector was considered unemployed, but with the emergence of an unshakable faith in markets in the 1980s, the informal sector came to be seen as a site of heroic entrepreneurialism in the face of predatory and inefficient bureaucracies.[17]

Workers in the vast informal sector constitute a "new" urban poor. In Delhi, the new urban poor is an amalgamation of disadvantaged social groups who were squeezed—simultaneously pushed and pulled—into informal service-sector work. In the 2000s, the Indian Supreme Court ordered Delhi municipal authorities to close factories whose operations did not meet environmental standards and were deemed "hazardous industries." As many as two million factory workers were rendered unemployed, and although approximately fifty thousand returned to villages, the remainder were "pushed" into oftentimes precarious informal work.[18] Additionally, unemployed factory workers and rural migrants were "pulled" into the informal service-sector by growing demand for cheap services from members of the new middle class.[19] The consumption of services offered by the new urban poor is a marker of class membership among members of the new middle class, among whom there is an assumption that "households cannot be run without servants."[20]

It is not uncommon for affluent households to employ a number of domestic servants to help with household chores, such as a driver, a security guard, and so on. Oftentimes gated communities devise licensing schemes for workers whose services are consumed collectively, such as tailors, clothes washers, waste collectors, and fruit vendors. Thus, the labor of informal service-sector workers makes possible the very lifestyles that the new middle class associates with the world-class city. This explains why the new urban poor are particularly visible in areas of the city that have supposedly

and things on an everyday basis. In short, they make the city work. For example, as a result of construction and increased consumption in affluent areas, there is often an exponential increase in solid waste, which municipal authorities typically struggle to manage. Informal-sector waste collectors are a common sight outside of shopping malls, as they gather recyclable materials which they then sell to informal-sector recyclers. Parking attendants are another example. Some of Delhi's centrally located bazaars have undergone makeovers and attract affluent customers who arrive by car. Without a veritable army of parking attendants, the narrow streets leading to these areas would be hopelessly gridlocked.

In spite of the fact that the new urban poor enable the vision of world-class transformation, they remain perpetually out of place. There is no "proper" place for them in the world-class city vision, and many of the activities in which the new urban poor engage are fraught with risk. For example, street hawkers are legally required to obtain

The labor of informal service sector workers makes possible the very lifestyles that the new middle class associates with the world-class city.

undergone transformation and exhibit the world-class aesthetic, such as affluent neighborhoods with gated communities, office parks, and shopping centers. In addition to working for the new middle class, there are a host of informal service-sector occupations that work to reduce friction and ensure the uninterrupted circulation of people

a license, but this is nearly impossible, so they are forced to operate illegally and they run the risk of having their goods confiscated.[21] Waste collectors are locked in an ongoing struggle with private-sector firms over ownership of the most valuable recyclable waste, such as aluminum and plastic.[22] Cycle-rickshaw pullers must overcome insurmountable bureaucratic hurdles if they want to operate legally.[23] Together, street hawkers, waste collectors, and cycle-rickshaw pullers number over one million in Delhi. Most do not long to return to a village. On the contrary, they harbor a desire for a secure future in a just city where the value of their labor is recognized and they can earn decent livelihoods.

The vision of a city that generates livelihoods stands in stark contrast with the world-class city vision. Delhi's City Development Plan, for example, was developed in a bid to attract investment from the central government, and it envisions a postindustrial future in which information technology is followed by the "life style sector [sic]" as the driver of economic growth.[24] While the plan fails to formally define the "life style sector," it includes "personal care and home care," and the plan claims that "the inherent spending habits of the populace has placed the city in a preeminent position in the fashion industry."[25] It proceeds to narrate the transformation of a "low-end" area into "Life Style Mile," an agglomeration of enterprises offering "lifestyle" services to affluent clientele. The point is that this vision is focused on transforming the city in ways that allow for particular lifestyles, while the very people enabling this transformation—i.e., the new urban poor—envision a city that generates livelihoods.

While the new urban poor and the new middle class embrace competing visions for India's urban future, they are currently interdependent. India's urban future will be determined by the ways in which these visions are negotiated and reconciled. Both groups are heterogeneous and cross-cut by divisions such as religion and caste. Thus, they rarely act collectively in citywide mobilizations. While this does not mean that Delhi's future will be free of conflict, it makes an apocalyptic conflict between haves and have-nots unthinkable. Instead, Delhi's future will be shaped by a myriad of localized conflicts over access to space, resources, and services such as water, electricity, and waste management.

Access to space is the most important resource for most workers in the informal service sector because their comparative advantage is based on being in the right place at the right time. In order to sell services to the new middle class, they require access to "world-class" areas, the very places where they are most aggressively pursued by local authorities. In the case of street hawkers, municipal authorities raid places that are known to operate and confiscate their wares. In order to gain a measure of security, they are typically forced to pay rent to a local powerbroker—such as a middle-class resident association or a local gang—that can protect them from authorities. Occasionally, conflict erupts as multiple groups vie for control over slivers of land. In an extreme example that made headlines, residents of an upscale apartment complex tragically beat a young man to death for defecating in a public park.[26] He had been visiting relatives in a nearby slum that lacked toilets. Madhu Kishwar described the ongoing localized conflict between these two communities as a "mini civil war," which erupted as each group sought to impose a set of rules regarding how and by whom the park could be used.[27]

Conflicts also commonly erupt over access to resources. For example, in Mumbai some affluent communities enjoy uninterrupted access to water while other communities lack access altogether. Residents of Mumbai lacking access to water have no choice but to tap into the municipal water supply "illegally," and this prompts authorities to raid the area to disengage the "illegal" connections in a never-ending are permanently out of place in the city, they typically cannot make a lawful claim to resources or space. Instead, they are forced to purchase overpriced resources on the open market, "steal" them, or rely on the benevolence of bureaucrats and other Delhi residents. Indian cities bear witness to the latest evidence for what should be common sense by now: economic growth does not necessarily reduce inequality.

While the new urban poor and the new middle class embrace competing visions for India's urban future, they are interdependent.

cat-and-mouse game.[28] Intense conflicts erupt between communities as accusations of water "theft" are met with recriminations. In short, unequal access to public water has led to the criminalization of some communities and occasionally violent conflicts. In Delhi, waste management has become a battleground as the composition of waste changed and a higher percentage of it became recyclable. Private-sector waste management firms that have been awarded tenders to manage waste tend to use capital-intensive technology, and they cannot employ even a fraction of the city's informal-sector waste workers. As a result, conflicts erupt over access to solid waste between formal enterprises and informal-sector recyclers.[29]

The localized conflicts described above revolve around a micro-politics of who has lawful access to scarce space and resources, and who is "stealing" water and electricity from whom. Given the fact that the new urban poor On the contrary, growth can deepen inequality if the gains are disproportionately captured by a small segment of society. In the twentieth century, inequality was associated with epic ideological struggles as organized labor confronted industrialists in attempts to secure higher wages and better working conditions. India was witness to these bitter struggles—the Communist Party of India was swept into power in Kerela and West Bengal—which unfolded in factories and working-class neighborhoods.[30] Since so few people in the twenty-first century Indian city are formally employed, these struggles will become less salient. Instead, the primary antagonism that will shape Indian cities will be access to the materiality of the city itself. That is, the localized conflicts over the use of space and access to resources described above will intensify, and these conflicts can easily pit neighbor against neighbor. The Indian city of tomorrow will largely be shaped by the outcome of these conflicts, and whether they are decided in a manner that generates livelihoods or facilitates particular lifestyles. Policymakers cannot easily address these conflicts since they are oftentimes between non-state actors. The current strategy pursued by municipal authorities is to try and prevent the poor from "illegally" accessing land and resources. This fails to address the structural issues that render the poor unable to make lawful claims to land and resources. A more farsighted plan would be to ensure a more equitable distribution of urban space and reliable services. If Indian cities are to be livable in the twenty-first century, municipal authorities must improve public service delivery systems and develop fair regulatory frameworks that provide workers in the informal service sector with space and security.

NOTES

1 Colin McFarlane, "Postcolonial Bombay: decline of a cosmopolitan city?" *Environment and Planning D* 26, no. 3 (2008): 480-499, 486. *Also* Ashis Nandy, *An Ambiguous Journey to the City: The Village and Other Odd Ruins of the Self in the Indian Imagination* (New Delhi: Oxford University Press, 2001), 13.

2 William J. Glover, "The troubled passage from 'village communities' to planned new town developments in mid-twentieth-century South Asia," *Urban History* 39, no. 1 (2012): 108-127, 126.

3 Vivek Chibber, *Locked in Place: State-Building and Late Industrialization in India* (Princeton: Princeton University Press, 2003). *Also* Emmanuel Teitelbaum, "Was the Indian labor movement ever co-opted?: evaluating standard accounts," *Critical Asian Studies* 38, no. 4 (2006): 389-417.

4 Ramachandra Guha, *India after Gandhi: The History of the World's Largest Democracy* (New York: Harper Perennial, 2008). *Also* Robert Jenkins, Democratic Politics and Economic Reform in India (Cambridge: Cambridge University Press, 2000).

5 Yuko Aoyama and Balaji Parthasarathy, "Research and development facilities of multinational enterprises in India," *Eurasian Geography and Economics* 53, no. 6 (2012): 713-730.

6 Gavin Shatkin, ed., *Contesting the Indian City: Global Visions and the Politics of the Local* (Malden: John Wiley & Sons, 2014). *Also* Llerena Guiu Searle, "Conflict and commensuration: contested market making in India's private real estate development sector," *International Journal of Urban and Regional Research* 38, no. 1 (2014): 60-78.

7 K.C. Sivaramakrishnan, *Re-visioning Indian Cities: The Urban Renewal Mission* (New Delhi: Sage, 2011).

8 *Economic & Political Weekly*, Special Section: Suicides by Farmers 41, no. 16 (2006): 1523-1569.

9 Partha Chatterjee, Lineages of Political Society: Studies in Postcolonial Democracy (Ranikhet: Permanent Black, 2011), 227. *Also* Vinay Gidwani, *Capital, Interrupted: Agrarian Development and the Politics of Work in India* (Minneapolis: University of Minnesota Press, 2008).

10 "Are Rich Rural Jats Middle-Class?" in *Elite and Everyman: The Cultural Politics of the Indian Middle Classes* (New Delhi: Routledge, 2011), 140-63.

11 Seth Schindler, "A New Delhi every day: multiplicities of governance regimes in a transforming metropolis," *Urban Geography* 35, no. 3 (2014): 402-419. *Also* Veronique D.N. Dupont, "The dream of Delhi as a global city," *International Journal of Urban and Regional Research* 35, no. 3 (2011): 533-554. *Also* Michael Goldman, "Speculative urbanism and the making of the next world city," *International Journal of Urban and Regional Research* 35, no. 3 (2011): 555-581. *Also* Ananya Roy, "The blockade of the world-class city: dialectical images of Indian urbanism," in *Worlding Cities: Asian Experiments and the Art of Being Global* (Malden: Blackwell Publishing, 2011). *Also* D. Asher Ghertner, "Calculating without numbers: aesthetic governmentality in Delhi's slums," *Economy and Society* 39, no. 2 (2010): 185-217.

12 Ibid.

13 K.P. Kannan and G. Raveendran, "Growth sans employment: a quarter century of jobless growth in India's organised manufacturing," *Economic and Political Weekly* 44, no. 10 (2009): 80-91. *Also* Kalyan Sanyal, Rethinking Capitalist Development: Primitive Accumulation, Governmentality and Post-Colonial Capitalism (New Delhi: Sage, 2007).

14 National Commission for Enterprises in the Unorganised Sector, *The Challenge of Employment in Development in India: An Informal Economy Perspective* (New Delhi: National Commission for Enterprises in the Unorganised Sector, 2007). *Also* Government of India, *2002 Report of the Special Group on Targeting Ten Million Employment Opportunities Per Year over the Tenth Plan Period* (New Delhi: Planning Commission, 2002).

15 Seth Schindler, "A New Delhi every day: multiplicities of governance regimes in a transforming metropolis," *Urban Geography* 35, no. 3 (2014): 402-419. *Also* Dolf te Lintelo, "The spatial politics of food hygiene: regulating small-scale retail in Delhi," *European Journal of Development Research* 2, no. 1 (2009): 63-80. *Also* Kaveri Gill, Of Poverty and Plastic: Scavenging and Scrap Trading Entrepreneurs in India's Urban Informal Economy (New Delhi: Oxford University Press, 2010). *Also* Amita Baviskar, "Cows, cars and cycle rickshaws: bourgeois environmentalists and the battle for Delhi's streets," in *Elite and Everyman: The Cultural Politics of the Indian Middle Classes* (New Delhi: Routledge, 2011), 391-418. *Also* Ashima Sood, "A future for informal services?: the cycle rickshaw sector as case study," *Economic and Political Weekly* 47, no. 42 (2012): 95-102. *Also* Seemin Qayum and Raka Ray, "The middle classes at home," in *Elite and Everyman: The Cultural Politics of the Indian Middle Classes* (New Delhi: Routledge, 2011), 246-270.

16 Government of National Capital Territory of Delhi, *A Report on Unorganised Service Sector in Delhi* (New Delhi: Directorate of Economics and Statistics, 2005).

17 Keith Hart, "Informal income opportunities and urban employment in Ghana," *The Journal of Modern African Studies* 11, no. 1 (1973): 61-89. *Also* Hernando De Soto, The Other Path: The Invisible Revolution in the Third World (New York: Harper and Row, 1989).

18 Nevedita Menon and Aditya Nigam, *Power and Contestation: India Since 1989* (Hyderabad: Orient Longman, 2007).

19 Ministry of Urban Development, *City development plan: Delhi* (New Delhi: IL&FS Ecosmart Limited, 2006).

20 Seemin Qayum and Raka Ray, "The middle classes at home," in *Elite and Everyman: The Cultural Politics of the Indian Middle Classes* (New Delhi: Routledge, 2011), 246-270.

21 Seth Schindler, "The making of 'world-class' Delhi: relations between street hawkers and the new middle class," *Antipode* 46, no. 2 (2014): 557–573.

22 Seth Schindler, Federico Demaria, and Shashi

NOTES

B. Pandit, "Delhi's waste conflict," *Economic and Political Weekly* 47, no. 42 (2012): 18-21.

23 Amita Baviskar, "Cows, cars and cycle rickshaws: bourgeois environmentalists and the battle for Delhi's streets," in *Elite and Everyman: The Cultural Politics of the Indian Middle Classes* (New Delhi: Routledge, 2011), 391-418. *Also* Ashima Sood, "A future for informal services?: the cycle rickshaw sector as case study," *Economic and Political Weekly* 47, no. 42 (2012): 95-102.

24 Ministry of Urban Development, *City development plan: Delhi* (New Delhi: IL&FS Ecosmart Limited, 2006).

25 Ibid., 17.4.2.

26 Amita Baviskar, "Between violence and desire: space, power, and identity in the making of metropolitan Delhi," *International Social Science Journal* 55, no.175 (2003): 89-98.

27 Madhu Kishwar, *Deepening Democracy: Challenges of Governance and Globalization in India* (New Delhi: Oxford University Press, 2006).

28 Stephen Graham, Renu Desai, and Colin McFarlane, "Water wars in Mumbai," *Public Culture* 25, no. 1 (2013): 115-141.

29 Seth Schindler, Federico Demaria, and Shashi B. Pandit, "Delhi's waste conflict," *Economic and Political Weekly* 47, no. 42 (2012): 18-21.

30 Chitra Joshi, *Lost Worlds: Indian Labour and its Forgotten Histories* (Delhi: Permanent Black, 2003).

Tackling Inequality

Part and Parcel of Kenya's Fight Against Poverty

Hannah Kim & Thomas O'Brien

Tackling poverty is arguably Kenya's most pressing developmental challenge—and indeed the nation's story encapsulates much of what one sees throughout the rest of Africa. On the one hand, the country holds great potential from its expanding and youthful population, dynamic private sector, new constitution, recent peaceful elections, and pivotal role within East Africa and beyond. Yet four out of ten Kenyans live in poverty. Income inequality is high, and there are significant disparities in income between urban centers, agriculturally rich areas in the west, and the arid and semi-arid areas in the northeast.

We argue that for Kenya to make inroads in its fight against poverty, it must redouble its efforts to tackle economic inequality as a complement to its long-established drive for growth. In this article, we highlight several facets of inequality in Kenya beyond those related solely to income, and emphasize the importance of addressing geographic inequality. We examine how devolution—which is a tectonic change in Kenya's institutional landscape brought about by the new constitution—can be a key instrument in tackling deeply entrenched geographic disparities. This approach combines the introduction of decentralization of political

Hannah Kim is an Operations Officer of the East Africa Department at the World Bank. She previously worked as a Technical Advisor for the Institutional Capacity Strengthening Fund at the Inter-American Development Bank.

Thomas O'Brien is the Task Manager of the Independent Evaluation Group (IEG) at the World Bank. He has also served as Senior Economist in the Europe and Central Asia region, and as Country Manager for Bulgaria.

power to the newly created counties and equitable sharing of national revenue. We conclude by looking at some of the steps needed in the coming years to push this agenda forward, including considerations in how best to manage the nation's new oil discoveries (in remote localities) for shared prosperity.

The Poverty Picture. The good news is that Kenya's poverty rate has been different regions. In the remote, arid, sparsely populated northeastern parts of the country (Turkana, Mandera, and Wajir), poverty rates are above 80 percent. Poverty rates are high because agroclimatic shocks impact vulnerable livelihoods that depend on livestock and low-productivity agricultural activities. Furthermore, people's assets, including educational opportunity and achievement, are very limited. At the other end

Addressing geographic inequality, which has been an almost decades-long bugbear, must be one key component of Kenya's strategy to defeat poverty.

falling—from 47 percent in 2005/06 to about 39 percent (on best estimates) in 2012/13.[1] The recent reductions in poverty in Kenya have been driven by solid GDP growth, along with improvements in social safety nets targeting the poor, continuing migration to urban areas, and better access to health and education services. However, poverty has not been lowered by any concerted efforts to reduce income inequality. In fact, income inequality remains quite stark, with the richest 10 percent of the population receiving 40 percent of the nation's income and the poorest 10 percent of the population receiving only 2 percent. Indeed, Kenya's income inequality—as measured by the Gini coefficient—is above that of neighboring countries including Ethiopia, Tanzania, and Uganda.[2]

Despite progress, the bare fact remains that nearly four in every ten Kenyans live in extreme poverty. And the experience of poverty among the population is also highly unequal across of the spectrum, Nairobi—the nation's capital and a growing metropolis whose population could reach 8 million by 2030—has been a growth pole and has seen its poverty rate drop to 22 percent.[3] This illustrates how addressing geographic inequality, which has been an almost decades-long bugbear, must be one key component of Kenya's strategy to defeat poverty.

The Scale of the Challenge: Why Inequality Matters. Kenya's government aims to end extreme poverty in one generation, and this goal is consistent with the vision of institutions such as the World Bank, which has established such a target at a global level to be reached by the year 2030. Looking ahead, however, our simulations show that GDP growth at historic rates (about 4.6 percent annually over the last decade) will not suffice; at that pace, the poverty rate would still be around 27 percent by 2030 if the inequality rates remain unchanged. However, if inequality could be curtailed sharply, then these historic growth rates would coincide with a poverty rate drop to 11 percent by 2030.[4] And if such progress in reducing inequality can be combined with some acceleration in growth (to 6 percent per annum), the goal of eliminating poverty is indeed in sight.[5] Calling for this GDP growth and income inequality curtailment is, of course, a tall order since the growth agenda alone calls for raising investments in infrastructure, enhancing firm-level productivity, and continuing prudent macroeconomic policy.[6]

A Key Focus on Inequality: The Geographic Dimension. Narrowing income inequality on the aforementioned scale requires addressing the geographic inequalities that have come to characterize Kenya. At one end of the spectrum, Kenya's growth poles have been concentrated along the Northern Corridor, from Mombasa to Nairobi and onward to Kisumu and Kakamega, where the majority of Kenyans live. These areas are rich in natural endowments and have relatively high population density that has helped develop a growing concentration of economic activity. Modern enterprises—such as those found in the "Silicon Savannah" around Nairobi—are shaping a growing middle class, and more broadly the population in these growth centers experiences relatively low levels of poverty and better access to services.

At the other end of the spectrum, however, other parts of the country have not shared in the nation's growing prosperity. This discrepancy manifests itself in many ways, not least in a highly uneven allocation of social benefits made possible by national economic growth. For example, only one in five children are of adequate height-for-age in Wajir county (population: 661,941), compared to more than eight in ten children in Mombasa (population: 1.4 million).[7] In the sparsely populated northeastern parts of Kenya, only 17 percent of women deliver at health facilities, in sharp contrast to Nairobi, where the rate is 90 percent. In the remote and sparsely populated Mandera county, one in ten children is born at a health facility, and this ratio declines to a dismal one in twenty in Wajir, compared to eight in ten in Kirinyaga.

In terms of education, significant differences creep in at primary and secondary schools, where enrollment rates and testing scores are much lower in arid and semi-arid areas compared to urban centers. The primary school net enrollment rate is 35 percent in Wajir and 25 percent in Turkana compared to 87 percent in Nairobi and 81 percent in Mombasa. Disparities in education outcomes persist in secondary school, where net enrollment rate is a low 7 percent in Wajir and 8 percent in Samburu compared to 48 percent in Nairobi and 32 percent in Mombasa.[8] National and regional assessments, including the National Systems for Monitoring Learning Achievements and the South African Consortium for Monitoring Educational Quality, consistently reveal the northeastern and western regions as underperformers over the years.[9] In Isiolo, only 8 percent of students received a passing average score on secondary school examinations, compared to 30 percent in Nairobi.

A range of factors influence these

contrasts, including agglomeration and economies-of-scale effects, which typically make public services easier to provide in urban locations. But arguably there is another effect at work—the influence of weak governance, which can be magnified in disadvantaged locations. Take the issue of absenteeism in public service institutions. As a detailed World Bank-supported survey shows for Kenya, in a standard work period some 28 percent of healthcare workers are absent from front-line delivery of services.[10] This problem is most severe in rural areas, where public facilities hold an absenteeism rate as high as 38 percent—and where the poverty rate is higher than the national average. Similarly, in the education sector, teachers tend to be more absent in rural areas (47 percent) than in urban areas (34 percent), and in public schools (47 percent) more than in private schools (31 percent). This stratification may in part explain why children in cities have a much greater chance of advancing than those in rural areas. One can see that the poor face a disproportionate burden that arises from these inequalities and lack of effective governance mechanisms that should hold health providers and teachers accountable to their clients. This reinforces the need to make targeted improvements in attendance by healthcare workers, schoolteachers, and other essential public servants in rural areas to avoid exacerbating existing disparities, and hopefully improve the prospects for upward mobility for the most vulnerable groups.

The Big-Picture Response: How the New Constitution Can Be a Game-Changer. So, what is the answer to tackling the geographic and other inequalities that have hampered the economic development of Kenya? For the people and their elected representatives, a big part of the solution is vested in a new constitution. Approved in 2010, the constitution—by far the most significant change since Kenya's birth as an independent nation over fifty years ago—seeks to tackle these longstanding and deeply entrenched spatial inequalities through gradual devolution. The principal ingredients are the creation of an entirely new set of forty-seven counties (and the elimination of a lower level of administration), a decentralization of political and administrative power and responsibilities to these counties, and the introduction of a more equitable sharing of national revenue and resources from the center to the local level.

The motivation behind the decentralization of political power to the newly created counties is an attempt to give Kenyans more equal access to institutions that can hold public servants accountable and meet local needs. Each of the forty-seven counties (with an average of around one million residents) has a governor and a county assembly that are democratically elected, and each takes on key responsibilities such as healthcare. Because Kenyans can now directly vote for their governors, they have more input on how resources are used and can better hold governors accountable for the delivery of key services. In this way, Kenyans can participate more directly in the fight against poverty in their own counties.

This also means government spending will not necessarily go towards developing the same infrastructure across the entire country; rather, government spending may support more tailored investments in health, education, and other key services that can better address existing inequities.

The new constitution also provides an avenue for a clearer and more equitable allocation of national revenues across locales. It introduces devolved, or geographically earmarked, funds transferred from the national government, which are raised from national taxes such as the Value Added Tax. Currently, resources are allocated based on a weighted formula: population, 45 percent (so that counties have sufficient resources to deliver services on a per capita basis); poverty rate, 20 percent (to promote redistribution); land area, 8 percent (to compensate for higher cost of delivering services); fiscal responsibility, 2 percent (to provide incentives for prudent fiscal management); and a basic equal share of 25 percent (to provide each county with resources to cover the fixed costs of running county administrations).

As a result of this formula, the allocation of national revenue to counties will show wider variations on a per capita basis. Marginalized counties in arid and semi-arid areas are now receiving significantly higher shares than the more developed urban growth poles.

For example, per capita revenue allocation is $92 in Turkana and $96 in Wajir compared to $37 in Nairobi and $51 in Mombasa.[11] This provides more capital for less developed counties, which will then allow them to finance key infrastructure and public services that have historically been underfunded in these areas. However, translating this new system into on-the-ground impact is easier said than done. Many of the poorer counties that stand to benefit from larger national revenue transfers may have modest administrative capabilities and be less readily equipped in practice to make efficient and transparent use of their resources. Conversely, Nairobi and Mombasa are currently facing a squeeze of inherited wage and debt obligations combined with smaller per capita transfers from the central government, which limits their ability to make new investments in urban infrastructure.

Few countries have attempted a political and economic decentralization process on this scale or speed. This truly historic transition, if implemented correctly and successfully, has the potential to have a positive impact on combating inequality and high levels of poverty in the long term. There have already been some positive early signs, such as the fact that Kenya's general election in 2013 passed off smoothly and peacefully (in contrast to the experience in 2008), suggesting the breadth

For the people and their elected representatives, the solution is vested in a new constitution.

of support for the changes introduced to the political system in 2010. And for the first time in over twenty years, Kenya's economic growth did not dip following an election.

Looking Ahead. Moving forward, tackling poverty will be an increasingly multifaceted endeavor. Beyond policies together. That dividend will be manifested through greater citizen engagement, direction, and oversight of public authorities to fundamentally deliver better services to ordinary people and build better local-level business environments. Here, there are many practical challenges, including establishing core county planning, public finan-

Few countries have attempted a **political and economic decentralization process** on this scale or speed.

to merely promote GDP growth, multiple measures can still be considered to protect the poor and help them develop their potential—and indeed lead to a stronger, more holistic contribution to GDP. This is key to reducing inequalities and promoting shared prosperity over the long term. For example, in addition to well-targeted investments in education and health, an expansion of a fiscally sound social safety net program will stand Kenya in good stead. Steps to raise productivity in the rural sector—which could include market and financial sector reforms as well as simple infrastructure improvements such as functioning rural roads—can pay off hugely. And initiatives to help specific segments of the population, notably the burgeoning youth population, are a pressing social imperative.

Perhaps the most enticing challenge is to deliver a "devolution dividend"— to reap the benefits of decentralizing power, accountability, and resources to the new county administrations—by making the new county and central government structures work effectively

cial management, and human resources systems. The needs and opportunities differ between the larger, more urbanized counties and the historically marginalized counties in arid and semi-arid regions; therefore, the responses must be tailored accordingly. The trends found in the Kenya Ethics and Anti-Corruption Commission county level corruption index remain to be fully analyzed, but might be worth following closely to track progress in governance improvements.

The principles behind Kenya's revenue sharing mechanism are also shaping how revenues from the recent oil discoveries in Turkana county will be shared between the central government and oil-rich county authorities. This is part of an overall approach to ensure that local counties will have the capacity to manage their share of oil revenue and channel it towards long-term investments in education, health, and savings that can benefit future generations. Doing so will be key to avoiding the potential obstacles that have plagued resource-rich countries, including weak institutions, inadequate macroeconomic policies, poor governance, and lack of profit-sharing mechanisms among relevant stakeholders (local communities, central government, current and future generations, and national and international private-sector investors) that could threaten to derail the effective use of these resources to fight poverty and, at worst, lead to exacerbating ethnic tensions that have been problematic in the past.

There are risks on the horizon and uncertainties remain to be managed. However, partnerships inside and outside Kenya—between citizens and the government, the private sector, and international development institutions such as the World Bank—can be a powerful agent for change. It appears as if the ingredients are increasingly coming together to make Kenya an African success story.

NOTES

The authors have also received invaluable contributions from Diariétou Gaye, Borko Handjiski, Christopher Finch, John Randa, Jane Kiringai, Kathleen Whimp, George Larbi, and Wolfgang Fengler. The views expressed in this paper are solely those of the authors, and should not be attributed to The World Bank, its Board of Directors, or the countries they represent.

1 Poverty is defined as the percentage of the population living on less than $1.25 a day in 2005 Purchasing Power Parity (PPP) at 2005 prices. The international poverty line at PPP is converted to local currencies in 2005 price and is then converted to the prices prevailing at the time of the relevant household survey using the best available Consumer Price Index. For more information, visit http://iresearch.worldbank.org/Povcal/Net/index.htm and see World Bank, *Prosperity for All: Ending Extreme Poverty* (2014).

2 As measured at 47.7 by the Gini coefficient, a statistic often used as a summary indicator by economists.

3 This is not to disregard the experiences of poverty in Nairobi, however, including that endured by poor families living in the informal settlements of almost one million people where living conditions can be harsh. World Bank, "Kenya Informal Settlements Improvement Project Appraisal Document" (2011).

4 In our simulations this is a reduction in the inequality measure of the Gini coefficient by 1 percentage point per year.

5 The Government's Second Medium-Term Plan 2013-2017 has an ambitious target of accelerating growth rates to an annualized 10 percent.

6 This is analyzed in more detail in O'Brien and Kim, *South Africa Journal of International Affairs* (forthcoming in 2015) and in World Bank Group, *Country Partnership Strategy for Kenya* (2014).

7 World Bank, *Devolution without Disruption: Pathways to a Successful New Kenya* (2012), 25.

8 "Exploring Kenyan Education," Internet, http://devseed.com/kenya-bank/ (date accessed: 29 November 2014).

9 World Bank, *Kenya Global Partnership for Education Primary Education Development Project* (2014).

10 World Bank, "Kenya Service Delivery Indicators," Internet, http://www.sdindicators.org/kenya/ (date accessed: 29 November 2014).

11 Mwangi Kimenyi, "Kenya Devolution and Resource Sharing Calculator," Brookings Institution (2013).

The Veil Ban in Europe
Gender Equality or Gendered Islamophobia?

Shaista Gohir

The wearing of the face veil by Muslim women is a topic of much controversy and heated debate throughout Europe, which has resulted in numerous bans or considerations to limit its use. This article seeks to examine the reasons routinely provided to justify the face veil restrictions. Are all of these motivations genuine, and are Muslim women denied procedural fairness during the processes leading to legislation? Can any legitimate concerns be addressed without legislation?

The leading voices against the veil are also considered: Is the opposition really concerned about gender equality, or are they simply exploiting this issue? Restrictions prohibiting Muslim women from wearing the veil produce widespread repercussions and recurring discourse against the veil. Putting aside the issue of whether religious freedom is violated—as the veil is a contested issue within Islam anyway—this article argues that prohibitions do control how some women choose to express their personal identities. While these women's dress choices may limit their full participation in society, state restrictions not only undermine gender equality, but also fuel gendered Islamophobia.

Shaista Gohir is the former Executive Director of Muslim Women's Network UK. She is also the founder of the Big Sister website, which highlights inspirational Muslim women globally from past to present.

Justifications to Ban the Veil.

The female Muslim population in Britain has not always displayed such strict adherence to its religious attire. First-generation Muslim women, for example, have typically donned a *dupatta*, or loose scarf worn in a relaxed manner that does not necessarily cover all of the hair. Moreover, the *dupatta* was worn often as part of the main South Asian outfit, the *shalwar kameez*, which consisted of baggy pants and a long top. Second- and third-generation Muslim women and girls have appeared to be even more relaxed in their choice of attire, routinely declining to wear any form of head covering. The intensification of anti-Muslim sentiments after 9/11 and the London bombings, however, has led to a dramatic rise in the number of Muslim women and girls, including those born in Britain, that wear the headscarf (*hijab*) at schools, colleges, universities, and at work, with some that also choose to wear the full body cloak (*jilbab*) in addition to the headscarf. A tiny minority has also adopted the face veil (*niqab*) or the *burqa*, a long garment covering the entire body from head to foot, including the face.[1] This phenomenon is not surprising because when any population feels threatened, it reacts by visibly defending its culture or faith, hence a stronger attachment to said culture or faith; however, this public display of an Islamic identity has now put many Muslim women in Britain as well as in other European countries under intense social pressure to conform rather than make autonomous choices about their lives. While mainstream society tends to view Muslim women as isolated from the general public, the more religiously fervent sections of Muslim communities accuse the women of not being "Muslim" enough if the women choose not to wear the various forms of clothing associated with their faith.

The wearing of the *niqab*, or veil, has become an emotive and controversial issue in Europe, with some politicians intent on criminalizing its use. In some Muslim countries, face veils are enforced to make women invisible and anonymous so that men may not be aroused or tempted, thereby absolving the men of their moral responsibilities. However, the wearing of the veil could also be seen as limiting women's mobility and freedom.

Some politicians believe that allowing the veil to be worn in Western countries is synonymous with accepting the religious enforcement that makes women invisible and isolates them from society. As non-verbal signals, such as facial expressions, play a major role in social interaction, the veil could certainly restrict personal, social, and economic activities. However, some women wearing the veil argue that viewing the face is no longer a necessity in a world where we spend more time interacting with people over the Internet, whether it is through Facebook, Twitter, emails, and

State restrictions not only undermine gender equality, but also fuel **gendered Islamophobia.**

other online forums, rather than via face-to-face interactions. They argue that many people on these platforms also hide their identities and there is no compulsion for people to show what they look like or even reveal who they are. These veiled Muslim women, therefore, cannot understand why people are so concerned about their anonymity.

So why are certain politicians, media, and some members of the public giving a disproportionate level of attention to the way Muslim women dress? The most common arguments used to justify prohibiting the veil in public are irrational. Some say concealing the face is a threat to security, even though Muslim women do show their faces for identification purposes required at colleges, universities, banks, and airports.[2] The use of odd cases such as Mohammed Ahmed Mohamed, who escaped disguised in a *burqa*, to suggest that men will start dressing up as Muslim women to commit crimes is disingenuous.[3] Another common objection is that not being able to see the face is a barrier to integration.[4] While the veil could indeed impede communication and therefore full participation in society, preventing a few thousand women in Europe from covering their faces would not help the majority of Muslim women who do not wear the face veil to integrate. If such concerns were genuine, then politicians would be attempting to tackle the real barriers to integration such as high unemployment rates and the multiple forms of discrimination these women experience.[5]

The debate over the veil ban for Muslim women in public settings is often framed as that of "saving Muslim women from oppression." Because the religiously-affiliated veils are part of the dress code enforced in countries such as Afghanistan, Saudi Arabia, and Iran, Muslim women's clothing is perceived as a symbol of subjugation in the West.

As foreign as the veil may appear to others, Muslim women in Europe are voluntarily choosing to cover their heads and a small minority is even willingly choosing to conceal their faces too. Undoubtedly, there will be women who are forced or pressured to do so, but many choose to wear the veil with varied motivations. While some do so out of religious obligation, others simply view it as taking an extra step to feel closer to God. There are also those who wish to make a political or fashion statement, or are simply going through a fad. Many also claim they feel liberated behind the veil. While it could be difficult to understand how the veil is seen as liberating, that is less important. It does *not* matter that some people find it intimidating, frightening, or offensive because it is unfamiliar to them. Hearing two hundred witnesses unfamiliar to them. During a Commons debate on International Women's Day, British member of Parliament Philip Hollobone said: "This is Britain; we are not a Muslim country. Covering one's face in public is strange, and to many people it is intimidating and offensive. I seriously think that a ban on wearing the *niqab* or the *burqa* in public should be considered."[6] These are not sufficient reasons to justify legislation banning it. Yet laws continue to be imposed or proposed in a number of European countries to forbid the veil—even though the vast majority of Muslim women do not wear it.[7]

Remarkably, the debates about veil bans are based on assumptions about the experiences and motives of women who wear the face veil rather than factual support. No effort is made to consult these women in the process leading up to the ban. For example, the Parliamentary Commission of Inquiry in France produced a report before the ban on face veils was adopted. This was based on hearing 200 witnesses and experts. The Commission had not planned to hear a single woman who actually wore a face veil. The only person whom they did interview who wore a face veil, Kenza Drider, was only heard upon her own request.[8] It is important that lawmakers are sufficiently informed on minorities' interests and needs when enacting legislation that pertains to said minorities. They must also act impartially which requires informed decision making based on accurate information. Denial of procedural fairness is therefore sending the signal that Muslim women are marginal in society and not valued members of society.[9]

So, how many Muslim women have actually adopted the veil into their own lives? There are no official statistics and those banded around to date are based on guesswork and even exaggeration. For example, while the exact number of women veiling in the Netherlands is unknown, estimates have varied from only a few dozen to about 300 from the 900,000 Muslims.[10] Belgium states that only a few hundred adopt it from a Muslim population of 650,000.[11] France estimates the number anywhere between 367 and 2,000 of its 5 million Muslims.[12] Britain has a Muslim population of 2.7 million and there have been no attempts to assess how many women may be wearing the veil, but the numbers are considered to be very small—perhaps in the hundreds or even thousands, but certainly not tens of thousands.[13] Despite veiling being such a minor phenomenon, the number of politicians calling on their governments to proscribe it is growing.

The Leading Advocates Against the Veil in Europe.

In April 2011, France, which had already passed a law in 2004 prohibiting the wearing of religious symbols—including the headscarf—in schools, became the first European country to pass a national law preventing the wearing of garments in public that conceal the face.[14] This has paved the way for other nations, such as Belgium and Holland, to enact similar bans.[15] Although other European nations have not imposed national laws restricting veils, some have opted to implement local prohibitions. For example, half of Germany's sixteen state governments prohibit teachers from wearing both headscarves and face veils. The German state of Hesse became the first state to forbid civil servants wearing headscarves and veils.[16] While it could be argued that the covering of the face is not appropriate for these roles, it is difficult to imagine how wearing a headscarf could hinder the civil servants from performing their duties. Some cities in Spain, including Barcelona, have also passed local laws that prevent the wearing of face veils in public, although in February 2013 Spain's Supreme Court ruled the laws as unconstitutional.[17]

Does Muslim women's clothing pose a threat to the Western way of life, or are these bans just about political point-scoring? Given the rise of Islamophobia across Europe, politicians seem to be in competition with one another to show who can be the toughest on Muslims. It is interesting to note that in this widespread campaign against the face veil, the leading voices have been male figures (with the exception of Pia Kjærsgaard, Co-founder of the Far Right Danish People's Party).[18] Some notable politicians include Nicolas Sarkozy of the right wing Union for a Popular Movement (France), Denis Ducarme of the center-right Reformist Movement (Belgium), Geert Wilders of the far right Freedom Party (Holland), Heinz-Christian Strache of the far right Freedom Party (Austria), Oskar Freysinger of the far right Swiss People's Party (Switzerland), and Mazyar Keshvari of the right wing Progress Party (Norway).[19] While the veil has not been banned in Britain, male politicians have been among the leading

face coverings in public has made little progress since then with no prospect of becoming legislated.

It is clear that the men most opposed to the face veil tend to be from right wing political parties, particularly from the far right. Their propaganda has been so successful that people who previously did not care about what Muslim women wore are now slowly also turning against the veil. Last year, yet another male, this time from the British coalition government, called for a national debate on face veils. Junior Minister and Liberal Democrat Jeremy Browne member of Parliament suggested that a ban on the face veil in schools and public places should be considered.[21]

Instead of allowing far-right rhetoric to influence policy, those in power should be removing the conditions in which such political parties thrive. Thankfully, the views supporting veil bans are currently restricted to the

Does Muslim women's clothing pose a threat to the Western way of life, or are these bans just about
political point-scoring?

voices in the debate against it, especially Nick Griffin of the far-right British National Party (UK), Nigel Farage, leader of the right wing populist UK Independence Party, and Philip Hollobone, member of the center-right Conservative Party (UK).[20] Last year Philip Hollobone even put forward the Face Coverings (Prohibition) bill to be debated in Parliament. His stance, however, did not represent the policy of the Conservative Party, and his proposal to prohibit the wearing of certain

fringes of British politics. However, the current economic recession, cuts in welfare benefits, and rise in unemployment and poverty has led voters to be disenchanted with the main political parties across Europe. Far-right parties are taking advantage of current political conditions and adopting xenophobic discourse arguing that immigrants are to blame for social and economic conditions. Instead of challenging this discourse, ruling parties are pandering to the far-right agenda and also trying to tap into people's fears. For example, the UK's Conservative-led coalition government launched an advertising campaign using billboards on vans to tell illegal immigrants to "go home." The words "go home" resonate racist slogans used to attack immigrants.[22] By

judge Peter Murphy concluded correctly when he ruled that a Muslim woman must remove her veil when giving evidence.[24] It is unfortunate that sometimes the odd Muslim woman may be unreasonable and refuse to remove it. Such attitudes only contribute towards

One cannot claim to protect the rights of women and then dictate their dress.

portraying themselves as the only ones defending the "white working class," politicians on the far right are successfully building their profiles, and increasing their respectability and acceptability. This became apparent in the European elections that took place in May 2014, which saw a surge of parties propagating racist and xenophobic ideas and policies. In effect, politicians who regularly promote fear and hatred are becoming a legitimate political voice supported by taxpayers' money.[23]

Despite the unwarranted attacks led by right-wing male politicians, there are particular legitimate circumstances in which it is necessary to reveal one's full face. For example, pupils and teachers in schools should not be allowed to wear the face veil, not only for security reasons in verifying identity, but also because such clothing would interfere with the child's learning and interaction with the teacher and fellow classmates. Providing testimony in a courtroom would also be another situation in which the veil is inappropriate. When questioned in court, the face is an essential part of the communication process and should be visible to ensure justice can be done. Hence, the British

portraying their own faith negatively, whereas Islam is not rigid but flexible. Yet, all of these legitimate concerns can be managed without imposing discriminatory laws. The campaigns to curtail what some Muslim women wear can only therefore be about Islamophobia and misogyny rather than about gender equality. One cannot claim to protect the rights of women and then dictate their dress. Men who ban certain types of clothing or enforce particular dress codes are using their own culture to control women's bodies. Whether it is fanatical Muslim men who use religion to insist that women hide their faces or Western men who disapprove of the way some Muslim women choose to assert their identity, it is the same patriarchy at work.

When dress is governed in any society, the rules always disproportionately impact women because men tend to control social, political, and religious institutions which construct social pressures and pass laws. Men use this power to regulate women's bodies both in the public and private spheres, often limiting women's freedom to choose how they dress.[25] Women are then victimized for violating these man-made rules. Men across various cultures have dictated how women should look or behave throughout history. For example, Jewish women have been battling to wear the prayer shawl that Jewish men wear when they pray at the wall in Jerusalem. The women who have dared to defy the rules by wearing the prayer shawl have had stones thrown at them by male worshippers and have been arrested by the police.[26] In Malawi, a Christian country, a former male president made it unlawful for women to wear skirts and trousers. Although the law has since been repealed, men have attacked and beaten women for wearing trousers and skirts. Women have also been attacked for wearing trousers in Kenya, South Africa, and Zimbabwe in recent years.[27] Even in Western countries, women were previously not allowed to wear trousers. In fact, a 200-year-old law that made it illegal for women to wear trousers in Paris was only revoked in 2013. Introduced in 1799, this ban stipulated that any woman wishing to "dress like a man" must seek special permission from the police and provide medical justification for showing her legs. Although the law had not been enforced for decades, it was repealed after several failed attempts.[28]

So why should men in any society dictate the discourse on what women wear? The current debate therefore should not be questioning what women are or are not wearing, but should be contesting male influence on women's dress codes. Regardless of the way women dress, their faith, ethnicity, or cultural background, women will be subject to sexism and misogyny that manifest in different forms.

Impact of the Veil Ban on Women.

People express their identities in numerous ways—through mannerisms, opinions, language, culture, and values. What they wear is an external expression of that internal identity. Everyone should therefore be free to exercise their own preferences over the matter of clothing, as long as it does not infringe on anybody else's rights. Women affected by the veil bans in Europe are claiming that their freedoms of religion and expression are being violated. However, they should not even have to prove that veil prohibitions are a violation of religious freedom; the *niqab* is a contested issue within Islam anyway. It should not matter if there is no requirement in Islam to cover the face, as women should be able to wear whatever they choose, regardless of the reasons for doing so.

One 24-year-old French woman did take her case to the European Court of Human Rights (ECHR). On 1 July 2014, however, the Strasbourg based court rejected her argument and upheld the French law banning the veil, ruling that "the face plays a significant role in social interaction."[29] While face veils do discourage social interactions on some level, it is a poor excuse to use in support of the veil ban because one cannot force others to socially interact. Many human rights and women's organizations have criticized the decision as discriminatory, as this over-reaction undermines the rights of women and may even make the veil more popular in Europe. Muslim women are already facing unprecedented levels of discrimination and hostility, including verbal abuse and physical assaults.[30] This decision will only further fuel gendered

Islamophobia. Subtle or overt, the distress caused by Islamophobia will negatively affect the psychological well-being and mental health of Muslim women. The ruling has already re-ignited the discussion amongst European countries, which had previously considered banning the veil but had not passed any laws due to the risk of being censured by the ECHR. Norway, Denmark, and Austria are now considering revisiting the issue.

The current environment in Europe is clearly very hostile towards veiled Muslim women, so what advice could be given to them? Some women who cover their faces manage to strike a balance between their personal freedom and full participation in British society. They simply wear the veil on a part time basis and acknowledge that it is appropriate to remove it in certain situations. Such women, however, are a minority within the minority. Muslim women who have opted to don the veil should, therefore, consider the consequences of their choice such as limitations to civic participation or not being able to readily access the job market. They should also reflect on how their decision contributes to the scrutiny the wider Muslim community faces. For women who are convinced that concealing the face is a religious duty, how informed is this choice? After all, the interpretation of religious scripture is controlled by men, for the benefit of men. Despite reservations about the veil, it is important to continue to vociferously speak out on the right of women, including those who choose to cover their face, to be able to make independent choices about their bodies. If women and girls are to live in this world with dignity and equality, their bodies and emotions must belong to them and them alone, and therefore women too must have a right to dress as freely as men.

NOTES

1 Fariha Sikondari, "Burka Ban: Why Muslim Women Cover Up," Internet, http://www.huffingtonpost.co.uk/fariha-sikondari/burka-ban-why-muslim-women-cover up_b_5585196.html (date accessed: 15 July 2014).

2 "Birmingham college makes U-turn on face veil ban," Internet, http://www.theguardian.com/uk-news/2013/sep/13/birmingham-college-uturn-veil-ban (date accessed: 19 July 2014).

3 "Calls for tougher terror controls after 'absurd' escape," Internet, http://www.itv.com/news/topic/mohammed-ahmed-mohamed/?page=2 (date accessed: 5 August 2014).

4 "Full face veil: should it be banned in public places?" Internet, http://www.secularism.org.uk/full-face-veil-should-it-be-bann.html (date accessed: 5 August 2014).

5 Hannah Furness, "Women 'remove hijabs to get work' as ethnic minorities face more discrimination," Internet, http://www.telegraph.co.uk/news/uknews/9728869/Women-remove-hijabs-to-get-work-as-ethnic-minorities-face-more-discrimination.html (date accessed: 6 August 2014). Also "Muslims discriminated against for demonstrating their faith," Internet, http://www.amnesty.org/en/news/muslims-discriminated-against-demonstrating-their-faith-2012-04-23 (date accessed: 9 August 2014).

6 "Hollobone introduces veil ban bill," Internet, http://www.islamophobiawatch.co.uk/hollobone-introduces-veil-ban-bill/ (date accessed: 15 September 2014).

7 Maleiha Malik, "Full-face veils aren't barbaric – but our response can be," Internet, http://www.theguardian.com/commentisfree/2013/sep/17/full-face-veil-not-barbaric-debate-muslim-women (date accessed: 15 September 2014).

8 Eva Brema, "Face Veil Bans in the European Court of Human Rights: The Importance of Empirical Findings," Internet, https://biblio.ugent.be/input/download?func=downloadFile&recordOId=4411976&fileOId=4412002 (date accessed: 8 November 2014).

9 Saïla Ouald Chaib and Eva Brems, "Doing Minority Justice Through Procedural Fairness: Face Veil Bans in Europe," Internet, http://www.academia.edu/3361920/Doing_Minority_Justice_Through_Procedural_Fairness_Face_Veil_Bans_in_Europe (date accessed: 8 November 2014). Also "Netherlands to ban burka, says anti-Islam MP," Internet, http://www.telegraph.co.uk/worldnews/europe/netherlands/8035778/Netherlands-to-ban-burka-says-anti-Islam-MP.html (date accessed: 9 August 2014).

10 "The Islamic veil across Europe," Internet, http://www.bbc.co.uk/news/world-europe-13038095 (date accessed: 6 August 2014).

11 Soeren Kern, "The Islamization of Belgium and the Netherlands in 2013," Internet, http://www.gatestoneinstitute.org/4129/islamization-belgium-netherlands (date accessed: 15 September 2014).

12 "Women immigrant outreach groups steer clear of burqa debate," Internet, http://www.france24.com/en/20100309-women-immigrant-outreach-groups-steer-clear-burqa-debate/ (date accessed: 10 August 2014).

13 "How many women wear the niqab in the UK?" Internet, http://www.theguardian.com/politics/reality-check/2013/sep/20/how-many-wear-niqab-uk (date accessed: 15 September 2014).

14 "French scarf ban comes into force," Internet, http://news.bbc.co.uk/1/hi/world/europe/3619988.stm (date accessed: 7 August 2014). Also Angelique Chrisafis, "Full-face veils outlawed as France spells out controversial niqab ban," Internet, http://www.theguardian.com/world/2011/mar/03/niqab-ban-france-muslim-veil (date accessed: 7 August 2014).

15 Jelle Flo and Jogchum Vrielink, "The constitutionality of the Belgian burqa ban," Internet, https://www.opendemocracy.net/jelle-flo-jogchum-vrielink/constitutionality-of-belgian-burqa-ban (date accessed: 7 August 2014). Also Katrina Nikolas, "Netherlands to ban the burqa in 2013," Internet, http://www.digitaljournal.com/article/318703 (date accessed: 8 August 2014).

16 "Germany: Headscarf Bans Violate Rights," Internet, http://www.hrw.org/news/2009/02/26/germany-headscarf-bans-violate-rights (date accessed: 8 August 2014).

17 "The Islamic veil across Europe," Internet, http://www.bbc.co.uk/news/world-europe-13038095 (date accessed: 9 August 2014).

18 Jennifer G. Andrade, "Denmark may enact French niqab ban," Internet, http://www.muslimnews.co.uk/newspaper/islamophobia/denmark-may-enact-french-niqab-ban/ (date accessed: 9 August 2014).

19 "Nicolas Sarkozy pushes for burqa ban in France," Internet, http://www.telegraph.co.uk/news/worldnews/europe/france/6556300/Nicolas-Sarkozy-pushes-for-burqa-ban-in-France.html (date accessed: 8 August 2014). Also "Belgian Parliamentary Panel Approves Draft Law Banning Full Veil In Public," Internet, http://www.rferl.org/content/Belgian_Parliamentary_Panel/1999090.html (date accessed: 10 August 2014). Also 25 "Dutch to Ban Full-Face Veils," Internet, http://www.nytimes.com/2011/09/17/world/europe/dutch-to-ban-full-face-veils.html?_r=0 (date accessed: 8 August 2014). Also "Austrian far-right party makes Islamophobic poster," Internet, http://www.worldbulletin.net/news/140006/austrian-far-right-party-makes-islamophobic-poster (date accessed: 10 August 2014). Also "Swiss Muslims Stand Against Islamophobia," Internet, http://www.onislam.net/english/culture-and-entertainment/media/454502-swiss-muslims-rise-up-against-islamophobia-.html (date accessed: 8 August 2014).

NOTES

Also "Norway braced for new burqa ban debate," Internet, http://www.thelocal.no/20140702/norway-braced-for-burqa-ban-debate (date accessed: 9 August 2014).

20 Mehdi Hassan, "Thinly veiled threat: Mehdi Hasan on the niqab," Internet, http://www.newstatesman.com/religion/2010/05/face-veil-muslim-women-ban (date accessed: 9 August 2014). *Also* "UKIP chief Nigel Farage calls for Burka ban," BBC News, Internet, http://news.bbc.co.uk/1/hi/8464124.stm (date accessed: 9 August 2013). *Also* George Eaton, "Tory MP's ban the burqa bill reaches parliament," Internet, http://www.newstatesman.com/politics/2013/09/tory-mps-ban-burqa-bill-reaches-parliament (date accessed: 10 August 2014).

21 "Head teachers against face veils in school," Internet, http://www.bbc.co.uk/news/education-24109186 (date accessed: 6 August 2014).

22 Ned Simons, "Home Office Immigration 'Racist Van' Under Investigation By Advertising Watchdog," Internet, http://www.huffingtonpost.co.uk/2013/08/09/home-office-racist-van_n_3730414.html (date accessed: 7 August 2014).

23 Sarah Isal, "Alarming rise in support for far-right European parties," Internet, https://www.theparliamentmagazine.eu/articles/news/alarming-rise-support-far-right-european-parties (date accessed: 15 September 2014).

24 Owen Boycott, "Judge compromises over niqab for Muslim woman in dock," Internet, http:// www.theguardian.com/world/2013/sep/16/muslim-woman-niqab-judge-ruling (date accessed: 6 August 2014).

25 Donna Hughes, "Men Create the Demand; Women Are the Supply," Internet, http://www.uri.edu/artsci/wms/hughes/demand.htm (date accessed: 7 August 2014).

26 Marcy Oster, "Women arrested for donning prayer shawls at Western Wall," Internet, http://www.jta.org/2012/08/19/news-opinion/israel-middle-east/women-arrested-for-donning-prayer-shawls-at-western-wall (date accessed: 7 August 2014).

27 "Malawian women protest over trouser attacks," Internet, http://www.bbc.co.uk/news/world-africa-16645594 (date accessed: 7 August 2014).

28 Henry Samuel, "Paris trouser ban for women could be lifted," Internet, http://www.telegraph.co.uk/news/worldnews/europe/france/7677686/Paris-trouser-ban-for-women-could-be-lifted.html (date accessed: 8 August 2014).

29 "European Court upholds French full veil ban," Internet, http://www.bbc.co.uk/news/world-europe-28106900 (date accessed: 15 July 2014).

30 Haroon Siddique, "Muslim Women more likely to suffer Islamophobic attacks than men — study," Internet, http://www.theguardian.com/world/2013/nov/20/muslim-women-islamaphonic-attacks (date accessed: 10 August 2014).

Closing the Gap in Indigenous Disadvantage

A Trajectory of Indigenous Inequality in Australia

Megan Davis

In recent years, the situation of indigenous peoples in Australia has been the subject of coordinated intergovernmental attention with occasional moments of recognition such as the reconciliation bridge walks, "closing the gap" (a coordinated intergovernmental agreement addressing disadvantage), and symbolic gestures such as the Apology to the Stolen Generation in 2008. While these have been important steps in Australia's "coming to terms" with its past treatment of Aboriginal and Torres Strait Islander peoples, the reality of Australia's relationship with its first peoples is more complex. Despite the recent attention, the disparity between Aboriginal and non-Aboriginal peoples continues to widen on indicators such as life expectancy and unemployment.[1]

The chasm may lie with competing notions of equality. For example, although lauded by the nation as a gesture of reconciliation, the Apology is widely critiqued in indigenous communities for its failure to provide appropriate compensation. Moreover, these incremental improvements have been piecemeal and ad hoc. There has been no overarching agreement about the impact of colonization or about how it has manifested itself in inequality.

This paper will argue that Australia's failure to close the

Megan Davis is a Professor of Law and Director of the Indigenous Law Center at the University of New South Wales. She also serves as a UN expert member of the United Nations Permanent Forum on Indigenous Peoples.

gap is due to its inability to come to terms with its past. The legal frameworks used throughout Australian history have perpetuated inequality. This paper will explain how blindness to past disparities hinders progress, using five historical periods to illustrate how legal frameworks at a constitutional, legislative, and policy level entrench inequality in the present day.

A Trajectory of Law and Policy Entrenching Inequality. Integral to understanding the inequality of indigenous communities today is the historical trajectory of indigenous-non-indigenous relations. Such an approach remains controversial in Australia. While there has been the occasional gesture of recognition such as the Redfern Speech or the Apology to the Stolen Generations, there has been no formal ventilation of competing historical narratives.[2] That the state is unwilling to come to terms with the past is demonstrated by the fact that few of the recommendations of the Royal Commission into Aboriginal Deaths in Custody, the Australian Law Reform Commission's inquiry into Aboriginal Customary Law, or the "Bringing Them Home" inquiry have been implemented. Contemporary inequality is best understood as being inextricably linked to the historical treatment of Aboriginal and Torres Strait Islander peoples.

I have divided the historical trajectory into five distinct periods: frontier, protection, self-determination, practical reconciliation, and new paternalism. Although these categories are neither comprehensive nor precise, each provides a useful counterpoint to Australia's disinclination to regard contemporary behaviors and disadvantages as a manifestation of past action and past practices.

The Frontier Period. The frontier wars, which occurred roughly from the early 1800s to the early 1900s, reflected the political economy of the dispossession of land. With rapid urban expansion of the new colony, land was needed for the pastoral industry. Aboriginal people occupied these lands, so the colony engaged in killings and massacres to obtain them. In many of the colonies, the massacres were sanctioned by law.[3] In Tasmania, the killing led to the near-extinction of the Aboriginal race.[4]

By the time the colony moved towards federation and the drafting of Australia's constitution, the Aboriginal population had dramatically lessened. The declining population coincided with the popularity of social Darwinism, which proved a convenient justification for the political exclusion of Aboriginal peoples from the nascent state.[5] This was reflected in the lack of participation in and paucity of discussion about Aboriginal people during the constitutional conventions that led to the Australian constitution. The text of the constitution reflects the dying race theory, meaning it was expected that Aboriginal people would not survive white settlement because of massacres and disease.[6]

There were two sections relevant to Aboriginal people in the new constitution. Section 127 excluded Aboriginal people from the census. As a dying race, it was argued that counting the numbers of Aboriginal people was unnecessary. Sir Edmund Barton, Australia's first prime minister, reflected this sentiment when he noted that it would "not be considered fair to include the Aborigines in population counts."[7] In Section 51 (xxvi) of the constitution (also known as the "races power"), the Commonwealth Parliament was empowered to make laws for "the people of any race, other than the Aboriginal race in any State, for whom it is deemed necessary to make

The Protection Era. The protection era lasted from roughly the late 1890s or early 1900s to 1968. It is distinguished by draconian statutes of compulsory segregation aimed at protecting Aboriginal people from mixing with the Europeans and from preventing further violence, dispersals, and spread of disease.[10] The reserves and missions were confined areas of land on which Aboriginal people were to live. Management of each reserve was delegated

Australia's failure to close the gap is due to its inability to come to terms with its past.

special laws."[8] The express exclusion of Aboriginal people from the legal domain of the Commonwealth meant that the new states would be responsible for crafting their laws.

Federation in 1901 meant the end of the frontier period. Aboriginal numbers were now severely depleted and the states had begun to forcibly remove Aboriginal populations from their traditional country and to reserves (institutions run by the state) or missions (institutions run by religious authorities) for their "own protection." This development is critical to understanding contemporary inequality. No Aboriginal group consented to British settlement or ceded land to the colonists. The silence in the constitutional arrangements on this fact has had an enduring impact on the way in which the polity views indigenous issues. The failure to resolve this fundamental issue in the frontier and federation period is a prominent feature of contemporary Aboriginal political discourse.[9]

to a superintendent. Every aspect of Aboriginal peoples' lives was regulated, including marriage, employment, freedom of movement, regulation of work, and pay from that work.[11] The superintendent had the control of the affairs of all Aborigines on a reserve relating to care, custody, and education. A permit was required to leave a reserve or to work, sale of liquor was prohibited, and Aborigines were denied possession of their own earnings.[12] The minimum wage for Aborigines set out in the 1901 regulations was one-eighth the white rate.[13] In effect, Aboriginal people were denied equality in almost every aspect of their lives.

There are two important features of this era that are critical to understanding contemporary indigenous inequality: the stolen generations and stolen wages. "Stolen generations" refers to the "half-caste" children of white colonists and Aboriginal women who were removed from their families by the state. Evidence today suggests that stolen-generation children continue to suffer from this policy of removal.[14] Many stolen-generation children were sexually abused or experienced violence in state- or church-run institutions.[15] Also, the policy of adoption into white families meant that many stolen-generation children experienced serious psychological problems stemming from dislocation and identity issues.[16]

The National Inquiry into the Separation of Aboriginal and Torres Strait Islander Children From Their Families ("Bringing Them Home") attempted to by Indigenous workers was taken by the government and held in trust for Aboriginal people, thus reflecting the paternalism of the era in which "Aborigines could not be trusted with money."[18] Each state and territory had different regimes; however, the regimes shared some common characteristics. For example, much of the money in these trust funds was spent by the state or misused by state officials. In addition, there is extensive evidence of administrators stealing indigenous workers' pocket money. The states also

Evidence today suggests that stolen-generation children **continue to suffer** from this policy of removal.

bring closure to this issue, yet it proved a contested ground. The findings of the inquiry were the subject of heated national debate, particularly in regards to the conclusion that genocide had been committed.[17] The controversy over the inquiry's findings and the failure of government to implement most of its recommendations has been a subject of criticism in the indigenous community. The "Bringing Them Home" inquiry is the closest the state has come to an official ventilation of the history; however, the government's inertia on the implementation of its recommendations is a powerful demonstration of the state's reluctance to acknowledge the past.

The other feature of the protection-era legislation is "stolen wages," a term used to describe government control over any wages earned by indigenous workers from 1897 to 1972. In every state and territory, money earned misapplied federal welfare benefits, including child endowment.

Draconian protection laws coupled with mismanagement by protection officials meant that Aboriginal people did not develop financial management skills and could not pass down money in inheritance to their children.[19] Rosalind Kidd, the leading Australian historian in this field, says that "the failure to provide for intergenerational wealth is an explanation for contemporary inequality."[20]

The treatment of Aboriginal people in reserves and missions did not go unnoticed internationally. With the development of international norms of racial non-discrimination as well as Australia's significant participation in the United Nations, pressure to address the protection regime grew. Moreover, there was a growing sense that the conditions of Aboriginal people were unacceptable and that they should have the same rights as other Australians. The protection period ended with a referendum in 1967 to amend the constitution. It removed the exclusion from the races power in Section 51 (xxvi), which had prevented the Federal Parliament from enacting laws for Aboriginal people. In addition, indigenous peoples were now to be counted in the national census, reversing the effects of Section 127 of the Australian constitution.

One might view the successful referendum as a defining national moment of recognition. The new Commonwealth authority to make laws for indigenous peoples did herald the end of the protection era. Yet, the Commonwealth continued to defer to the states on matters pertaining to indigenous communities. The federal government did not use it new powers, nor were

new government and declared a new policy era of "self-determination."

The Self-Determination Era. The
era of self-determination is characterized by the Commonwealth using the power granted to it in 1967 to develop policies aligned with indigenous political aspirations. Although the Whitlam government was only in office for a short time, the measures for which it legislated, including specialist indigenous legal and medical services as well as land rights for the Northern Territory, had far-reaching implications for the lives of indigenous Australian people.

In addition, the Whitlam government ratified the International Convention on the Elimination of All Forms of Racial Discrimination and implemented it into Australian law via the Racial Discrimination Act 1975

The treatment of Aboriginal people in reserves and missions did not go unnoticed internationally.

there new policies to realize political aspirations such as land rights or greater participation in Australian democracy that would designate parliamentary seats. As a result, there was growing discontent among Aboriginal people that they would not receive land rights. This discontent led to the establishment of the Tent Embassy in 1972, a political protest outside Parliament House in Canberra. Later that year the government that had overseen the referendum and ruled for thirty years was voted out and a new government was elected. Prime Minister Gough Whitlam led the

(RDA). The RDA has been highly effective in addressing inequality and preventing a challenge to *Mabo v. Queensland*, which saw the High Court rule in favor of the existence of native title.[21]

The other significant use of the races power during the self-determination era was the creation of a new representative body known as the Aboriginal and Torres Strait Islander Commission (ATSIC) in 1989.[22] It had a representative function, providing for non-compulsory elections. Its also advised the government on indigenous issues, advocated for the recognition of indigenous rights, and delivered and monitored some of the Commonwealth Government's indigenous program.[23] The objects of the ATSIC Act were to ensure participation of indigenous peoples in government policy formulation, to promote indigenous self-determination, to further indigenous development, and to ensure coordination of government policy affecting indigenous people.[24] These were important steps in Australia's coming to terms with the past. However, the end of the self-determination era is an equally important story because it illustrates the ad hoc and piecemeal nature of these measures and the lack of continuity that exists in indigenous law and policy from one government to the next.

The year 1996 witnessed a change of government. The new Howard administration was philosophically opposed to ATSIC and self-determination, regarding it as separatist.[25] The self-determination era therefore ceased in 2005 with the abolition of ATSIC, which was regarded as advocating "symbolic" measures such as human rights, a treaty, constitutional reform, and a bill of rights. The Howard conservative government discouraged Aboriginal rights and eschewed an apology to the stolen generations on the basis that Australians could not be blamed for the actions of previous governments.

ATSIC represents a pattern that continues in Aboriginal affairs: the making and unmaking of laws affecting indigenous rights. The insecurity of indigenous rights is inextricably linked to the vast difference in policy positions of the two major parties. Moreover, due to legislative inertia, very few recommendations from the Royal Commis-

sion into Aboriginal Deaths in Custody were implemented.[26] The same goes for the recommendations of the Australian Law Reform Commission law and the Council for Aboriginal Reconciliation.[27] The report of the National Inquiry into the Separation of Aboriginal and Torres Strait Islander Children has attracted sustained criticism. Only a few of its recommendations have been implemented, the Apology being the most publicised one.[28]

Practical Reconciliation. Howard introduced the concept of Practical Reconciliation as a counter narrative to the "symbolism" of the rights agenda. The focus would instead be on practical and pragmatic measures such as employment, housing, land tenure reform, and education. Elected representation was declared a failure for indigenous communities, and the government introduced a handpicked advisory group. This major shift in policy was called "mainstreaming," transferring all indigenous-specific programs to already existing government departments and agencies.

Aside from these developments in policy and legislation, there were significant constitutional developments during the practical reconciliation period that further highlight the inequality of legal frameworks in Australia. Two High Court decisions and the Northern Territory Emergency Response (NTER) demonstrated the vulnerability of indigenous rights to repeal or suspension by the Commonwealth. The two decisions were *Wik People v. Queensland*, related to native title, and *Kartinyeri v. Commonwealth*, also known as the Hindmarsh Island Bridge Case. Both cases revealed the unintended legal consequences of the 1967 referendum.[29] The *Wik* decision held that pastoral leases do not necessarily extinguish native title as found by the High Court in *Mabo*.[30] The Howard government responded to the decision by amending the Native Title Act.[31] To carry out this decision, the Howard government suspended the operation of the RDA, the only existing legal protection from racial discrimination. This meant the diminution of native title rights. Indigenous peoples were being singled out for adverse treatment in favor of the rights of pastoralists. The suspension of the RDA demonstrates the lack of checks and balances on the federal Parliament's power when it comes to the rights of Aboriginal peoples.

Another High Court decision during the "practical reconciliation" era came in 1998. One of the Howard government's first acts when it came to power in 1996 was to introduce legislation to Parliament (Hindmarsh Island Bridge Act 1997) that relied on Section 51 (xxvi) to prevent the Ngarrindjeri Aboriginal women in South Australia from invoking the Aboriginal and Torres Strait Islander Heritage Protection Act 1984 to stop the construction of a bridge over a sacred site. The Ngarrindjeri women challenged the act in the High Court on the basis that the Commonwealth could not use the races power (as amended in 1967) in an adverse manner. The Commonwealth argued that there are no limits on the races power so long as the consequence of the law was race, meaning that the Commonwealth could use the races power to pass discriminatory laws. In the High Court during oral argument,

the Commonwealth's lawyer argued that the races power "is infused with a power of adverse operation," with "direct racist content," and "a capacity for adverse operation." The High Court rejected the claims of the Ngarrindjeri women and left open the proposition that the Commonwealth can use the races power to impose racially discriminatory laws upon Aboriginal people. The constitutional power that promised so much in 1967 could now be used by the state to discriminate against Aboriginal peoples. The United Nations Committee on the Elimination of All Forms of Racial Discrimination was so disturbed by these developments that it placed Australia on its early warning urgent action list, the first Western country to be so named.

The Northern Territory Emergency Response (NTER), initiated in 2007, serves as a third example of the inequality of legal frameworks in Australia. The NTER was the Federal Government's emergency response to the findings of the 2007 "Little Children Are Sacred" report, which found evidence of widespread abuse of Aboriginal children and women in remote Northern Territory Aboriginal communities. The "emergency response" banned alcohol and pornography and instituted compulsory acquisition of Aboriginal land by the Commonwealth, the exclusion of customary law as a relevant factor in sentencing and bail, welfare income management, and the denial of review by the Social Security Appeals Tribunal of income management decisions.[32] The relevant Aboriginal communities including Aboriginal traditional owners and land councils were not consulted on these measures. Aboriginal people argued that the NTER was a "Trojan horse" designed to open up Aboriginal land to non-Aboriginal interests. This lack of consultation was used as evidence of the specious motives of the federal government manipulating women and children's welfare as a ruse for a grab of Aboriginal land.

As with the Wik amendments, the NTER was the subject of a complaint by a number of Aboriginal Territorians to the UN Committee on the Elimination of Racial Discrimination. The complaint emphasized the lack of prior consultation in the design and implementation of the NTER. They pointed out that many of the prescribed communities live in poverty and experience serious alcohol-related violence and abuse. Accordingly, the violence in communities was the manifestation of poverty and state neglect.

New Paternalism.

The current government has not been around long enough for scholars to determine whether the current iteration of indigenous law and policy will require a new category. Prime Minister Abbott has coined the phrase "new paternalism" to describe the current Commonwealth's approach to Aboriginal communities. In many ways, it is an extension of the practical reconciliation era. It does, however, feature many of the hallmarks of the protection era. In some communities, welfare spending is controlled.

A distinguishing feature of this government is the constitutional recognition reform process. Inherited from the previous Labor government, constitutional recognition emerged from the Prime Minister's Expert Panel on the Recognition of Aboriginal

and Torres Strait Islander Peoples in the constitution. It was established, in part, to address the discriminatory nature of Section 51 (xxvi) as discussed above in the Kartinyeri decision. The panel recommended a constitutional non-discrimination provision, stating that an entrenched non-discrimination clause is an integral part of recognizing Australian first peoples' rights. The practical need for this is based on real experiences of discrimination that indigenous people have felt at the hands of the Commonwealth Parliament as discussed above.

The submissions to the Panel from Australians overwhelmingly supported a racial non-discrimination provision.[33] Of course, most submissions argued there must also be measures to address disadvantage and ameliorate the effects of past discrimination. National surveys of Australians on the issue confirmed that 80 percent of respondents were in favor of amending the Constitution with a new guarantee against laws that discriminate on race, color, or ethnic origin.[34] However the Prime Minister, conservative politicians, and conservative constitutional lawyers are rejecting such a reform as a "back door" or "one clause" bill of rights. Their main argument against a non-discrimination provision is that such a clause would place too much power in the hands of unelected judges and that Parliament is the best protector of indigenous peoples' rights. They also argue it will lead to the fragmentation of the state on ethnic grounds. Yet, given the lengthy historical discrimination traversed in this article, it is unsurprising indigenous peoples are arguing for a constitutionally entrenched racial non-discrimination clause. This highlights the competing notions of equality. Indigenous peoples see the Government's rejection of such a constitutional provision as a rejection of the racial inequality in Australian history: a failure to come to terms with the past.

Conclusion. Chronicling indigenous inequality by reference to five distinct periods in Australian history provides an imperfect but compelling portrait of the ad hoc nature of laws, insecure rights and the disruptive manner with which law and policy is applied to indigenous communities. The piecemeal fashion in which indigenous peoples have been considered by the polity is partly a consequence of the failure to negotiate a treaty between indigenous peoples and the state. Australia is the only Commonwealth nation that has failed to negotiate this type of treaty. Australia also stands alone as the only common law country without a bill of rights that protects the fundamental rights and freedoms of citizens. As a result, indigenous people have suffered considerably, as illustrated by the ease with which the federal Parliament suspended the operation of the Racial Discrimination Act 1975.

Indigenous peoples have never attained the degree of political legitimacy required to influence public institutions. This means that indigenous rights are vulnerable to legislative repeal, which has manifested itself in a lack of autonomy that has had far reaching implications for indigenous well-being.

Moreover, the unresolved issue of sovereignty remains a source of friction. The decision in *Mabo* remains unsatisfactory for indigenous peoples who question the High Court's retrofitting of contemporary land law to the facts of settlement. The finding of the acquisition of Australia by way of peaceful settlement ignored the facts of history.[35] This resulted in the domestic law's complete denial of sovereignty of Aboriginal peoples the abrogation of Aboriginal customary law. When the Prime Minister's Expert Panel travelled across Australia in 2011, it found that sovereignty was the "top priority" in indigenous communities.[36] This was despite more than a decade of practical reconciliation eschewing the symbolism of rights. The lack of resolution of this unfinished business and the insufficient acknowledgement of the existence of first peoples has had a deep impact on indigenous identity and has manifested itself in distrust of public institutions. If Australia is to close the gap in the disparity between indigenous and non-indigenous Australians, it needs to come to terms with the antecedents of present day inequality and accept them as a continuing factor in disadvantage.

NOTES

1 Council of Australian Governments, *National Indigenous Reform Agreement* (Closing the Gap), 2009, Internet, http://www.federalfinancialrelations.gov.au/content/npa/health_indigenous/indigenous-reform/national-agreement_sept_12.pdf (date accessed: 25 November 2014). *Also* Council of Australian Governments, *Closing the Gap Prime Minister's Report*, 2014, Indigenous Chamber, Internet, http://www.indigenous-chamber.org.au/2014-closing-the-gap-report-from-the-prime-minister/ (date accessed: 25 November 2014).

2 Paul Keating, "Opportunity and Care, Dignity and Hope," (Redfern Park, Sydney, 10 December 1992), Internet, primeministers.naa.gov.au/galleries/audio/transcript-m3983-749.aspx (date accessed: 25 November 2014). *Also* Commonwealth, Parliamentary Debates, House of Representatives, 13 February 2008, 167 (Kevin Rudd).

3 Raymond Evans et al., *1901: Our Future's Past*, (London: Pan Macmillan, 1997), 27. *Also* Henry Reynolds, *The Other Side of the Frontier* (Ringwood, Vic: Penguin Books, 1982).

4 Benjamin Madley, "Patterns of Frontier Genocide 1803–1910: the Aboriginal Tasmanians, the Yuki of California, and the Herero of Namibia," *Journal of Genocide Research*, Volume 6, Issue 2 (2004), 167–192.

5 Russell McGregor, *Imagined Destinies: Aboriginal Australians and the Doomed Race Theory: 1880–1939* (Melbourne: Melbourne University Press, 1997).

7 Gordon Reid, *That Unhappy Race: Queensland and the Aboriginal Problem, 1838–1901* (Melbourne: Australian Scholarly Publishing, 2006), xii.

8 Edmund Barton, "Official Record of the Debates of the Australasian Federal Convention: 1891–1898," 8 February 1898, Melbourne, 713.

9 Australian Constitution Section 51 (xxvi), later amended by Constitution Alteration (Aboriginals) 1967 (Cth) Section 2.

10 Expert Panel on Constitutional Recognition of Indigenous Australians, *Recognising Aboriginal and Torres Strait Islander Peoples in the Constitution: Report of the Expert Panel* (2012), 205-213.

11 Reid, *That Unhappy Race*, ix.

12 Aboriginal Protection Act 1869 (Vic), Aborigines Protection Act 1886 (WA) Aboriginal Protection and restriction of the Sale of Opium Act 1897 (QLD), Aboriginal Protection Act 1909 (NSW), Aborigines Act 1910 (Vic), Aborigines Protection (Amendment) Act 1940 (NSW).

13 Rosalind Kidd, *Trustees on Trial: Recovering the Stolen Wages* (Canberra: Aboriginal Studies Press, 2006), 72.

14 Kyllie Cripps, "Indigenous Children's 'Best Interests' at the Crossroads: Citizenship Rights, Indigenous Mothers and Child Protection Authorities," *International Journal of Critical Indigenous Studies*, Vol. 5, No. 2 (2012), 25-35.

15 "Royal Commission into Institutional Responses to Child Sexual Abuse" (2013), *About the Royal Commission* (Sydney: Royal Commission).

16 *Bringing Them Home: Report of the National Inquiry into the Separation of Aboriginal and Torres Strait Islander Children from Their Families*, April 1997, Human Rights and Equal Opportunity Commission, Commonwealth of Australia 1997.

17 Ibid., 270–5.

18 Kidd, *Trustees on Trial*, v.

19 Rosalind Kidd, *The Way We Civilise* (Brisbane, Que: University of Queensland Press, 1997).

20 Kidd, *Trustees on Trial*.

21 *Mabo v. Queensland* (1988), 166 CLR 186.

22 *ATSIC Act*.

23 *ATSIC Act* §3.

24 *ATSIC Act* §3.

25 Andrew Gunstone, "The Howard Government's Approach to the Policy of Indigenous Self-Determination," *MAI Review*, Vol. 1 (2006), Internet, http://ojs.review.mai.ac.nz/index.php/MR/article/viewFile/3/3 (date accessed: 30 November 2014).

26 *Royal Commission into Aboriginal Deaths in Custody, National Report: Overview and Recommendations* (Canberra: Australian Government Publishing Service, 1991).

27 Australian Law Reform Commission, *Report into the Recognition of Aboriginal Customary Laws*, Report No. 31 (Canberra: Australian Government Publishing Service, 1986). *Also* Council for Aboriginal Reconciliation, *Recognising Aboriginal and Torres Strait Islander Rights*, (Canberra: Australian Government Publishing Service, 2000).

28 Human Rights and Equal Opportunity Commission (HREOC), *Bringing Them Home: A Guide to the Findings and Recommendations of the National Inquiry into the Separation of Aboriginal and Torres Strait Islander Children from their Families*, (Canberra: Australian Government Publishing Service, 1997). *Also* Christopher Pearson, "Conscience has the Final Say," *The Australian*, 23 July 2003. *Also* Ron Brunton, *Betraying the Victims: The "Stolen Generations" Report* (1998). *Also* Institute of Public Affairs Backgrounder, http://www.ipa.org.au/files/IPABackgrounder10-1.pdf (date accessed: 25 July 2005). *Also* Reginald Marsh, *"Lost," "Stolen" or "Rescued"? Australian Policy Towards Part-Aboriginal Children* (Quadrant, Vol. 15, 1999).

29 Wik Peoples v. Queensland (1996), 187 CLR 1, 185. *Also* Kartinyeri v. Commonwealth (1998), 195 CLR 337.

30 *Mabo v. Queensland* (1988), 166 CLR 186.

31 Native Title Amendment Act, 1998.

32 Social Security and Other Legislation Amendment (Welfare Payment Reform) Act, Sch 1. *Also* Northern Territory National Emergency Response Act, Pt 2. *Also* Families, Community Services and Indigenous Affairs and Other Legislation Amendment (Northern Territory National Emergency Response and Other Measures) Act, Sch 1. *Also* Northern Territory National Emergency Response Act, Pt 4. *Also* Northern Territory National Emergency Response Act, Pt 6. *Also* Social Security and Other Legislation

NOTES

Amendment (Welfare Payment Reform) Act, Sch 1. *Also* Social Security (Administration) Act 1999 (Cth), s 144(ka).

33 Expert Panel on Constitutional Recognition of Indigenous Australians, *Recognising Aboriginal and Torres Strait Islander Peoples in the Constitution: Report of the Expert Panel* (2012), xiv.

34 Ibid., 169.

35 Mabo v. Queenslan, No. 2 (1992), 175 CLR 1.

36 Expert Panel on Constitutional Recognition of Indigenous Australians, *Recognising Aboriginal and Torres Strait Islander Peoples in the Constitution: Report of the Expert Panel* (2012), 210.

Food Security

Fragility, Responsibility, and the Future

An Interview with Lester Brown

GJIA: In the past, grain price spikes have led to conflict and even revolution. People have argued that the Arab Spring was largely a result of this phenomenon—just how fragile do you think our world is right now?

Brown: We could be just one poor harvest away from chaos. We have carry-over stocks—the amount that is in the bin when the new harvest begins—that amount to about one hundred days of consumption. The amount of stocks that we carry was determined decades ago, but these numbers do not take into account climate change. They were determined long before the term "climate change" even existed. But with climate change, I think we need to be much more food-security conscious. I have been working on these issues for more than half a century now, and what we have seen is that historically when things get tight, people start cutting down their food consumption to one meal a day. But now we have seen a more serious stage develop where families have food-less days. There are hundreds of millions of families now in this category. For example, in Nigeria around 27 percent of all families now plan foodless days. They get together and say: "Well, we can only eat five days this week, that's all we

Lester Brown is the founder of the Worldwatch Institute, as well as the founder and president of the Earth Policy Institute. He previously worked at the U.S. Department of Agriculture as both an international analyst and the head of the department's International Agricultural Development Service.

can afford, so we'll skip Wednesday and Saturday."

GJIA: Are foodless days a regional problem, or is this something that occurs globally?

Brown: It varies country to country, but the problem is becoming widespread. In India, 24 percent of families plan for foodless days. Pakistan is 22 or 23 percent. Peru is 14 percent. The subcontinent—the area of India, Pakistan, and Bangladesh—is generally 22 to 24 percent.

assume the responsibility for India's food security, that's something they're going to have to do."

GJIA: So food security is something that individual countries need to take responsibility for in terms of their own specific capacities?

Brown: Right. And some can take responsibility just by expanding production. Others have to do it by making

We could be just **one poor harvest** away from chaos.

GJIA: Is this due to the inaccessibility of arable land or because the governments of these states are not doing enough to feed their populations?

Brown: The problem is partly a function of land availability. We think developing countries have a lot of potential ratios, but in fact most of them have already used that potential. Between 1965 and 1972, for example, India doubled its wheat harvest, but that situation only resulted from the monsoon failure of 1965. The United States acquired a great deal of political leverage over India because the United States was the only country that could even think about filling the gap between supply and demand after that monsoon. It would have taken about 12 million tons of wheat. And President Lyndon Johnson said: "Wait a minute, we can't

sure they have the purchasing power to import what they need. So it has many different dimensions. What we did in the 1965 monsoon situation was look at Indian agriculture. The food price policy was a ceiling price on grain, a price above which you could not sell. The ceiling catered to urban consumers, but did not help farmers. They knew that ceiling was there and that the margin might not have been that great. So we sat down with the leaders of the government in India. We said: "If you want us to bail you out, you are going to have to reform your agriculture." And we had a list. There were four important things, but the most important by far was to reverse the food price policy and institute price supports, so farmers could count on a price at harvest time. Then they could invest in irrigation pumps, fertilizer, or better seeds. We used that, and in the next seven years India doubled its wheat harvest. It was the culmination of irrigation, fertilizer, higher-yielding varities, and so on. No country had ever done that with a major crop before, not even the United States.

GJIA: If fifty years ago India managed to find a solution, why then is it still experiencing such a high level of food insecurity?

Brown: India has greatly increased its grain harvest—probably tripled or quadrupled it since 1950. But its population has grown about that much during that same period. So it's not that they have not been running pretty quickly, but they have not been running quickly enough to get ahead of the population growth. Some of the growth in the last decade or two has been unsustainable. It is based on over-pumping, and the World Bank estimates that 190 million people in India today are being fed mostly for wheat. But, as the aquifers were depleted in each of the four countries, the wells started going dry and the harvest started shrinking.

The four of them now import much of their grain. Fortunately, they also were oil countries so they could afford it. But they cannot keep operating this way indefinitely because their populations are growing. There is no effort to coordinate population policies and water policies, so populations are growing and water tables are falling. You do not need a PhD in math to understand that that is not a winning combination. But the Saudis, for example, who are very up front about this, have projected that by 2016, they will be out of the grain production business entirely. They have no water left, and if you do not have water in Saudi Arabia, you do not have anything. Fortunately they are

---

With climate change, we need to be much more food-security conscious.

---

with grain produced by over-pumping. By definition, this is an unsustainable situation. India is kind of borrowing from the future. In almost every state in India today, water tables are falling and wells are starting to go dry, and with each passing year there will be more. That is the big problem in a nutshell— the big risk in India. The major threat to India's future is food security. India is over-pumping and at some point the wells start to go dry. This happened in the Arab Middle East with Saudi Arabia, Syria, Iraq, and Yemen. All four countries have been over-pumping in order to expand their grain harvest, an affluent society so there is no short-term threat, at least to their security. But these are the kinds of things that are happening in the world. In the United States, we have the Ogallala Aquifer, which is a fossil aquifer that does not recharge. So once you pump it out, like an oil field, it is gone. And, it is now partly gone. But it is not that much of a threat to us, because irrigated grain production is low. We grow most of our grain in the Corn Belt: Ohio, Indiana, Illinois, and Iowa.

GJIA: Is food security a luck-of-the-draw kind of thing? Is that kind of the system that we are in at the moment?

Brown: Yes. I do not know who drew the boundary lines between the United States and Canada, but I think we must have had some geologist on our side of the table. During the glacial period, the last Ice Age, as the glaciers moved south, they pushed a lot of soil in front of them. When they retreated, they left that soil there. Iowa was on the southern edge of the path. So Iowa is just an extraordinary piece of agricultural real estate. Around most of the world, topsoil is about six inches thick. In Iowa, topsoil is six feet thick. This is exceptional, and so the United States is the agricultural superpower in the world.

The United States and China produce about the same amount of grain. China actually produces a little more than we do, but we only have 300 million people and they have 1.3 billion people. We are the world's leading exporter of grain. There is no other country close to the United States in terms of potential influence in the world if we want to use food for political purposes.

GJIA: Do you think that the United States is doing that right now, leveraging its ability to produce on a global scale?

Brown: We have, as a country, had a policy of not using food for political purposes. That does not mean it might not be in the background at some point in some negotiations, but it is never put on the table. But if we wanted to, we certainly could use it.

GJIA: Do you think that there are any

environmental constraints on production?

Brown: We used to think you had to plow every year but we now know that it is better if you can farm without plowing. As a result, zero tillage is widespread in this country. But the water issue is the one that is emerging as the principal constraint on efforts to expand world food production. There is another constraint, which is the photosynthetic constraint. Even if you have developed high-yielding seeds, and even if you make nutrient constraints and moisture constraints with irrigation, the only constraint left is photosynthesis. I call it the glass ceiling. We cannot see it, but we know it is there. And I have identified about forty crops in major countries like rice in Japan and China, wheat in France, Germany, and the U.K., where countries have hit this glass ceiling. They cannot go any higher. It is not that farmers in Japan do not want to raise rice yields more, but that there is nothing more they can do to raise rice yields. And the interesting thing is that it took Japan a century before they plateaued. China's plateau is starting much later and is now within 4 percent of Japan with rice yields. I am pretty sure they are not going to go beyond Japan, so they are about to plateau as well.

GJIA: Do you think a point will come where enough people are food insecure that there will be widespread revolution?

Brown: This could very well translate into political instability. The rising food prices were a factor in the Arab

Spring. They were not the only factor, but one of them. Remember it was a food vendor in Tunisia who set himself on fire and triggered the whole thing. For most of history, the world had never been in a situation where there was not a lot of potential for expanding food production. The year 1950 was a kind of hinge point—up until that time, almost all growth in production had come from expanding the area. But suddenly there just was not much new land to go to, as it was almost all under the plow. So, and it is remarkable how precise it is, since 1950 we have tripled the world grain harvest, and almost all of it has come from raising yields. The area grain today is almost exactly the same as it was in 1950.

differences, the lines of potential fragmentation begin to surface. The Arab Middle East is an example right now. All of these countries are true deficit countries now, and have serious water problems with no solution in sight. Iran is not one of the Arab countries but it is in that region and it is going to lose probably 20 percent of its irrigated land in the next five years or so because water tables are being depleted.

GJIA: Is there a nexus that a country must reach in order for it to become unstable? Can you predict that once grain hits X amount of dollars that we are going to see rumblings?

Brown: You would have to do it on a country-by-country basis because

We have, as a country, had a policy of not using food for political purposes.

GJIA: The issues that the world is facing seem to be caused by the failure of governments: the failure to find land and then farm it appropriately, also the failure to find and cultivate water in environmentally friendly ways. How do we address all of these problems if we want to create a sustainable future?

Brown: There is not a strong commitment to equity in these developing countries. One of the great strengths of the United States was this sense of equity, social openness, and social mobility. It is easy to create an unstable situation and not always easy to recreate a stable one. So once things begin to come apart on ethnic or religious

incomes vary, the urban share of the population varies, and migration patterns vary. These would all be things you would have to have to take in to account. We are probably going to see in a few decades around 100 million environmental refugees. Some of the refugees and people moving in the Middle East in Syria are environmental refugees. In many Arab countries, the soil and water resources have deteriorated and the wells have gone dry because the aquifers have been depleted. Grain production is declining in every one of them as a result.

GJIA: If you had to make any policy recommendations for the United States or for international organizations that are working to combat these issues, what is the best way to move forward if there are so many different problems that are at play? How do we make world food security as stable as possible?

Brown: We cannot just look at the last twenty years and project that into the

Agency for International Development and the United States Department of Agriculture who work in technical assistance programs. It does not take a genius to do these things that we are talking about, as they are fairly straightforward. But it is knowing what is needed and then figuring out a way of getting it, like I mentioned in the case

The question is whether we have the political will and are willing to push.

future because it is not going to play out that way. We need analysts, we need hydrologists, and we need a team of people doing the predictions. We need hydrologists, meteorologists, agronomists, and demographers to look at the demand side and at the whole package so that we can look at all the things that will be affecting future food supplies and food security. It would not hurt to have a nutritionist or two on the team as well to look at where we maximize nutrition on this scale. The first thing I would do would be to diversify the team making the projections to get all these things on the table. Specifically, instituting a support price would be the first single thing I would look at. Without a support price, prices go up and down and farmers do not invest in expanding production in a meaningful way because they cannot count on stability.

GJIA: Do you think there is an international organization that is equipped to handle something like that at this point?

Brown: There are people in the U.S.

of India. We changed Indian agriculture. We changed the whole philosophy, which continues today. They still have a support price, which is as it should be, and which is why India is actually exporting wheat now.

GJIA: It seems as if when one problem is fixed, there is yet another problem that must be taken into consideration. Can you describe a situation in which things have really come together correctly?

Brown: When we were looking at the monsoon failure in India in 1965, I calculated that the country needed about 12 million tons of wheat, but it had never gotten more than 4 million tons through the port in one year before. It just physically was not possible. But there were some people in the Department of Agriculture who had been in the Army Quartermaster Corps in World War II. These were the people who figured out what to do when the military wanted to move something from here to there. So to get the grain to India, they leased the Manhattan, which was the largest supertanker afloat at the time and was owned by Esso, now Exxon-Mobil. They cleaned it out and cut all the oil stains out. They anchored it in the Bay of Bengal so two U.S. ships a day would unload on one side, and on the other side all these all these boats called *dhows* could then take the grain and go up the Ganges and its tributaries to get it to the villages that needed it. We happened to have the World War II experience and logistics — these guys were the best. There is no question about whether we have the intellectual capacity to manage these issues. The question is whether we have the political will and are willing to push.

Globalization and Its Discontents

David Gow

At 9:00 p.m. on 4 August 2014, thousands of British homes switched off their lights in memory of the declaration of war against Germany a century earlier. It was a poignant recollection of the words of then-Foreign Secretary Sir Edward Grey that very day, one hundred years earlier, "the lamps [were] going out all over Europe."[1] Europeans all paid tribute to the 16 million military members and civilians killed in the First World War. That savage conflict triggered a wave of economic nationalism and revanchism exacerbated by the Great Depression; the result was mass unemployment and violent social tensions. Now, twenty-five years after the collapse of communism brought unprecedented growth and redistribution of global wealth, a failure of leadership and wave of economic nationalism threatens a return to the dark ages of protectionism, isolationism, and xenophobia.

This can be traced back to the unwillingness of governments to embrace the anti-protectionist policies that they initially adopted in 2008. Instead, they pursued strict austerity measures that fostered social exclusion rather than solidarity, and the bulk of Europeans have yet to see their incomes return to pre-2008 levels.[2] We shall see that this increase in social inequality comes with mounting insecurity.

David Gow was Scotland's first EU correspondent before joining the Guardian in 1985. He served as Germany Correspondent, Business News Editor, Industrial Editor, and others before serving as European Business Editor. He now writes for, *inter alia*, the EIU, Bertelsmann Stiftung, The Guardian and Huffington Post and is consultant editor at EuropeWatch. He is also a senior advisor to cabinet DN, a Brussels-based consultancy.

Yet the social democrat left, both in the United States and Europe, has failed to articulate an alternative narrative or promote a more equitable solution. As a result, *politikverdrossenheit* (German for being fed up with politics) is a new buzzword to describe widespread alienation.

This growing frustration with politics is dangerous for the very cross-border institutions—such as the EU and the WTO—that are designed to manage globalization and ensure its benefits are shared equitably. The EU could face break-up rather than further integration, and so too could states such as the United Kingdom and Spain, with Scotland illustrating how economic decline can align with an overall identity crisis to succor a more benign national-

the forces that ravaged Europe and the world in 1914 and, above all, from 1933 to 1945.

Rage against the machine: The rising toll of inequality and insecurity.
Mounting inequalities in wealth and incomes have brought widespread sociopolitical alienation. Globalization has undoubtedly brought hundreds of millions out of poverty in developing countries. International supply chains have been a boon to consumers in the developed world. But the systemic risks associated with globalization have engendered financial chaos and economic instability. Worse, they have caused serious social fissures and undermined faith in political institutions. Some commentators now argue

This growing frustration with politics is dangerous for the very cross-border institutions that are designed to manage globalization and ensure its benefits are shared equitably.

ism. In this article, we shall show how economic nationalism is asserted to fend off foreign direct investment and to defend "local jobs for local workers." We argue that authorities need to start treating the origins of economic nationalism and political extremism. Promoting social solidarity and fairness, curtailing the untrammeled powers of transnational corporations, and ensuring greater devolution of political power are all vital ingredients of the struggle to ensure that the benefits of globalization are retained, spread, and enhanced. The alternative is a return to

that the heyday of globalization is over; the world has demonstrably retreated back into economic nationalism.[3]

The collapse of investment bank Lehman Brothers in the fall of 2008 prompted a series of panicky meetings within the G8, G20, EU, and elsewhere to restore stability and, above all, avoid the protectionist policies adopted in the 1920s and 1930s (including the Smoot-Hawley Tariffs and others) that deepened the Depression.[4] But this initial effort soon petered out, ushering in a return to neoliberal policies and, worse, brutal austerity programs.

What economist Nouriel Roubini has described as the "backlash against globalization" spread because people perceived that they—not the bankers or the big transnational corporations—were being made to pay for the systemic failures that caused the worst recession in eighty years.[5] They detected a swift return to business as usual. Banking excesses, including willful rigging of markets and grandiose tax-evasion schemes, simply continued. The new, innovative companies of the global market exhibited similar traits, with Google, Amazon, and others manipulating fiscal residences in order to maximize profits.

The glaring income and wealth inequality highlighted by Professor Thomas Piketty and others lies behind the revolt against globalization. The High Pay Center in the United Kingdom cites evidence that in 1997, an FTSE-100 chief executive received 47 times more than their average employee; by 2012 this had risen to 133 times (still far short of equivalent U.S. levels).[6]

This rising inequality is far from the only reason for the backlash. The European Commission forecasts that unemployment in Europe will be 10.4 percent in 2015 and will remain 11.7 percent in the Eurozone—compared with 6.8 percent in the pre-crisis first quarter of 2008.[7] This masks levels of around 25 percent in Spain and Greece, where youth unemployment is above 50 percent. As this author pointed out in *Basta!*, this is the direct result of Eurozone policymakers "taking a sledgehammer to crack the wrong nut," choking off nascent but fragile recovery, and clamping down on state

spending when stimulus, especially in the form of social investment capital, was required.[8] The weak—including those denied access to good education, to learning new skills, to unions, and to the labor market—became scapegoats. The EU, set up not only to prevent any recurrence of war on the continent but also to ensure equitable sharing of the fruits of peace and prosperity, disappointed its 500 million citizens when it failed to do the latter. The record low turnout in the May 2014 elections to the European Parliament—43.09 percent—underscores the degree of alienation citizens now feel.[9] Even inchoately, these voters sense that the fruits of greater economic and political integration have been, and will remain, much less bountiful than promised. The harvest of insecurity and inequality is propelling them into the arms of nationalists who offer economic revival behind closed borders.

Europe isn't working: Why the EU's failed response to the new global competitive challenge threatens its shared institutions.

This deepening disenchantment with globalization has not yet created a dominant extremist movement on the scale of the 1930s. There is not a homogeneous, coherent far-right bloc within EU institutions, including the European Parliament (EP). But the most successful far-right leader, Marine Le Pen of France's *fascisant* Front National, has alarmingly emerged in some polls as the most popular French presidential candidate for 2017.[10] She and other right-wing extremists expound views—anti-immigrant, protectionist, authoritarian—that were anathema a decade ago, but now feed on popular discontents.

Unemployment, especially among the white working-class, is one source of this far-right revival—as is the squeeze on social benefits. But Europe's problems are more deep-rooted in an existential crisis that predates 2008-09 and has been exacerbated by globalization, radical changes to the international division of labor, and the emergence of the BRICs and other rivals. Europe, and the EU in particular, has been unable to adapt to the new world order, and the continent seriously risks being left behind in the struggle for resources, skills, and innovative thinking. Bruegel, a Brussels-based think tank, calculates that 54 percent of European jobs are at risk through computerization.[11] The EU has 7 percent of the world's population, but is in the throes of a demographic crisis. Its 25 percent share of global economic output is declining rapidly. It cannot

Growing numbers of Europeans now view the common currency, the euro, as the root of continued economic decline and the EU as the cause of dismal prospects. Even the European Commission is forecasting just 1.2 percent Eurozone growth this year and 1.8 percent in 2015—with the Eurozone trending at half the expansion rate of the United States, according to the OECD.[12] The IMF—which has cut its world growth forecast to just 3.2 percent—sees the Eurozone expanding just 1.5 percent next year and suffering from prolonged "lowflation."[13] Amid worries about the impact of tit-for-tat Russian sanctions against the West, there are fears that the European recovery is so fragile that it could easily be punctured. The one federal institution that carries trust—at least among markets—is the European Central Bank (ECB), which "saved" the euro in mid-2012 but has since been slow to react, only belatedly taking measures to combat deflation and

Anger at **uncontrollable economic hardship** and social change has morphed into rage against foreigners.

carry on financing more than half of global welfare spending as it does now. But, rather than buttressing the search for shared solutions, this multifaceted crisis is tempting political leaders to revert to nationalistic solutions.

The Eurozone crisis has accelerated the retreat to the nation state. There is now a renewed risk of recession in the wake of that crisis and the Great Recession, as most countries in Europe are recovering more slowly than ever.

stagnation.

Other EU institutions, and the ECB itself in debtor countries like Greece, are demonized for exacerbating poverty. It is hardly surprising then, that anger at uncontrollable economic hardship and social change has morphed into rage against foreigners. Even in relatively peaceful countries like the United Kingdom, the success of the U.K. Independence Party (UKIP) in channeling anti-EU, anti-immigrant, and anti-globalization sentiments has hardened mainstream political demands for brakes on the freedom of movement of labor inside the EU. This has come with an alarming recrudescence of anti-Semitism, notably since the latest Gazan conflict.[14] Overtly Nazi parties are gaining support in parts of Scots finally voted to stay in the United Kingdom, but remain at the forefront of a new constitutional settlement in the British Isles.[15]

This is not just a question of economics. Scotland is better off (in GDP per capita) than most United Kingdom regions outside London, though

The overwhelming evidence today is of a resurgence of the **ugliest forms of economic nationalism.**

Europe as the feelings of a "lost decade" intensify.

Scotland changes the goal posts: A benign economic nationalism.
Unlike their much bigger English neighbors, Scots are largely pro-EU and pro-immigrant. The run-up to the 18 September referendum on independence was rarely marked by some of the uglier xenophobic tones of the EU debate south of the border. Rather, the two-year-long debate was a mature discussion of identity and polity, and of how to handle rapid social and economic change and adapt to globalization. It was almost as if there were not two competing versions of nationalism on offer: the Scottish National Party's came with the Queen, NATO, and the Pound; the cross-mainstream party Better Together came with enhanced Scottish political institutions and fiscal powers. The two sides even embraced a similar social democratic vision of the future: one stridently anti-Tory and pro-Nordic (the SNP); the other, a softer, more traditional embrace of the empowering state. The 5.2 million

its own victims of globalization—the old industrial working class—often face poverty and early death.[16] There is, undoubtedly, a widespread feeling that it can emulate small countries, like Finland, in combining competitiveness and innovation with greater social solidarity—not the hallmarks of current Westminster thinking.[17] The British state, "captured" by an inward-looking, self-satisfied metropolitan elite, is no longer viewed as the guarantor of shared prosperity. Moreover, Scots, including pro-Union ones, are weary of the prolonged post-war identity crisis among the English and are eager to foster a more vibrant local, unique culture that is simultaneously outward looking. At the very least, this suggests that all forms of economic nationalism are not necessarily malign.

A Dwindling Globe.
In spite of this, the overwhelming evidence today is of a resurgence of the ugliest forms of economic nationalism across the globe. For the West, one of the most worrying forms is the impact of the Ukrainian conflict, with Russia imposing tit-for-

tat sanctions via bans on imported food and other agricultural produce in response to targeted measures against bodies and individuals close to Putin.[18] The G8 is an empty shell, while the Doha round of trade liberalization talks is virtually a corpse. Even the Bali Trade Facilitation Agreement (TFA) has fallen foul of Indian protectionism orchestrated by Narendra Modi, the Hindhu nationalist premier.[19] Bilateral trade deals either pending or under negotiation such as the TTIP and TPP (that exclude China and Russia) could be derailed because of the perceived need to protect local industry and agriculture. The BRICs, angry at their lack of voting power in the multilateral Bretton Woods bodies like the IMF, are setting up parallel/rival institutions such as a BRICs development bank.[20] According to the McKinsey consultancy, cross-border capital flows, which grew rapidly in the heyday of globalization, have declined 67.5 percent since mid-2007.[21]

As Mark Leonard of the European Council on Foreign Relations writes:

Many saw global trade relations as a prelude to global government, with rising powers such as Russia and China being socialized into roles as 'responsible stakeholders' in a single global system. But multilateral integration now seems to be dividing rather than uniting.[22]

As world trade growth sits below half its pre-crisis levels of 6 to 8 percent, countries like France consistently challenge the rules of economic behavior with an often *démodé* form of economic nationalism. Securing even moderate reforms is rendered almost impossible by mighty unions, yet union density is just 8 percent (compared with 74 percent in Finland).[23] The French state takes up around 53 percent of GDP. Though many, if not most, of the companies listed in the *Cotation Assistée en Continu* (CAC-40, a benchmark French stock market index) are majority-owned by foreigners, state intervention enshrined in law is the norm—as in the center-right government decision to make yogurt a strategic national asset in the proposed 2005 takeover of dairy giant, Danone, by PepsiCo.[24] The recent tussle over GE's acquisition of Alstom echoes a similar disagreement a decade ago and is equally designed to defend jobs against *délocalisation* to cheaper regions. It prompted Joaquin Almunia, the socialist European competition commissioner, to warn about "serious signals of an increase in protectionist threats in Europe."[25] Trapped in a cycle of low growth, high unemployment, weak productivity, and long since overtaken by its neighbor *outre-Rhin*, France fails to respond to emerging-market competition—and Le Pen's authoritarian *dirigisme* becomes attractive to millions by issuing false promises of keeping jobs and capital at home.

A new grand bargain? "The two tectonic shifts in the global economy—slower GDP growth and increased emerging-market competition—have created a fault line that runs through Europe," writes Ashoka Mody, visiting professor of International Economic Policy at Princeton University.[26] That fault line risks turning into a violent political chasm unless policy-makers restore faith in institutions and start to grapple with the deep-rooted anger throughout Europe and the world. This requires a fundamental shift away from austerity politics and further self-enrichment of asset wealth holders. Equally, it requires the center-left to finally abandon the policies of state-engineered redistribution of wealth via punitive income taxes and top-down welfare provision. In Europe, the EU should encourage greater growth, innovation, and new skills so that the wealth of nations is shared more equitably while old-style redistribution via state spending becomes impossible. Rather than embark upon quantitative easing, which disproportionately benefits the rich, the ECB and other policymakers should combat deflation and depression, and revisit the concept of redemption bonds to counter severe imbalances in the Eurozone economy. This has to be a rooted recovery based on investment in human and social capital, including infrastructure, rather than more debt-fueled consumption.

And, it has to come from below, with new forms of democratic participation, as power is devolved downwards.

With America in retreat, Russia at war with the West, China pursuing ultra-nationalist overseas goals, and the Middle East rent by reactionary religious and tribal conflicts, the world is a much darker place post-2008 and is increasingly unable to deal with the uneven development of globalization. The nation-state is even more incapable of providing the required new social contract based on fairness and investment. Carrying on as before is a recipe for even more political extremism and social violence. Economic nationalism is a dangerous, dead-end path that may lead to a reprise of conflict and further trampling on Enlightenment values. But it simply requires courage, vision, and confidence in human ingenuity to break the vicious circle.

NOTES

1 James Cronan, "The Lamps are Going Out all over Europe," Internet, http://blog.nationalarchives.gov.uk/blog/lamps-going-europe/ (date accessed: 5 August 2014).

2 J Bradford DeLong, "Securing the Middle Class in the Internet Age," Internet, http://www.social-europe.eu/2014/08/middle-class-in-the-internet-age/ (date accessed: 6 August 2014).

3 Ian Bremmer, "The New Rules of Globalization," *Harvard Business Review*, January-February 2014, http://hbr.org/2014/01/the-new-rules-of-globalization (date accessed: 6 August 2014).

4 David Gow, "Don't Expect Miracles...," Internet, http://www.theguardian.com/business/2009/feb/18/european-union-recession-policy (date accessed: 6 August 2014).

5 Nouriel Roubini, "The Great Backlash," Internet, http://www.todayonline.com/commentary/great-backlash-against-globalisation (date accessed: 31 May 2014).

6 High Pay Centre, "High Cost of High Pay," Internet, http://highpaycentre.org/files/High_Cost_of_High_Pay1.pdf (date accessed: 20 January 2014).

7 European Commission Economic and Financial Affairs, "EU Economy: Recovery Gaining Ground," Internet, http://ec.europa.eu/economy_finance/eu/forecasts/2014_winter_forecast_en.htm (date accessed: 25 February 2014).

8 Hannes Swoboda and David Gow, *Basta! An End to Austerity* (Brussels: European Parliament 2013).

9 Cynthia Kroet, "2014 European Parliament Election Turnout was Lowest Ever," Internet, http://www.europeanvoice.com/article/european-parliament-elections-2014-reveal-lowest-voter-turnout-ever/?preview_id=176546 (date accessed: 5 August 2014).

10 Hugh Carnegy, "Marine Le Pen Takes Poll Lead in Race..," Internet, http://www.ft.com/intl/cms/s/0/6a09af64-18a7-11e4-a51a-00144feabdc0.html#axzz3H4yMRS5r (date accessed: 7 August 2014).

11 Jeremy Bowles, "Risks of Job Computerization Across EU-28," Internet, http://www.bruegel.org/nc/blog/detail/article/1399-chart-of-the-week-54-percent-of-eu-jobs-at-risk-of-computerisation/ (date accessed: 31 May 2014).

12 OECD, "What is the Global Economic Outlook?" Internet, http://www.oecd.org/eco/economicoutlook.htm (date accessed: 31 May 2014).

13 IMF, "An Uneven Global Recovery Continues," Internet, http://www.imf.org/external/pubs/ft/weo/2014/update/02/ (date accessed: 31 May 2014).

14 Jon Henley, "Antisemitism on Rise Across Europe in 'Worst Timers Since the Nazis,'" *The Guardian*, Internet, http://www.theguardian.com/society/2014/aug/07/antisemitism-rise-europe-worst-since-nazis (date accessed: 7 August 2014).

15 Mure Dickie and Kiran Stacey, "Scotland Opens Issue of Autonomy Across UK," *Financial Times*, Internet, http://www.ft.com/intl/cms/s/0/e4c80e1a-1e4e-11e4-9513-00144feabdc0.html#axzz39zKrE5FA (date accessed: 7 August 2014).

16 Scottish Government, "Scotland's International GDP Per Capita Ranking," Internet, http://www.scotland.gov.uk/Resource/0044/00446013.pdf (date accessed: 7 August 2014).

17 Paavo Teittinen, "WEF: Finland tops Europe in Competitiveness," Internet, http://www.helsinkitimes.fi/business/10901-wef-finland-tops-europe-in-competitiveness.html (date accessed: 12 June 2014).

18 Dirk Kaufmann and Deutsche Welle, "Russia Retaliates Against EU Sanctions," Internet, http://www.dw.de/russia-retaliates-against-eu-sanctions/a-17833608 (date accessed: 5 August 2014).

19 Times of India, "India hopes to convince WTO...," Internet, http://timesofindia.indiatimes.com/india/India-hopes-to-convince-WTO-on-food-subsidy-by-September/articleshow/39782382.cms (date accessed: 7 August 2014).

20 Sameer Dossani, "BRICS Bank: New bottle, how's the wine?" Internet, http://www.brettonwoodsproject.org/2014/02/brics-bank-new-bottle-hows-wine/ (date accessed: 27 February 2014).

21 Ralph Atkins and Keith Fray, "Capital Flows: Powered Down," Internet, http://www.ft.com/intl/cms/s/0/6754e5da-76e6-11e3-a253-00144feabdc0.html#axzz39zKrE5FA (date accessed: 29 May 2014). *Also* Jonathan Wheatle, "Capital flows: the EM push-me-pull-you," *Financial Times*, Internet, http://blogs.ft.com/beyond-brics/2014/05/29/capital-flows-the-push-me-pull-you/ (date accessed: 29 May 2014).

22 Mark Leonard, "Clashes with Russia Point to Globalization's End," Internet, http://www.ecfr.eu/content/entry/commentary_clashes_with_russia point_to_globalizations_end293 (date accessed: 1 August 2014).

23 L. Fulton, "Trade Union," Internet, http://www.worker-participation.eu/National-Industrial-Relations/Across-Europe/Trade-Unions2 (date accessed: 1 August 2014).

24 Anon, "CAC 40," Internet, http://en.wikipedia.org/wiki/CAC_40 (date accessed: 1 August 2014).

25 Tom Fairless, "France Feeds New European Economic Nationalism," Internet, http://online.wsj.com/articles/france-feeds-new-european-economic-nationalism-1403869546 (date accessed: 1 August 2014).

26 Ashoka Mody, "The Global Economy's Groundhog Day," Internet, http://www.bruegel.org/nc/blog/detail/article/1413-the-global-economys-groundhog-day/?utm_source=Bruegel+Update&utm_campaign=bf42dbe3bf-Bruegel+Update_Week_32_2014&utm_medium=email&utm_term=0_cb17b0383e-bf42dbe3bf-273935242 (date accessed: 1 August 2014).

Conflict&Security

The Abe Factor

Sheila Smith

Since his election as prime minister in December 2012, Abe Shinzo has attracted global attention. Abe is not a new face on the global stage; this is his second time serving in Japan's highest elected office. But his bold agenda of reform has created the image of a newly assertive Japan. At home, Abe enjoyed wide support as he sought to institute broad economic, security, and diplomatic reforms.[1] Abroad, Abe's ambitions for Japan created particular worries in Northeast Asia, as China and South Korea were quick to see in the prime minister a revisionist impulse that harkened back to an earlier era of geopolitics. As Washington's closest ally in the Pacific, Japan's foreign policy choices have long shaped the United States' strategic goals, and Tokyo's tense relations with its neighbors in Northeast Asia pose particular challenges for the Obama administration.

While Abe's leadership may explain the new tenor of Japan's assertion of its strategic interests, it is insufficient to explain why the Japanese are reconsidering some of their past foreign policy choices. Indeed, there is a revival of strategic debate in Japan, a debate that began before Abe returned to office. A rising China posed considerable challenges for Tokyo policymakers, and the tensions that erupted over

Sheila Smith is currently the senior fellow for Japan studies at the Council on Foreign Relations (CFR). Prior to joining CFR, Smith worked at the East-West Center.

the disputed islands in the East China Sea in 2010, and again in 2012, only amplified Japan's anxiety over China's ambitions. Abe did not create this standoff with Beijing over the Senkaku Islands, but his cabinet had to cope with rising popular antipathy towards China. Moreover, Beijing's challenge to Tokyo's sovereignty islands raised confidence in the government plummeted as politicians bickered, failing to come together to set their country on a better path.

Prime Minister Abe and the Return of the LDP.
Abe's Liberal Democratic Party (LDP), Japan's ruling party for most of the postwar period,

Abe's ambitions for Japan created particular worries in Northeast Asia, as China and South Korea saw in the prime minister a revisionist impulse that harkened back to an earlier era of geopolitics.

the possibility of a clash between the militaries of Asia's two largest powers.[2] To make matters worse, when tensions with China were rising, South Korean President Lee Myun-bak visited a set of islands contested by his country and Japan, resulting in a severe deterioration in Japan-South Korea relations and posing yet another challenge for the new Abe government.

Abe's return to power stabilized politics at home, and this explains his strong domestic support. For almost a decade, politics in Tokyo were fractious as politicians pitted themselves against bureaucrats and realigned in an evolving array of political coalitions. A historic turning point came when a new contender for power, the Democratic Party of Japan (DPJ), emerged to win the Lower House in 2009. Three successive DPJ cabinets struggled to govern, and Japan was badly shaken by two unprecedented crises: escalating tensions with China and the Great East Japan Earthquake.[3] Japanese public

spent three years in opposition, chastened by their defeat. DPJ Prime Minister Noda Yoshihiko had attempted to forestall the widely publicized plan by Tokyo governor Ishihara Shintaro, a well-known anti-China nationalist, to purchase the islands in an effort to demonstrate Japanese sovereignty. But Noda's decision to have the Japanese government acquire them instead set off the intense protests in China, and the era of bilateral management of differences over the islands came to an end. Thus, in September 2012, Abe contended for his party's leadership as anti-Japanese demonstrators swarmed the streets of scores of Chinese cities including Beijing, Shanghai, Guangzhou, and even Hong Kong, and as the Chinese government sent maritime patrols to the Senkaku Islands to challenge Japan's control over them.[4]

The Japanese public was outraged at Chinese behavior, and this shaped the LDP leadership race. Four of the five contenders argued for defending their sovereignty against Beijing's challenge, with Abe going so far as advocating for permanently stationing Japanese officials on the islands. In the Lower House election that followed, Abe campaigned for a stronger national defense policy, with particular attention paid to the Senkaku Islands. It did not go unnoticed when China sent a small surveillance plane over the islands a day before the election, which further focused the Japanese voter's attention to the islands as they headed to the polls.

Once in office, the challenge for Abe over the island dispute remained, but his cabinet faced a host of other, more pressing policy priorities. The cabinet's top priority was to improve the Japanese economy, and it adopted an aggressive growth strategy dubbed "Abenomics."[5] In addition, Abe took on some of the defense reforms he had considered during his first term in office. He created a new National Security Council and passed a new secrecy protection law. He revamped the National Defense Program Guidelines and increased defense spending to allow for a more ambitious five-year defense procurement plan. Finally, he argued for relaxing the government interpretation over the use of force by Japan's postwar military, the Self Defense Force (SDF), to allow them to work alongside the militaries of the United States and other partners.[6]

A new diplomatic push was also high on Abe's agenda. His first priority was to solidify the U.S.-Japan alliance, and he visited President Obama in Washington in February 2013. There he promised to move forward with Japan's participation in the Trans-Pacific Partnership, a multilateral free trade initiative championed by the United States.

He also reassured the Obama administration that Japan would not do anything in the East China Sea to increase the risk of a military clash with China, and promised calm and steady management of the maritime tensions.

Abe's diplomatic outreach to South Korea, however, made little progress, as the new government openly criticized Abe and his conservative party's views on history. Senior officials in both countries also seemed mismatched. South Korea's new foreign minister was openly hostile to Japan while Aso Taro, Abe's emissary to President Park's inauguration, managed to offend the new president.

Eventually, growing concern over the estrangement between Seoul and Tokyo began to influence U.S. alliance planning. Secretary of Defense Chuck Hagel visited Seoul to celebrate the sixtieth anniversary of the U.S.-South Korea alliance. Following that, Hagel went to Tokyo for high-level security consultations with the Japanese government. The United States and Japan announced that they would review their bilateral defense cooperation guidelines to take into account the rapidly changing security situation in Northeast Asia. This provoked Korean media criticism, followed by the Korean government expressing concern that the United States was encouraging a role for the Japanese SDF in a Korean contingency. For the first time, the historical issues that hindered strategic cooperation between Seoul and Tokyo were beginning to impinge upon U.S. alliance management.

Despite Abe's focus on Japan's economic recovery and his success in reforming security planning institutions, the prime minister's views on Japan's past remained a focus of criticism. Early in his time in office, Abe gave an interview in the *Sankei Shimbun* suggesting doubts about Japan's statements of remorse for its behavior during the wars of the early twentieth century, raising concerns that he would abandon them in favor of a more revisionist view of Japan's past. A related concern existed over whether he would make an official visit to the controversial Yasukuni Shrine, which honors Japan's wartime deaths. During his first term in office, Abe emphasized the need to improve relations with both China and South Korea, and refrained from visiting the shrine.[7]

The second Abe cabinet, however, took a different tack. Abe did not immediately visit Yasukuni, but Deputy Prime Minister Aso visited in Abe's stead in April 2013, along with three other cabinet members. A week or so later, during Diet deliberations, the prime minister drew criticism when he appeared at Yasukuni Shrine to make a formal visit. Immediately and predictably, the governments of China and South Korea expressed their outrage. Less anticipated but perhaps even more striking was the statement of "disappointment" issued by the U.S. government. For the first time, Washington and Tokyo understood the strategic impact of this challenge to the postwar settlement differently. The refusal of Chinese and South Korean leaders to meet with Abe challenged Japan's regional diplomacy through the end of 2013.

The Postwar Settlement in Northeast Asia.

Sensitivities over the past and reactive nationalism across the region continue to be amplified by geostrategic shifts. The emphasis by Beijing and Seoul on Japan's legacy of war and expansion in the twentieth century still inhibits Tokyo's ability to forge close diplomatic relations with its neighbors. Moreover, Japan's internal debate over

Abe's first priority was to solidify the U.S.-Japan alliance.

stated that he was not convinced that Japan "invaded" China during World War II. From that point onwards, the Japanese press began to focus on whether the prime minister himself would go to the controversial shrine. The August 15 commemoration of the end of the war passed without a visit, but on October 19 Abe noted in the Diet that he "regretted" not visiting the shrine during his first term in office. Finally, on December 26, Abe suddenly its own legacy of war and occupation, as well as its postwar constitution, also shapes the shifting regional balance of interests. Advocacy of constitutional revision is interpreted by some in the region as a disavowal of Japan's postwar doctrine of limited military power, and Abe's own discomfort with national policy statements on the past only exacerbates regional concerns about Japan's future path.

Within and across nations in northeast Asia, the postwar settlement is being called into question, and in new ways. Questions about territorial sovereignty and control are now linked to questions about the legitimacy of the postwar peace. While the San Francisco Peace Treaty outlined the terms of peace with Japan, both South Korea and China were absent from that deliberative process. Separate peace treaties between Japan and South Korea in 1965 and between Japan and China in 1978 eventually outlined terms of peace, including compensation for wartime losses and generous postwar aid and investment treaties. Yet today in South Korea, that diplomatic treaty is being called into question through legal cases in the Constitutional Court. Three cases claim that the government of South Korea did not adequately represent those who were injured by Japanese wartime behavior. In 2011, the Constitutional Court judged that the South Korean government had failed to gain an adequate apology and compensation for the suffering of Korean women who worked in the wartime brothels of the Japanese army. Currently the court is hearing two more cases claiming the South Korean government did not gain full compensation for forced labor during wartime by two Japanese companies. The use of domestic courts to challenge wartime compensation is also beginning in China, and in April 2014, the Shanghai Maritime Court awarded damages to a Chinese company whose property was confiscated by the Japanese military during the war after a protracted court case.[8]

Japanese views on past efforts at reconciliation are also changing. Tensions with China over maritime boundaries,

food security, and the island dispute led to greater skepticism about the Chinese government. Emotions ran higher toward South Korea after 2012, with many Japanese expressing a sense of betrayal that Koreans would abandon their close relations with Japan in favor of a rising China. Today, nationalist advocates in Japan are willing to demonstrate their displeasure with both Chinese and South Korean critics. This diplomatic estrangement with Seoul created a new bitterness in the political debate in Tokyo and despite the Abe cabinet's repeated statements that Japan's door was open to political talks, there was little appetite for a renewed effort at reconciliation.

Washington also began to consider the diplomatic estrangement between Tokyo and Seoul differently. The costs to the U.S. of this deterioration in relations between its two allies in Northeast Asia were obvious. Coordination on North Korea, still the greatest potential challenge to regional security, had weakened. Furthermore, the refusal of leaders from both countries to sit down to resolve their differences made reconciliation impossible, and heightened the risk that the allies would be unprepared to cooperate should a crisis emerge. Eventually, the Park government's refusal to meet with Japanese officials and Abe's decision to visit Yasukuni Shrine prompted the Obama administration to act. In early 2014, through consultations with the staff of all three leaders, President Obama convened a meeting between Abe and Park on the sidelines of the Nuclear Security Summit at The Hague. While the purpose of this trilateral summit was to discuss North Korea and other shared security concerns, this first meeting between Park and Abe was also the much-needed opportunity to initiate talks on how to resolve differences over the legacies of war. This meeting, however, was only the beginning; the Japanese and Korean governments needed to find a way forward on resolving the continued demands of those who were dissatisfied with the terms of their 1965 postwar peace treaty.

Perhaps the most telling reflection of how much attitudes in Japan had changed came during the debate over the Kono Statement, the formal Japanese apology for the treatment of Korean women recruited for wartime brothels. Conservative critics in parliament began to demand a retraction of the statement, and parliamentary hearings were called to review the government's decision to issue the apology. The new Japan Restoration Party (*Ishin no Kai*) began this formal inquiry, although there were many inside Abe's own party who also wanted the statement rescinded. Chief Cabinet Secretary Suga Yoshihide created a review board of experts, and on June 20, the results were published. The report refuted the charge that the Japanese government had based its statement of remorse solely on hearsay. Additionally, it addressed other questions about the Asian Women's Fund, a fund established by private donations and government funds for atonement and support for the victims of this system of abuse, and outlined the deliberations with the South Korean government on how to best reach out to the women who had suffered. While this has satisfied the more pointed criticism within the Japanese legislature

for the moment, the policy review was immediately denounced by the South Korean government as evidence of the Abe cabinet's lack of "sincerity."

Abe and his party bring renewed attention to Japan's own postwar settlement, and two issues in particular motivate Japan's conservatives. The first is how to honor Japan's war dead, and here opinion is divided.[9] Abe's decision to visit Yasukuni at the end of 2013 was not made through consultations among party leaders or with the rank-and-file members of his party. While some conservatives advocate for visiting Yasukuni, others advocate for different venues for honoring Japan's war dead. The second issue, however, is less divisive within the LDP, and is contained in its manifesto: the desire to revise the Japanese constitution, particularly to remove the limitations on the SDF. In his New Year's address in 2014, Abe argued for change, pointing out that in the half-century or more since the Japanese constitution was promulgated, Japan had gone through tremendous social change. Amending it to reflect those changes would, in Abe's words, restore "a Japan we can be proud of."[10]

Short of formal revision, however, Abe has already begun to remove some of the limits on the SDF. After consultations with his coalition partner, the Komei party, the Prime Minister announced on July 1 that his government would reinterpret the Constitution to allow for the right of collective self defense. This would allow the SDF to do more with other militaries to ensure Japan's security.[11] For the United States, Japan's willingness to consider relaxing this constraint on the SDF was seen as an important step towards enhancing allied military cooperation. Washington's policy planners did not hesitate to endorse the Abe cabinet's goal of considering a reinterpretation of Article 9.[12]

But, there is a broader debate in Japan over whether its postwar strategy will continue to serve its needs in a changing Asia. Abe returned to office with a far different parliamentary balance than when the LDP lost power in the 2009 election. Today, there are political parties to the right of the LDP advocating constitutional revision and a stronger national military strategy. To be sure, the cabinet has done much to improve decision-making on Japanese security. Crisis management and alliance coordination is expected to improve under the new National Security Council, and the national secrets law that accompanied it should help as well. The cabinet has also presided over an unprecedented shift in Japanese policy towards arms transfers in the region. And, finally, the prime minister has pursued strategic partnerships with a host of regional partners.

critics, both within and outside Japan, sensitive to his views on Japan's prewar past. But the Abe factor is only part of the explanation. As China's influence raises questions about the postwar order, Japanese politicians are seeking to revitalize their nation's economy and enhance its defenses.

Those who see a long overdue decision to "normalize" defense policy in Abe's security reforms rarely link these policy changes to a revisionist narrative on Japan's past. Likewise, those who focus on Japan's revisionists tend also to see evidence of militarism in all security policy decisions. These two ways of looking at Japan are also reflected in the way Abe himself is portrayed. For some, he is a conservative nationalist, while for others he is a much-welcomed leader with strategic vision.

But Abe may very well be both, and in today's Northeast Asia he is not alone. Revisionist nationalism is closely attended by a renewed interest in asserting strategic interests, and Japan is no exception. Labeling Abe as a rightist or a nationalist, in fact, obscures the more complicated reality. Popular sen-

Labeling Abe as a rightist or a nationalist, in fact, obscures the **more complicated reality.**

Abe: Nationalist or Strategist?

The combined effect of geostrategic change and a growing demand to question the terms of the postwar peace within Japan, South Korea, and China fuels nationalist impulses across the region.

Almost two years after his election, Abe continues to serve as a lightning rod for

timents are volatile across the region, and political leaders see opportunity in advocating for nationalist causes as a means of gaining support for strategic aims. This is as true for Japan as it is for South Korea and China. The use of a nationalist narrative that draws on the suffering caused by the wars of the twentieth century has been irresistible as these three nations reorient their strategic focus; but these narratives are also used to isolate Japan.

The fusion of historical legacy with strategic reorientation has profound implications for the United States. Not only is the United States a treaty ally of Japan and South Korea, but it is also trying to build a new strategic relationship with a rising China. As tensions outside of Asia such as the Ukraine crisis and the rise of the Islamic State divert U.S. attention, Japanese perceptions about the reliability of the United States as a global leader are again changing. As the postwar settlement in Northeast Asia is being reconsidered, so too is the U.S. role in ending World War II and establishing the terms of the postwar peace. As next year's celebration of the seventieth anniversary of the end of World War II approaches, Tokyo and Washington need to think carefully about how their past will inform Asia's future and how the U.S.-Japan alliance can speak more directly to the popular demand for a reexamination of the postwar settlement in Northeast Asia.

NOTES

1 Prime Minister Abe's popular support peaked in April 2013 with an approval rating of 74 percent, and even at its lowest point has not dropped below 48 percent, according to monthly polls conducted by the *Yomiuri Shimbun* on 16 April 2013 and 4 July 2014, respectively.

2 *See* Sheila A. Smith, "A Sino-Japanese Clash in the South China Sea," *Council on Foreign Relations*, April 2013.

3 The first in 2010 pitted the new government against Beijing when a Chinese fishing trawler captain rammed two Japan Coast Guard vessels, setting off the worst diplomatic confrontation between the two nations in postwar history. A year later, the Great East Japan Earthquake and accompanying tsunami caused the meltdown of nuclear reactors at the Fukushima Daiichi plant and a tremendous loss of life. According to the latest figures from Japan's National Police Agency, 2,601 people remain "missing," separate from the 15,899 killed. *See* National Police Agency of Japan, "Damage Situation and Police Countermeasures associated with 2011 Tohoku District," Internet, http://www.npa.go.jp/archive/keibi/biki/higaijokyo_e.pdf (date accessed: 29 November 2014).

4 NPR, citing Kyodo, reported up to 85 cities in all. *See* Louisa Lim, "Second Day of Anti-Japan Protests Rock China," Internet, http://www.npr.org/2012/09/16/161228298/chinese-flood-streets-in-anti-japan-demonstrations (date accessed: 29 November 2014).

5 "Abenomics" was a policy combination of government stimulus; inflation targeting by the Bank of Japan; and structural reform that encompassed a broad array of institutional reform including agricultural reform, increasing the participation of women in the economy, and upping the incentives for investment in Japan.

6 *See* Office of the Prime Minister and His Cabinet, *Cabinet Decision on Development of Seamless Security Legislation to Ensure Japan's Survival and Protect its People* (Tokyo, Japan: Cabinet Public Relations Office, Cabinet Secretariat, 2014), Internet, http://japan.kantei.go.jp/96_abe/decisions/2014/__icsFiles/afieldfile/2014/07/03/anpohosei_eng.pdf (date accessed: 29 November 2014).

7 Past Japanese prime ministers who had sought to normalize visits to the shrine were met with criticism from Beijing and Seoul; but there was also growing resentment of this criticism within Japan, and a group of parliamentarians from the LDP, DPJ and other parties visited the Shrine to note their displeasure with what they openly criticized as "foreign" pressure in the domestic affairs of Japan. *See* Sheila A. Smith, *Intimate Rivals: Japanese Domestic Politics and a Rising China* (New York: Columbia University Press, 2015).

8 *See* "China Court Releases Japanese Ship after 28.5 mln USD Payment," *Xinhua*, 24 April 2014, Internet, http://news.xinhuanet.com/english/china/2014-04/24/c_133286549.htm (date accessed: 29 November 2014). *Also* Mitsui O.S.K. Lines, Ltd, "Chinese Authorities Impound MOL Vessel", Internet, http://www.mol.co.jp/en/pr/2014/14021.html (date accessed: 29 November 2014).

9 For a fuller examination of the politics of prime ministerial visits to Yasukuni Shrine, see Sheila A. Smith, *Intimate Rivals: Japanese Domestic Politics and a Rising China* (New York: Columbia University Press, 2015), chapter three.

10 Shinzo Abe, "New Year's Reflection," Internet [English translation available], http://japan.kantei.go.jp/96_abe/statement/201401/newyear_e.html (date accessed : 29 November 2014).

11 The Advisory Panel on Reconstruction of the Legal Basis for Security, tasked with making recommendations to the prime minister on how to rationalize the laws that organized Japan's security planning, argued for far greater changes than Abe ultimately proposed. In its report, the advisory panel argued for allowing Japan to play a far greater international role through collective security arrangements in the United Nations, as well as to open up the possibility of greater military cooperation with other partners in the Asia-Pacific. In addition, the commission also took another careful look at the limitations imposed on Japan's military exercising the right to self-defense on their own, arguing that technology and the changing military balance in Asia required a relaxation of limitations imposed on the SDF in a far earlier and less dangerous time. *See* the The Advisory Panel for Reconstruction on the Basis of Security, *Report of the Advisory Panel on Reconstruction of the Legal Basis for Security*, the Prime Minister's Office website, Internet [English translation available], http://www.kantei.go.jp/jp/singi/anzenhosyou2/dai7/houkoku_en.pdf (date accessed: 29 November 2014).

12 At a 2+2 meeting in Tokyo between the U.S. Secretaries of Defense and State and their Japanese counterparts in October 2013, the Joint Statement read:

Japan's security policy continues to reflect its long-standing commitment to regional and global peace and stability, as well as its intention to make more proactive contributions to addressing the challenges faced by the international community. At the same time, Japan will continue coordinating closely with the United States to expand its role within the framework of the U.S.-Japan Alliance. Japan is also preparing to establish its National Security Council and to issue its National Security Strategy. In addition, *it is re-examining the legal basis for its security including the matter of exercising its right of collective self-defense,* expanding its defense budget, reviewing its National Defense Program Guidelines, strengthening its capability to defend its sover-

NOTES

eign territory, and broadening regional contributions, including capacity-building efforts vis-à-vis Southeast Asian countries. The United States welcomed these efforts and reiterated its commitment to collaborate closely with Japan (*emphasis added*). See the full Joint Statement at: http://www.state.gov/r/pa/prs/ps/2013/10/215070.htm.

Collective Insecurity in the Sahel

Fighting Terror with Good Governance

Richard Downie

On 14 April 2014, gunmen from the Nigerian Islamist extremist group Boko Haram seized more than 250 girls from their school dormitory in the remote northeastern town of Chibok as they prepared to take their final examinations. The attack was only the latest in an escalating series of bombings, murders, and kidnappings committed by the group—a nihilistic, fragmented coalition of Islamists, criminals, political agitators, and embittered young men nominally committed to overthrowing the Nigerian government in the name of fundamentalist Islam. It prompted a typically lethargic response from the authorities, who took no action despite a campaign of daily demonstrations in Abuja led by Nigerian civil society activists. Unofficial campaigning for the 2015 national elections continued without pause. For nearly three weeks, President Goodluck Jonathan offered no public comments about efforts to retrieve the girls. Parents of the missing girls, exasperated by the Nigerian military's inertia, risked their own lives by pursuing the attackers into the forest.[1]

While Nigeria's political class appeared unmoved by the tragedy, it struck a chord with the global media, which propelled the story to the top of the news headlines. Pressure

Richard Downie is the Deputy Director of the Africa Program at the Center for Strategic and International Studies.

mounted on the Nigerian government to accept international help. Soon, the United States, France, the United Kingdom, China, and others were providing assistance, including surveillance assets, intelligence-sharing resources, hostage negotiators, and military advisors. But while expectations surged that the girls would soon be freed, more than three months later there was little sign of progress. Not a single girl had been released and Boko Haram's attacks continued apace.

Why is it that Nigeria, urged on by its international partners, has been unable to make a breakthrough in tackling Boko Haram? This article argues that overcoming regional terrorism is an arduous, long-term endeavor requiring a combination of elements that have been absent from Nigeria's response so far. They include the deployment of professional security forces that respect human rights, community engagement, and cooperation with neighboring states. Most of all, defeating regional terrorists requires genuine political commitment to tackle some of the underlying governance challenges and economic grievances that provide the motivation—and recruitment tools—for violent extremist organizations (VEOs). The international community must also rethink its strategy for supporting African allies confronted with terrorism. Too often, efforts are confined to tackling the symptoms of violence through military "train and equip" programs rather than focusing on terrorism's root causes. By doing so, countries like the United States and France buttress governments whose incompetence and venality help fuel and sustain insurgencies. Similar lessons apply to countries

confronted by terrorism in the broader Sahel region, the band of fragile states spread precariously below the Sahara Desert. They include Mali, where a corrupt civilian government was toppled for bungling its response to a nationalist uprising that was subsequently hijacked "by extremist groups," including al-Qaeda in the Islamic Maghreb (AQIM). International actors—the key bilateral partners in this region being France and the United States—must resist the temptation to pursue quick fixes to deep-seated security problems and must balance engagement with governments with strategies to encourage broader governance reform. In tandem with these efforts, a long-term strategy must be devised to foster sustainable, African-led solutions to insecurity that draw in regional and sub-regional organizations like the African Union (AU) and the Economic Community of West African States (ECOWAS).

The Rising Terrorist Threat in Nigeria and the Sahel. Parts of

Africa have encountered terrorism for many years, but the threat has traditionally been confined to two distinct areas: coastal east Africa and the Maghreb. During the past decade, however, the zone of terrorist operations has expanded to include the Sahel, an impoverished region incorporating all or part of ten countries extending from Senegal in the west to Eritrea in the east. This region is now the epicenter of extremist activity, and a glance at its political, economic, geographic, and demographic features helps explain why.

The Sahel is one of the poorest regions in the world. It contains fast-growing populations with few economic opportunities. Its people have learned to survive in a hostile, food-insecure environment, but their coping strategies are coming under intolerable pressure from climate change, which is accelerating the southward push of the Sahara. The core states of the Sahel—Mauritania, Mali, and Niger—are near the bottom of the UN Human Development Index, with Niger occupying the very last position, at 187.[2] Nigeria

While countries like Mali and Nigeria appear to have little in common, they share a woeful record of public governance that has helped add extra fuel to the flames of violent insurgencies.[6] Since independence, their ruling elites have governed in bad faith, operating unofficial networks and favoring special interest groups, whether regional or ethnic. Corruption has run rampant. Security forces have acted with impunity, protecting incumbent

Overcoming regional terrorism is an arduous, long-term endeavor requiring a combination of elements that have been absent from Nigeria's response.

is an exception. It has Africa's largest population, largest GDP, and is the largest oil producer on the continent.[3] These riches produce a different set of problems, breeding a political elite dependent on oil rents and overseeing public corruption on an industrial scale. When the head of Nigeria's Central Bank, Lamido Sanusi, accused Nigeria's national oil company of failing to account for almost $20 billion of revenue, he was threatened with prosecution and forced out of office.[4] Nigeria's headline GDP figure obscures its deep economic inequalities. The six states that comprise Nigeria's northeast are the most impoverished in the nation, with high unemployment, poor educational outcomes, and non-existent public services.[5] It is a political backwater, neglected by a central government cocooned in Abuja and content to see an opposition stronghold wither. It is no coincidence that this is the region that produced Boko Haram.

regimes rather than the public. Economic mismanagement and a lack of strategic vision have combined to deny opportunities for their increasingly young populations, whose aspirations for education and employment have been unmet. These conditions provide fertile ground for the growth of VEOs and organized crime networks that prey upon the thwarted ambitions of the region's young people.

For both countries, the results have been catastrophic. In Nigeria, Boko Haram has morphed in the space of a decade from an obscure religious sect into a vicious insurgency that has captured territory and murdered more than two thousand civilians in the first half of 2014 alone.[7] In Mali, the government's failure to quell an uprising in the north led to a mutiny in 2012, a coup d'état, and the transformation of the northern security crisis into a terrorist insurgency that rapidly engulfed two-thirds of the country before the

French military intervened. Terrorism, therefore, is a manifestation of deep-seated problems in these African societies.

The Response So Far: Halfhearted and Ineffective.

Efforts by Nigeria and its neighbors in the Sahel to deal with terrorism have failed. In Nigeria, Boko Haram poses a more potent threat than at any time in its existence. In Mali, the terrorist grip on the north of the country was only loosened by a French intervention that was supported by West African states. The Malian authorities were mere observers.

A number of factors explain this ineptitude. First, the scale and complexity of the threat must be recognized. Western nations and civil society activists who chastise the Nigerian government for failing to rescue the Chibok girls do not sufficiently acknowledge that any attempt to rescue such a large number of hostages, held in multiple locations by merciless fighters, would inevitably result in mass casualties. More broadly, conducting successful counterterrorism operations is a challenging task requiring patience, skill, and a long-term strategy—as the United States learned to its cost in Iraq and Afghanistan. Even so, Nigeria's counterterrorism efforts have been woefully inadequate, even counterproductive. There are major doubts about the commitment of the Nigerian authorities to tackle Boko Haram. As Nigerians in the northeast have been attacked, kidnapped, and had their homes destroyed, the ruling elite in faraway Abuja has shown more interest in using the crisis to trade accusations and seek advantage over their political opponents than in coming up with a serious response. The indifference shown by the Nigerian government to its own population illustrates just how detached Nigeria's political class has become from its citizens.

In neighboring Cameroon, a desire for self-preservation explains why the authorities were so slow in taking the offensive to Boko Haram. President Paul Biya was only jolted into action when his close confidante narrowly escaped a kidnap attempt in July. In Mali, the former government of Amadou Toumani Touré was long suspected by its neighbors of turning a blind eye to the activities of AQIM in the north, perhaps out of fear that a military assault would upset a fragile rapprochement with former rebel groups. Whatever the reasons for this inactivity, it turned out to be a costly miscalculation when the group overran vast swathes of the country in 2012.

In light of this official indifference, it comes as no surprise that populations in the region have sometimes displayed ambivalent attitudes toward the nonstate actors operating in their midst. This is particularly true in Mali, where groups like AQIM gained a foothold in communities by offering public services that the state was either unwilling or unable to provide. The almost total absence of any social compact between the state and its people is further illustrated by the way state security forces have interacted with civilians in areas affected by terrorism. In Nigeria, the federal Joint Task Force has almost matched Boko Haram in its brutal treatment of civilians, meting out collective punishment of communities suspected of harboring Boko Haram members, detaining young people at random, and doing little to minimize civilian casualties. Human rights groups have made allegations, backed up by apparent video evidence, of extrajudicial killings carried out by the Nigerian military and officially sanctioned vigilante groups.[8]

The general incompetence of the military response has been staggering. The security forces in most of the Sahel lack training and leadership; they are demoralized, unprofessional, and in some cases deliberately under-resourced by coup-fearing civilian leaders.[9] In Nigeria, regular troops with the 7th Division have on several occasions refused to fight in Borno state, claiming their superiors have siphoned off funding that was meant to feed and equip them.[10] As a result, they are poorly prepared to launch counter-insurgency operations against a brutal, committed enemy.

Among the governments of the region, there is little appetite to think beyond military responses to terrorism and confront its root causes, because that would involve reflecting upon their own governance shortcomings. While Nigeria's National Security Advisor, Colonel (ret.) Sambo Dasuki, attempted to outline a more comprehensive approach to Boko Haram, including de-radicalization programs, community engagement, and efforts to address economic grievances, the Nigerian government has made little apparent effort to implement the plan.[11] Time and again, requests for international assistance involve little more than the submission of wish lists for military equipment.

A final, missing ingredient in Africa's response to the terrorist threat posed by groups like Boko Haram is the failure of states to work effectively together. The relationship between Nigeria and Cameroon highlights these shortcomings. Close cooperation between these two neighbors is critical for countering Boko Haram, which moves with ease over the poorly guarded international border, launching attacks on both sides. However, Nigeria denies Cameroon's military the right to pursue terrorists into its territory. In Cameroon, there are strong suspicions that the authorities, despite their denials, have fueled the insurgency by colluding with European powers in paying ransoms to free European hostages held by Boko Haram.

Embryonic efforts are underway to boost regional cooperation through the Lake Chad Basin Commission security initiative, including moves to set up a Regional Intelligence Fusion Unit.[12] These plans offer some cause for optimism, but it has yet to be seen whether this unit will be more effective than other regional efforts. A program to tackle AQIM—which involved establishing a Joint Operational General Staff Committee in southern Algeria with participation from Algeria, Mali, Niger, and Mauritania—has had negligible impact. Meanwhile, the African Union is years away from developing the kind of sustainable, rapidly deployable peace enforcement or peacekeeping capacity that would deter and defeat armed terrorist groups. Its planned African Standby Force is way behind schedule and an interim mechanism, the African Capacity for Immediate Response to Crises, is only just getting off the ground. The Mali security crisis demonstrated that the regional

ECOWAS body was willing to act but incapable of doing so effectively.

Searching for Solutions: International Engagement, its Shortcomings, and Ways Forward.

There are no easy solutions to the scourge of Boko Haram and other VEOs. What is clear, however, is that the countries and regions in which they reside bear primary responsibility for dealing with them. Their governments could start to salve some of the grievances that provide the extremists with their recruitment message by ruling in a professional, accountable, just, and transparent manner. Unfortunately, the worst-affected countries lack the leadership, the political will, and—in some cases—the resources to achieve this. The international community faces a quandary. It must deal with the terrorist problem in the short-term in order to protect its own security interests while trying to nurture homegrown institutions in these regions that will be able to tackle the problem in the long run.

While an assortment of actors is engaged in Nigeria and the Sahel—both bilaterally and multilaterally—the United States and France are two of the most important. French involvement has been mainly security-focused. In July, it unveiled a new regional security strategy called Operation Barkhane to follow its military offensive in Mali. The United States has a range of programs, including broad-based security, development, and diplomatic engagement with Nigeria and an ambitious—and stuttering—civil-military effort to address the causes and symptoms of vio-

lent extremism in the Sahel, the Trans-Sahara Counter Terrorism Partnership (TSCTP).

These efforts are well-meaning but overly focused on technical fixes that do not sufficiently appreciate the political economies of the countries in which they operate. It is all very well to try to build strong institutions, but these are countries that are led by dominant individuals or groups, ruling through informal networks. Institution-building, important as it is, must be accompanied by pragmatic strategies to work with, and through, political elites. The key challenge is finding ways to work with these elites, whose buy-in is required in order for anything productive to happen. A careful balance must be struck between addressing their self-interests without undermining core objectives of long-term stability and sustainable development. A perpetual problem for the United States and other donors is that flashy military equipment and training is gladly accepted by African governments who then block or subvert additional support that runs against their interests, such as assistance to countervailing institutions like legislatures and civil society. The result of this engagement is to strengthen incumbent regimes whose very continuance acts as a powerful recruitment tool for armed opposition. One wonders whether Western counterterrorism objectives in the Sahel are best served by programs that enable increasingly illegitimate leaders, like Paul Biya of Cameroon and Blaise Compaore of Burkina Faso, to remain in office even longer.

Too often, it appears that short-term, reactive responses to terrorism trump longer-term efforts targeting its root causes. The demand for quick wins means it is easier to fire off a Hellfire missile than devise a long-term approach to counter-radicalization that may take years to bear fruit or fail to produce measurable outcomes of the type demanded by budget-makers in Congress.

It is partly for these reasons that the United States privileges military approaches over civilian ones. While there are merits in increasing the capacity of African military institutions (although police should not be ignored), these efforts merely empower the next generation of coup-makers if they are not subordinate to civilian authority. In Mali, a military that benefited from generous U.S. support mutinied in the face of an armed threat,

appears to be broken, but few alternatives have been put on the table. President Obama's announcement at the U.S.-Africa Leaders' Summit last August of a new fund to develop a rapidly deployable peacekeeping capacity was more of the same. Of the six countries chosen to receive funding worth $110 million for each of the next three to five years, Ethiopia, Rwanda, and Uganda show no interest in establishing democratic rule.[13] Meanwhile, the United States Agency for International Development has no mission in Burkina Faso, Chad, Mauritania, and Niger; neither Cameroon nor Niger has U.S. ambassadors due to Congressional delays in approving President Obama's nominations. The absence of key personnel makes it harder for

The general incompetence of the military
response has been staggering.

and a U.S.-trained officer, Mamadou Sanogo, took the opportunity to overthrow the civilian government. Should the United States be strengthening the security forces of countries where civilian rule is shaky, such as Mali, Niger, and Nigeria, nevermind non-democratic regimes like those in Chad and Cameroon? The security services in these countries may be incapable of fighting VEOs, yet they are still the most powerful domestic institutions, influencing politics and gobbling up funds in the name of national security that could be used to improve education and health outcomes.

The "train and equip" approach to developing Africa's security institutions

the United States to demonstrate its seriousness in tackling the diplomatic and developmental challenges of this complex region and weakens efforts to energize host countries into taking a regional approach to insecurity.

The United States has tried to take on board some of these critiques through its flagship engagement program in the Sahel, TSCTP. This State Department-led program spreads a relatively small amount of money across a large, ten-country region. It has also been weakened by interagency coordination issues and policy differences. However, the TSCTP at least signals an attempt to take a more comprehensive approach to extremism and its underlying causes.

The United States and its international partners should be offering a similarly comprehensive menu of support to Nigeria in its fight against Boko Haram. This should include economic assistance to the northeast, education reform, counter-radicalization strategies, community engagement, security sector reform, and more accountable, inclusive governance. All of these ingredients are required to turn the tide against Boko Haram and all depend upon the buy-in of a Nigerian government that to date has shown little interest. For the time being, however, limited deployments of advisors and intelligence-gathering assets appear to be the order of the day, although they have done little to bring back the Chibok girls or tackle the wider scourge of terrorism that wreaks an ever-greater toll on the citizens of Nigeria.

NOTES

1 Drew Hinshaw, "In Nigeria, Parents Tormented by Stumbling Search for Girls Kidnapped By Boko Haram," *Wall Street Journal*, 8 May 2014, Internet, http://online.wsj.com/news/articles/SB10001424052702304655304579550050970946552 (date accessed: 29 November 2014).

2 United Nations Development Program, *"Human Development Reports 2014,"* Internet, http://hdr.undp.org/en/data (date accessed: 29 November 2014).

3 U.S. Energy Information Administration, "Nigeria Country Analysis Brief Overview," 30 December 2013, Internet, http:// www.eia.gov/countries/country-data.cfm?fips=ni (date accessed: 29 November 2014).

4 BBC, "Nigeria Central Bank Head Lamido Sanusi Ousted," 20 February 2014, Internet, http://www.bbc.com/news/worldafrica-26270561 (date accessed: 29 November 2014).

5 *See* International Crisis Group, "Curbing Violence in Nigeria (II): The Boko Haram Insurgency," 3 April 2014, Internet, http://www.crisisgroup.org/~/media/Files/africa/west-africa/nigeria/216-curbing-violencein-nigeria-ii-the-boko-haram-insurgency.pdf. haram-insurgency.pdf (date accessed: 29 November 2014). *Also* Ambassador John Campbell, "Why Nigeria's North South Distinction Is Important," Council on Foreign Relations, 7 February 2011, Internet, http://www.cfr.org/nigeria/why-nigerias-north-south-distinction-important/p24029 (date accessed: 29 November 2014).

6 Since independence in 1960, Mali has experienced two coup d'états, a revolution, and three Tuareg rebellions. Nigeria suffered four successful coups and a civil war before an aborted civilian handover in 1992 led to yet another military takeover. Civilian rule was restored in 1999, but the country has since endured insurgencies in the Niger Delta and northeast as well as serious bouts of communal violence in the Middle Belt.

7 Human Rights Watch, "Nigeria: Boko Haram Kills 2,053 Civilians in 6 Months," 15 July 2014, Internet, http://www.hrw.org/news/2014/07/15/nigeria-boko-haram-kills-2053-civilians-6-months (date accessed: 29 November 2014).

8 Heather Murdock, "Amnesty International: 'Gruesome' Videos Show Human Rights Abuses in Nigeria," 5 August 2014, Internet, http://www.voanews.com/content/amnesty-international-gruesome-videosshow-human-rights-abuses-in-nigeria/1971726. html (date accessed: 29 November 2014).

9 For an overview of the challenge of professionalism facing militaries in the region and specific examples of the Malian military's shortcomings in responding to the northern rebellion, see Emile Ouedraogo, "Advancing Military Professionalism in Africa," *Africa Center for Strategic Studies*, July 2014, Internet, http://africacenter. org/wp-content/uploads/2014/07/ARP-6- EN.pdf (date accessed: 29 November 2014). *Also* Philippe Leymarie, "The Sahel Falls Apart," *Le Monde Diplomatique*, April 2012, Internet, http://mondediplo.com/2012/04/05sahel (date accessed: 29 November 2014). *Also* Oladiran Bello, "Quick Fix or Quicksand? Implementing the EU Sahel Strategy," *FRIDE* Working Paper 114, November 2012, Internet, http://fride.org/download/WP_114_Implementing_the_EU_Sahel_Strategy.pdf (date accessed: 29 November 2014).

10 *See* Sahara Reporters, "Near Mutiny at Army Barracks in Maiduguri Over High Number of Nigerian Troops Casualty in Gwoza," 7 August 2014, Internet, http://saharareporters.com/2014/08/07/near-mutiny-army-barracks-maiduguri-over-high-number-nigerian-troops-casualty-gwoza (date accessed: 29 November 2014).

11 International Crisis Group, "Curbing Violence in Nigeria (II): The Boko Haram Insurgency," 3 April 2014, Internet, http://www.crisisgroup.org/~/media/Files/africa/west-africa/nigeria/216-curbing-violence-innigeria-ii-the-boko-haram-insurgency. pdf (date accessed: 29 November 2014).

12 For more details, see Lake Chad Basin Commission, "Remarks of the Executive Secretary at the Meeting on Insecurity," 22-23 July 2014, Internet, http://www.cblt.org/en/ remarks-executive-secretary-meeting-security (date accessed: 29 November 2014).

13 White House factsheet, "U.S. Support for Peacekeeping in Africa," 6 August 2014, Internet, http://www.whitehouse.gov/the-press-office/2014/08/06/fact-sheetus-support-peacekeeping-africa (date accessed: 29 November 2014).

The Ukraine Invasion and Public Opinion

Harley Balzer

Russia has engaged in a "war without war and occupation
without occupation" in Ukraine, replicating its tactics in
Georgia in 2008 and Moldova for more than a decade.[1]
Media coverage worldwide emphasizes the tremendous surge
in Vladimir Putin's popularity while Russian government-
controlled media trumpet support for pro-Russian insurgents. The conflict in eastern Ukraine has made tacit
acceptance of Russia's annexing Crimea almost a given, with
few questioning the popularity of this development inside
Crimea itself or within Russia.

Ukraine is far more important to Russia's rulers than it
is to the United States or the European Union. A Eurasian
Union is the cornerstone of Putin's foreign policy, and that
union is a far less meaningful entity without Ukraine. Russian leaders refuse to admit that closer Ukrainian ties with
the EU might produce economic benefits for the entire
region.[2] Russia's military leadership perceives Ukraine's
closer economic relationship with the EU as a step toward
joining NATO. These concerns, voiced publicly, pale beside
a greater threat not to Russia but to Putin's regime: a prosperous and democratic Ukraine economically integrated
with Europe would exist in stark contrast to Putin's resource-

Harley Balzer is Associate Professor of Gov-
ernment and Interna-
tional Affairs and an
Associate Faculty Mem-
ber of the Department
of History at George-
town University.

based non-democracy. Ukraine's turn to Europe is not a threat to Russia and would almost certainly benefit the Russian economy over time, but it is an existential challenge to Putin and Russia's ruling elite.[3]

Given that the stakes are far higher for Putin than for Europe or America, and that Russia enjoys clear military superiority over Ukraine, what might

Russian speakers, prefer independence. In the Russian-speaking regions joined to Ukraine in 1954, over half of those voting favored independence (54 percent in Crimea and 57 percent in Sevastopol). In the heavily Russian-speaking Donetsk and Luhansk Oblasts, major centers of violent separatist activity in 2014, 84 percent voted for independence in 1991.[5]

Ukraine's turn to Europe is an existential challenge to Putin and Russia's ruling elite.

curb Russia's aggression? This article finds some basis for optimism in public opinion: Ukrainians, including Russian speakers in eastern Ukraine, have consistently expressed a preference for living in Ukraine, not Russia, and many are willing to fight for it. Russians have expressed opposition to direct Russian military involvement in Ukraine, and in September 2014 tens of thousands staged protests against Putin's policy.[4] Putin's ratings boost from seizing Crimea, while real, is not unusual in comparative perspective and may well be temporary.

Opinion in Ukraine. Surveys in Ukraine have consistently indicated a desire for independence and territorial integrity. Opinion has fluctuated over time, but even in Russian-speaking regions a majority has never favored separation or Russian military intervention.

The referendum on Ukrainian independence in December 1991 indicated that an overwhelming majority of Ukrainians, including a majority of

Surveys in 2014 produced results similar to those in 1991. In March 2014, just before Russia's invasion of Crimea, a clear majority of Ukrainian citizens stated that they prefer to live in a sovereign Ukraine, with 85 percent of respondents opposing Russian military intervention.[6] When asked whether the Russian army should be sent to protect ethnic Russians if they were threatened, ethnic Russians living in Ukraine were evenly divided in their response, with 43 percent on each side of the issue. The number of ethnic Russians strongly opposed to seeing Russian troops in Ukraine (32 percent) was greater than the number strongly in favor of such action (23 percent).

A poll by the Democratic Initiative of Ukraine conducted in March 2014 found that 8 percent of the residents of the country as a whole favored separating from Ukraine and joining another state, with the figures ranging from under 1 percent in western Ukraine to a high of 18 percent in the Donbass.[7] Fewer than 10 percent expressed support for southeastern Ukraine becoming part of Russia. Donbass respondents expressed the strongest support for separatism, at 27 percent.

The referendum Russia organized in March 2014 to ratify annexing Crimea officially claimed that 97 percent of Crimean residents supported separatism. This data is of questionable validity, as the atmosphere was fraught due to Russian provocations. The UN High Commissioner for Human Rights, Navi Pillay, noted "misinformation and hate speech used as propaganda," and urged the authorities in Crimea to account for killings, torture, and arbitrary arrests in the buildup to the referendum.[8]

The Russian president's Council for Development of Civil Society and Human Rights reported turnout of just 30 to 50 percent, well below the official 83 percent. Putin's own Council found that just 22.5 percent of registered voters in Crimea voted for Russian annexation.[9] CNN polled one thousand Ukrainians one day after the Russian-organized referendum and reported that just 19 percent expressed loyalty to Russia, while 67 percent supported sanctions against Russia and 56 percent felt loyalty to Europe.[10]

Surveys by the Kiev International Institute of Sociology in April 2014 produced results confirming the March International Republican Institute (IRI) data. Although majorities in both Luhansk (60 percent) and Donetsk (71 percent) accepted the Russian media claim that the events on Maidan were an armed coup sponsored by the West, this did not create a demand for separation. Just 16 percent of Luhansk residents supported unification with Russia, while 73 percent supported Ukrainian independence. Few supported armed intervention.[11]

A major pretense for Russian annexation of Crimea and support for separatists in eastern Ukraine has been ostensible threats to native Russians and Russian speakers living in these areas. Yet despite a barrage of propaganda from Russian media, surveys in Ukraine have provided no evidence that large numbers of Russian-speakers feel threatened or suffer discrimination. In the March 2014 IRI survey, there was no region of Ukraine where a majority of respondents agreed with the statement, "the rights of Russian-speakers are being encroached upon." The strongest support for this view was in Donetsk, where 40 percent agreed and 57 percent disagreed. In the entire eastern region, 72 percent disagreed. In eastern Ukraine, only 17 percent supported Russia sending military forces into Ukraine; in the south, Russian intervention was favored by 27 percent.[12]

Longitudinal data from Ukraine over the past twenty-three years indicate a consistent preference for continued sovereignty and a growing desire for closer ties with Europe. This trend has grown stronger during the months of conflict following Russia's annexation of Crimea. The two high points in support for an independent Ukraine were December 1991 and September 2014. After 1991, hyperinflation and the economic crisis caused support for independence to decline, reaching lows of 56 to 60 percent. Russia's armed incursion into Chechnya in 1994 caused support for independent statehood to increase, reaching 71 percent. Pro-independence sentiment declined again during the 1997-98 economic crisis. The second Chechen war produced another bump, accentuated by Russia's war with Georgia in 2008, resulting in 83 percent favoring independence. Support for independence declined again, but in 2014 it reached 90 percent, its highest level since 1991.[13]

As a result of Putin's aggressive policy, an overwhelming majority of Ukrainians now view Russia as their enemy and perceive affiliation with Europe as necessary. In 2009, just one-quarter of Ukrainians thought Russia exerted a negative influence on their country; now the figure is two-thirds.[14] According to a Pew Research poll in 2009, a majority of Ukrainians—51 percent—opposed NATO membership, while only 28 percent favored it.[15]

Two polls by the Ukrainian sociological group Rating illustrate the impact of Putin's policies.[16]

> July 2012: 17 percent for NATO membership, 70 percent opposed
> July 2014: 44 percent for NATO membership, 34 percent opposed

Continuing Russian pressure in fall 2014 induced more Ukrainians to support NATO membership. In Kyiv, a growing number of people now prefer to speak Ukrainian rather than Russian.[17]

Opinion in Russia. Analyzing opinion data from Russia requires interpretive nuance. The regime has portrayed Russia's people as nearly unanimous in supporting the annexation of Crimea and providing aid to separatists in Ukraine. While Russians are proud of regaining great power status, a growing number are not willing to pay the economic cost of rebuilding Crimea, much less sacrifice their sons for eastern Ukraine.

Most Russian citizens accepted their government's media message that Russian speakers in Ukraine were threatened (88 percent) and agreed that Russia's president should seek to further the interests of those Russian speakers (84 percent).[18] But this does not translate into support for armed intervention. While Russians believe that Ukraine would be better off with an economy oriented to Russia and its Customs Union, they do not agree that this is something warranting military action.[19]

A poll in June 2014 found that more than 90 percent of Russia's citizens approved of the annexation of Crimea, but they did not agree with the official Russian view that Russian speakers in Ukraine were threatened, or that Ukraine's relationship with Europe would damage Russia's economy. Polls at about the same time found that only 5 to 10 percent supported military intervention in Ukraine.[20]

At no point has a significant share of Russia's population expressed support for military intervention in Ukraine. In mid-July 2014, two-thirds of respondents in a VTsIOM (All-Russian Center for the Study of Public Opinion) poll said the conflict should be resolved

The costs of the Ukraine conflict will be a significant factor in a myriad of ways.

by diplomatic means. Another 22 percent favored "surgical strikes," and just 11 percent wanted to send Russian troops. In a later survey, only 13 percent thought Russia should send troops to Ukraine even if NATO intervened. A much larger number perceived the threat of war stemming from the activity of the separatists—groups armed and aided, if not organized and led, by Russian "volunteers."[21]

In August 2014, 60 percent of Russian citizens viewed the situation in Ukraine as an internal conflict. VTsIOM General Director Valery Fyodorov suggested this "explains why very few Russians want their army to help the federalist forces in the Donetsk and Luhansk regions."[22] An absolute majority of Russians said the Russian leadership should not privilege foreign-policy goals, including "interference" in Ukraine, over attention to "Russia's social and economic problems."[23]

Just as many Europeans do not want to pay the price for sanctions imposed on Russia, most Russians oppose paying to rebuild Crimea. Support for paying the cost of annexation has eroded significantly over time. A Levada Center poll conducted in August 2014 showed continuing support for annexation, but the number willing to pay for Crimea dropped from 26 percent in March to 17 percent in September. The share opposed to paying increased from 19 percent to 30 percent.[24]

Domestic public opinion explains Russian officials' persistent denial that Russian military personnel are participating in the conflict in eastern Ukraine (except "volunteers" and soldiers who have chosen to spend their vacation aiding Russian speakers in

Ukraine). President Putin in March 2014 denied that Russians were involved in the occupation of Crimea, but in May acknowledged that the "little green men" were from Russia. Despite this moment of frankness, Russian officials have consistently maintained that contingents in eastern Ukraine wearing identical unmarked uniforms and carrying identical equipment are not from Russia. The rationale for the invasion of Ukraine was what Russian sources describe as an illegal coup against the elected president Viktor Yanukovich, but planning for a possible invasion was done well ahead. One Russian acquaintance described the experience of a family member who served in the military in 2013. The contract soldiers in his elite unit were asked if they would be willing to fight in Ukraine, either officially or unofficially. Those who declined did not have their contracts renewed. This suggests that contingency preparations were underway well before President Yanukovich was forced from office.[25]

Russian authorities clearly are concerned about a potential backlash. They have been careful to conceal evidence of Russian casualties in Ukraine. Returned corpses are labeled "Cargo 200," a designation used in the Afghan War. Dmitri Gudkov, the lone opposition deputy remaining in the Russian parliament (Duma), inquired about thirty-nine Russian paratroopers from the 76th Airborne Division based in Pskov who likely perished in Ukraine. The Ministry of Defense responded that the Russian Federation is not involved in the conflict and that releasing information about specific individuals would violate their right to privacy.[26] The local Soldier's Mothers group also raised questions. When the St. Petersburg branch of this homegrown NGO joined in asking about the situation, they were denounced as foreign agents.[27] In August 2014, President Putin awarded the 76th Airborne Division the Order of Suvorov for its work in "local conflicts" in previous decades.[28] The timing caused many to believe the honor reflected recent service in Ukraine. The decree (*ukaz*) is not available on the Kremlin website. Journalists were told that it is not in the public domain.

One of the ways information about dead and injured Russian "volunteers" is reaching the public domain is from reports about individuals punished for divulging this information. In mid-October 2014, Liudmila Bogatenkova, a seventy-three-year-old human rights activist, was detained for reporting information about Russian casualties.[29] The web site most active in publicizing "Cargo 200" casualties was blocked at the end of September for "nationalism."[30] On September 26, the site posted an item by Konstantin Zel'fianov stating that the number of dead and wounded Russian soldiers and mercenaries was more than four thousand. Zel'fianov added that while some bodies were returned to Russia, many, if not most, were simply thrown into mine shafts.[31]

Intimidation of critics has been both direct and indirect. Levada Center Director Lev Gudkov suggested that the views expressed by Russians in many opinion polls reflect economic coercion: two-thirds of Russians live paycheck-to-paycheck, many on the government payroll, so fear of being fired has a strong influence on what they will tell reporters and sociologists.[32] A better-informed Russian public is likely to have a less positive view of the Ukraine invasion.

Putin's Rating. Russian media have trumpeted the enormous popularity of Putin's Ukraine gambit. Western media speak of his "skyrocketing" rating. Putin's favorable rating increased from about 60 percent to above 80 percent following the annexation of Crimea and remained high until the end of August 2014, when it dipped slightly. But is Putin's "bump" in popularity unusual for a leader when a conflict begins? And is it sustainable?

Putin's approval rating increased about half as much as that of George W. Bush following the attacks organized by Osama Bin Laden. A Gallup poll taken 7 to 10 September 2001 gave Bush a 51 percent approval rating, with 39 percent expressing disapproval. In a Gallup poll taken after the attacks, Bush's rating jumped to 90 percent approval.[33]

The rise in Putin's approval rating pales in comparison to the growth in his popularity during the first Chechen War. In July 1999, when he was appointed Prime Minister, Putin registered about 30 percent approval and 30 percent disapproval. By the end of the year, after vowing to "rub out" Chechen fighters "in the outhouse," his approval reached 80 percent.[34]

The annexation of Crimea remains popular in Russia, and Putin's ratings reflect this, though Putin's approval may have peaked in August 2014. A Levada Center poll at the end of the month indicated a drop from 87 percent to 84 percent approval, with a slight increase in disapproval.[35]

Job approval does not mean voters would support someone's re-election. George H. W. Bush reached a 90 percent approval rating during the first Gulf War in 1991, but lost the 1992 presidential election. In July 2014, the number of Russians who said they would vote for Putin again was just 52 percent.[36] By September it fell below 50 percent. Putin's officials still count the votes, but extensive falsification of vote counts was a major reason for the protests in 2011-12, and there is a risk this could be repeated.

The costs of the Ukraine conflict and rebuilding efforts will be a significant factor in a myriad of ways. Russia's economy was close to a no-growth situation before the annexation of Crimea resulted in economic sanctions. The ruble fell, stock market values dropped, and capital flight increased. Now many domestic constituencies will get

regions more quickly. Negative reactions to these economic consequences will take a further toll on Putin's popularity.

Policy Implications. Despite the dangerous precedent of using armed aggression to revise borders in Europe, neither Europe nor the United States has evinced willingness to pay a significant price to reverse Putin's annexation of Crimea or prevent the eastern regions of Ukraine becoming another frozen conflict.[38] European business interests and politicians receiving substantial financial benefits from Russian state-owned companies are leading the effort to rationalize Putin's behavior, arguing that Russia has legitimate interests in the region and emphasizing the economic costs to Europe from sanctions.

Targeted sanctions and efforts to

Public information is crucial to helping Russians understand the impact of Putin's policies on their own country.

less funding as a result of the war in Ukraine. Economic development projects in Chechnya and the rest of the North Caucasus are being cut to pay for Crimean development. Pensioners have been warned to prepare for increases in "communal services" costs (heat, water, electricity, etc.), and the pension fund has been confiscated to help pay the costs of Crimean annexation.[37]

While the macroeconomic problems are manageable in the short- to medium-term, negative effects are likely to be felt by individuals, enterprises, and

reduce European dependence on Russian hydrocarbons are important policies that should be maintained for an extended period. Sanctions rarely achieve results in the short term.

The most important area for Western action is the information space. Most Russian citizens appear to have forgotten the lessons of state-run media from the Soviet era. They are less cynical in part because Putin's regime has effectively chosen themes with popular appeal, but also because the regime continues to aggressively attack independent information sources.[39] Providing alternative Russian-language media could help balance Putin's propaganda. The European Union should finance this effort, with technical help

armed wings of nationalist organizations helped protect protestors on the Maidan and battled "volunteers" from Russia in eastern Ukraine. However, their presence and potential influence

---

Fear of conflict should not deter the United States and Europe from doing everything possible to stop Putin's aggression.

---

from the United States. Early 2015, when Polish Prime Minister Donald Tusk becomes EU President and Latvia assumes the presidency of the Council of the European Union, would be a good opportunity to establish a new "Radio Free Europe."[40]

Public information is crucial to helping Russian elites and ordinary citizens understand the impact of Putin's policies on their own country. The economic consequences of the Ukraine invasion will take time to develop, but they will be significant.[41] Non-Russians inside Russia and some Russian regions are already asking why they too should not have real federalism.[42] Putin's fixation on the potential consequences of Ukraine orienting its economy to Europe distracts Russia's policy focus from more serious threats.[43] When some of the North Caucasus fighters currently in Syria return to open an Islamic State front in Dagestan or Ingushetia, the need for a common effort will be more apparent but less achievable.[44]

Putin is winning the information war in part because the Ukrainian government genuinely does need to address concerns about Ukrainian nationalist groups and future policies. The

has allowed Putin to portray post-Yanukovich governments as neo-Nazis, so-called Banderovtsy. Russian television has persistently conveyed this message.[45]

Ukrainian leaders must clean up their economic system as well as their government. Fixing the damage bequeathed by Yanukovich and his cronies requires difficult measures that will be unpopular. The temptation to use ongoing conflict as an excuse to defer economic reform will be strong. Without steadfast efforts to fix the economy, Putin's effort to promote instability in the region will continue to be successful.

The United States and NATO need to develop greater capacity to respond to "war without war" and "new wars," where stealth and deniability obscure the nature of the conflict and insurgents perpetuate instability over an extended period as extortion, expropriation, and kidnaping become their income stream.[46]

The new NATO "rapid reaction" force should be accompanied by establishing "rapid response" peacekeeping groups that threatened governments could invite to areas when the sort of "invasion without invasion" practiced in Crimea and eastern Ukraine is initiated. The new units would be able to provide information about events and could interpose themselves between unidentified paramilitary fighters and local civilians and military units to deter violence. Halting the informal incursions at the outset will be far less costly than dealing with long-term occupations and frozen conflicts.

The appetites of nationalist revanchists rarely are assuaged by victories. They grow. High-level nationalist politicians in Putin's administration have produced monographs not only defending the Crimean annexation but also advocating Russia's right to recover Alaska.[47] Putin has said (even if taken out of context) that his forces could be in Kiev in two weeks. They could probably be in Tallinn, Riga, and Vilnius in a few hours. An attack on new NATO members may be precisely what Putin views as the way to undermine the alliance.

NATO should do what it can to raise the costs, both economic and military, of continued Russian aggression in Ukraine. Steven Pifer and Strobe Talbott have suggested providing defensive weapons to the Ukrainian government.[48] This is a good start. Enhancing current information sharing and making it clear that other options are under consideration could also help deter aggression.

Finally, it is time to separate Putin and Russia in our discourse. In the current situation, being anti-Putin, far from being anti-Russian, is to be in favor of a healthier and wealthier Russia that is less dangerous to Russians, non-Russians within Russia, and democratic governments now faced with a threatening alternative worldview.[49]

Conclusion. Putin's creeping annexation of former Soviet territory should not be allowed to escalate into a broader armed conflict, but fear of conflict should not deter the United States and Europe from doing everything possible to stop Putin's aggression. Numerous analysts have noted the broad range of issues on which U.S. and Russian cooperation is essential: terrorism, Iran's nuclear program, North Korea, Afghanistan, piracy, and others.[50]

If Putin extends the conflict to more of Ukraine or to the Baltics, cooperation on these areas of mutual interest could become impossible. The results of the 2014 U.S. elections will make it even more difficult for the Obama administration to work with Putin's government. If Putin's spokespersons continue to present cooperation on mutual interests like terrorism as "favors," there may be no hope of overcoming U.S. domestic political concerns.

Encouraging Russians who oppose the military conflict with brother Slavs is not only plausible but is also possible. They do not need a regime change but merely need to convince their leader that the current policy is unpopular as well as irrational for Russia's future. Opinion data indicate that an overwhelming majority of Ukrainians, including Russian speakers, favor independence, an overwhelming majority of Russians oppose military intervention in Ukraine, and Putin's approval rating has far outpaced his electoral rating as a result of his Ukraine policies. Both ratings have fallen since June. These data offer hope that the policies could be changed. Growing conflicts within Putin's elite as economic sanctions create competition and tensions could accelerate the process.

Levada Center surveys indicate that 85 percent of Russian citizens believe they have no influence on policy decisions.[51] The regime's extensive efforts to contain protest, control the media, and thwart civic activism suggest that Russia's rulers do not share this view: Putin and his cronies remain seriously concerned about public opinion. Doing more to open the information space will help.

NOTES

1 Elizabeth Cullen Dunn and Michael S. Bobick, "The Empire Strikes Back: War without war and occupation without occupation in the Russian sphere of influence," *American Ethnologist* 41, no. 3 (2014): 405-413.

2 Veronika Movchan and Mykola Tyzhenkov, "Economic impact of Ukraine-EU Association Agreement: quantitative estimates CGE model" (Kyiv: Institute for Economic Research and Policy Consulting), Internet, http://www.ier.com.ua/en/public_events/?e=147 (date accessed: 24 November 2014). *Also* Anders Åslund, "Ukraine's Choice: European Association agreement of Eurasia Union?" (Washington, DC: Peterson Institute for International Economics, September 2013). *Also* Gabrielle Tétrault-Farber, "EU Association Agreements Not Seen as Threat to Russian Economy," *The Moscow Times*, 26 June 2014, Internet, http://www.themoscowtimes.com/news/article/eu-association-agreements-not-seen-as-threat-to-russian-economy-/502590.html (date accessed: 24 November 2014).

3 For an excellent discussion of the ways Russia's elite pursues policies that fail to address the nation's economic and social needs, see Karen Dawisha, *Putin's Kleptocracy: Who Owns Russia?* (New York: Simon and Schuster, 2014).

4 For video of these protests, see: "Thousands protest Russia's Ukraine policy," *CNN*, Internet, http://www.youtube.com/watch?v=akleO4l-gw4 (date accessed: 24 November 2014). *Also* "Russians rally against Moscow role in Ukraine," *Aljazeera*, Internet, http://www.aljazeera.com/news/europe/2014/09/russians-stage-anti-ukraine-war-moscow-201492114729171223.html (date accessed: 24 November 2014). *Also* "Russian Anti-War Rally," *Ukraine Today*, Internet, https://www.facebook.com/uatodaytv/posts/297626593759526 (date accessed: 24 November 2014). *Also* "Russia Anti-War March: Tens of thousands in Moscow protest Kremlin's secret war in Ukraine," UkrStream.TV, Internet, http://ukrstream.tv/en/videos/russian_anti_war_march_tens_of_thousands_in_moscow_protest_kremlin_s_secret_war_in_ukraine#.VCDXUxbwoII (date accessed: 24 November 2014).

5 Andrew Wilson, *Ukrainian Nationalism in the 1990s: A Minority Faith* (Cambridge: Cambridge University Press, 1996), 128. 93 percent of those voting expressed support for Ukraine's independence, including 55 percent of Russian speakers in Ukraine. In Kharkiv Oblast, 86 percent favored independence, in Odessa 85 percent voted for independence, and in Mikolayiv 89 percent. In the nineteen regions of central and western Ukraine, more than 90 percent voted for an independent Ukrainian state. Of the total eligible electorate in Ukraine in 1991, 76 percent voted for independence. This was a sharp change from March 1991, when Mikhail Gorbachev insisted on a referen-

dum asking people in the Soviet Union whether they favored some type of union of the Soviet republics. About two-thirds of the residents of Ukraine who voted were in favor of the statement: "Do you agree that Ukraine should be part of a Union of Soviet sovereign states on the basis on the Declaration of State Sovereignty of Ukraine?" The difference in the outcomes in March and December 1991 is best explained by the failed putsch in August of 1991. When offered a choice between remaining in a Soviet Union where another coup might be staged or becoming independent, Ukrainian residents, including a majority of Russian speakers, voted decisively to go their own way.

6 "Public Opinion Survey: Residents of Ukraine" (Washington, DC: International Republican Institute, March 14-26 2014). The survey was conducted by Baltic Surveys and The Gallup Organization for the International Republican Institute, and involved fieldwork by Rating Group Ukraine.

7 "Чи властиві українцям настрої сепаратизму?" Democratic Institute of Ukraine, 24 March 2014, Internet [English translation unavailable], dif.org.ua/ua/events/nkdfkedlkrjg-kje.htm (date accessed: 24 November 2014). Also see the analysis in Paul Goble, "*Window on Eurasia*: Few in Ukraine — Including in the East — Support separatism or joining Russia, poll shows," 12 April 2014, Internet, http://windowoneurasia2.blogspot.com/2014/04/window-on-eurasia-few-in-ukraine.html (date accessed: 24 November 2014).

8 Nick Cumming-Bruce, "U.N. cites abuses in Crimea before Russia annexation vote," *The New York Times*, 15 April 2014. For the full text of the report, see United Nations, "Report on the human rights situation in Ukraine" (New York: Office of the United Nations High Commissioner for Human Rights, 15 April 2014).

9 Data from the Presidential Council cited in Dawisha, *Putin's Kleptocracy*, 319.

10 Richard Allen Greene, "Ukraine favors Europe over Russia, new CNN poll finds," CNN, 12 May 2014. 37 percent of Ukrainians in the eastern regions Donetsk, Luhansk, and Kharkiv favored an alliance with Russia, 14 percent wanted an alliance with the European Union, and half (49 percent) responded that Ukraine would be better off if it did not ally with either. Nationwide, a slight majority (54 percent) said it would be good for Ukraine to join the EU. More than eight out of ten (82 percent) said it would be bad for the country to have Russian troops in Ukraine. Two-thirds (67 percent) described Putin as "dangerous."

11 "The views and opinions of residents of South-Eastern Ukraine: April 2014," *Zerkalo Nedeli Dzerkalo Tyzhnia*, Internet [English translation unavailable], 18 April 2014, http://zn.ua/UKRAINE/mneniya-i-vzglyady-zhiteley-yugo-vostoka-ukrainy-aprel-2014-143598_.

NOTES

html#comment (date accessed: 24 November 2014).

A helpful summary is available in Steven Pifer and Hannah Thoburn, "Nuanced views in Eastern Ukraine," 28 April 2014, Internet, http://www.brookings.edu/blogs/up-front/posts/2014/04/28-nuanced-views-eastern-ukraine-pifer-thoburn (date accessed: 24 November 2014). Only Donetsk and Luhansk produced majorities supporting Yanukovich. The only region in Ukraine where a majority supported federalization was Luhansk. Strong support for armed seizures of administrative buildings was expressed by 12 percent of respondents in Luhansk. Nowhere else was the number favoring violence above 10 percent. 77 percent opposed the armed occupation of buildings. Intervention by Russian troops was supported by 19 percent of respondents in Luhansk and Donetsk. Russia military intervention was strongly opposed by 48 percent in Donetsk. Elsewhere in southeast Ukraine, at least 70 percent opposed the introduction of Russian troops.

12 International Republican Institute, 4-8.

13 Paul Goble, "Window on Eurasia: Ukrainians now almost unanimous in supporting independent Ukraine," 24 August 2014, Internet, http://windowoneurasia2.blogspot.com/2014/08/window-on-eurasia-ukrainians-now-almost.html (date accessed: 24 November 2014).

14 Marjorie Connelly, "Ukrainians favor unity, not Russia, polls find," The New York Times, 8 May 2014.

15 Sprehe, Kathleen Holzwart, "Ukraine Says 'No' to NATO," Pew Global, 29 March 2010. Internet, http://www.pewglobal.org/2010/03/29/ukraine-says-no-to-nato/ (date accessed: 24 November 2014).

16 "Maizhe polovina ukarintsiv khoche vstupu do NATO, sotsopituvannia (Less than half of Ukraininans want to join NATO)," Internet [English translation unavailable], http://tvi.ua/new/2014/07/22/mayzhe_polovyna_ukrayinciv_khoche_vtupu_do_nato__socopytuvannya (date accessed: 8 October 2014).

17 George Mirsky, "Kiev govorit po-Ukrainski (Kiev Speaks Ukrainian)," 2 November 2014, Internet [English translation unavailable], echo.msk.ru/blog/georgy_mirsky/1429814-echo/ (date accessed: 24 November 2014). One good indicator of the validity of Echo Moskvy reporting is the government's recent moves against the broadcaster.

18 "Oprosy: Bol'shinstvo rossiian uvereny chto v Ukraine sushchestvyet ugroza dlia Russkogovoriashchikh zhitelei (Surveys: A majority of Russians are certain that there are threats to Russian-speaking residents of Ukraine)," Nezavisimaia gazeta 152, (24 July 2014): 3.

19 Sergei Goriashko, "Rossiianam ne nravitsia evropei'skii' vybor Ukrainy (Russians do not like Ukraine's choice of Europe)," Kommersant Daily 227, (10 December 2013): 8. A poll by the Public Opinion Foundation found 59 percent thought Ukraine would be better off aligned with Russia than with Europe. 36 percent thought Ukrainian ties to Europe would harm Russia, just 11 percent thought it would be beneficial, and 34 percent thought it would have no impact on Russia. This corresponds with the Levada Center August data: Russians would prefer that Ukraine be in the Eurasian Union, but are not willing to sacrifice a significant amount to make this happen.

20 Thomas Sherlock, "With low popular support for escalation, Putin faces a sharpening dilemma," The National Interest, 21 August 2014, Internet, http://nationalinterest.org/feature/putins-public-opinion-challenge-11113 (date accessed: 24 November 2014).

21 ITAR-Tass, "Two thirds of Russians against sending troops to Ukraine - poll," VTsIOM, 29 July 2014, Internet, http://en.itar-tass.com/russia/742703 (date accessed: 24 November 2014).

22 "Most Russians see Ukrainian turmoil as civil war - poll," Russia Today, 26 August 2014, Internet, http://rt.com/politics/182860-russia-ukraine-civil-poll/ (date accessed: 3 November 2014).

23 Thomas Shurlock, "Putin's Public Opinion Challenge," Center for Geopolitical Analyses, 8 August 2014. Shurlock states that "with low popular support for escalation, Putin faces a sharpening dilemma."

24 Levada Center, "Prisoedinenie Kryma k Rossii (Uniting Crimea with Russia)," 2 September 2014, Internet [English translation unavailable], http://www.levada.ru/print/02-09-2014/prisoedinenie-kryma-k-rossii (date accessed: 24 November 2014). Respondents happy about regaining Crimea decreased from 23 percent in March to 16 percent in September. The number saying it gives them pride in their country dropped from 37 percent to 30 percent. In March, just 19 percent were against paying to develop Crimea; in August the number was 28 percent. The share willing to suffer for Crimea declined from 28 percent to 17 percent.

25 Interview by Balzer, St. Petersburg, June 2014. Reports in the Russian media have supported this account. Liudmila Bogatenkova was detained in October 2014 in part because she was advising families about their options when contract soldiers were forced to sign agreements to go to Ukraine. "A 73-year-old Russian woman investigating the deaths of Russian soldiers in Ukraine was thrown into an investigative isolation ward," Noyvi region, Internet [English translation unavailable], http://nr2.com.ua/News/world_and_russia/73-letnyuyu-rossiyanku-zanimavshuyusya-rassledovaniem-gibeli-voennyh-RF-v-Ukraine-brosili-v-SIZO (date accessed: 24 November 2014).

26 After the thirty-nine paratroopers were buried in Pskov in August, attempts to ascertain what happened to them produced unpleasant consequences for those asking the questions. Lev Shlosberg, a member of the Pskov regional legislature, sought an inquiry about the deaths and was subsequently attacked by three

NOTES

men who left him with injuries requiring hospitalization. More than twenty journalists in Pskov reported being attacked after they posed questions about the deaths. Members of a BBC news group in Astrakhan investigating reports of Russian soldiers' deaths were attacked and their cameras smashed. A human rights advocate reported that at least a dozen bodies arrived in Orenburg from Ukraine early in the second half of September. Local military authorities were outraged when they learned the men had been officially discharged from the army following their deaths.

27 Catherine Fitzpatrick. "Russia This Week: Kremlin advisor Speaks at Yalta Conference Amid Separatists, European Far Right (25-31 August)," Interpretermag.com, August 30, 2014, Internet, http://www.interpretermag.com/russia-this-week/#4035 (date accessed: 24 November 2014).

28 Anna Dolgov, "Defense Ministry dismisses reports of Russian paratroopers killed in Ukraine," *The Moscow Times*, 30 September 2014, Internet, http://www.themoscowtimes.com/news/article/defense-ministry-dismisses-reports-of-russian-paratroopers-killed-in-ukraine-as-rumors/508089.html (date accessed: 24 November 2014).

29 "Russian woman investigating deaths," *Noyvi Region*, Internet [English translation unavailable], http://nr2.com.ua/News/world_and_russia/73-letnyuyu-rossiyanku-zanimavshuyusya-rassledovaniem-gibeli-voennyh-RF-v-Ukraine-brosili-v-SIZO-82527.html (date accessed: 24 November 2014).

30 "The group 'Cargo 200 from Ukraine to Russia' has been blocked on the Classmates site," *Noyvi Region*, Internet [English translation unavailable], http://nr2.com.ua/News/politics_and_society/Na-Odnoklassnikah-zablokirovali-gruppu-Gruz- 200-iz-Ukrainy-v-Rossiyu-81061.html (date accessed: 24 November 2014).

31 "The number of dead and missing Russian soldiers in the Donbass has reached 4,000," *Noyvi Region*, Internet [English translation unavailable], http://nr2.com.ua/News/politics_and_society/Na-Odnoklassnikah-zablokirovali-gruppu-Gruz- 200-iz-Ukrainy-v-Rossiyu-81061.html (date accessed: 24 November 2014).

32 Echo Moskvy, "Rossiia, kotoruiu vybiraet bol'shinstvo—kakaia ona? (What kind of Russia would the majority choose?)," Interview with Lev Gudkov, 20 June 2014, Internet [English translation unavailable], http://echo.msk.ru/programs/year2014/1343750-echo/ (date accessed: 24 November 2014).

33 "Presidential Approval Ratings—George W. Bush," *Gallup*, Internet, http://www.gallup.com/poll/116500/presidential-approval-ratings-george-bush.aspx (date accessed: 24 November 2014).

34 Putin's 2014 jump in approval may resemble the effects from the war with Georgia in 2008. Mark Adomanis described Putin's approval numbers as a "sugar high." His approval rating was 88 percent in September 2008, down to 80 percent a year later, and at 68 percent in September 2010. Mark Adomanis, "Putin's poll numbers are skyrocketing, but they aren't going to last," Center on Global Interests, 10 April 2014, Internet, http://www.globalinterests.org/2014/04/10/putins-poll-numbers-are-skyrocketing-but-they-arent-going-to-last/ (date accessed: 24 November 2014).

35 Alexander Zemlianichenko, "Putin's approval rating falls for first time this year," *The Moscow Times*, 28 August 2014. Putin's rating has spiked several times over his career. Putin's lowest approval rating since he became President in June 2000 was either 50 percent or 61 percent in November 2013, depending on which polls are consulted. In early August 2014, Putin's approval reached 87 percent, comparable to his ratings in 2008 during the war with Georgia, and in 2000 when battling Chechnya. "Putin's approval rating soars to 87 percent, poll says," *The Moscow Times*, 6 August 2014, Internet, http://www.themoscowtimes.com/article/504691.html (date accessed: 24 November 2014).

36 Ivan Nechepurenko, "Crimea factor finite in Putin's rating," *The Moscow Times*, 13 August 2014, Internet, http://www.themoscowtimes.com/news/article/505076.html (date accessed: 24 November 2014).

37 Information about communal services price hikes derived from interviews in Moscow and St. Petersburg, June 2014. On the pension fund see Anastasiia Bashkatova, "Pensionnye nakopleniia grazhdan potracheny na Krym i bor'bu s krizisom (The Citizens' Pension Fund has been spent on Crimea and the struggle with the crisis), Internet [English translation unavailable], g.ru/economics/2014-06-26/1_pensii.html (date accessed: 24 November 2014).

38 Frozen conflicts refer to areas of the former Soviet Union where ongoing low-level violence has become the norm, with no political settlement in view. Russia has played a major role in preserving these regions as unstable pseudo-states, using them as leverage against former Soviet republics. Nagorno-Karabakh (leverage against Azerbaijan and influence with Armenia), South Ossetia and Abkhazia (stripped from Georgia), and Trans-Dniester (part of Moldova) have been the four most-cited cases. Eastern Ukraine might become the fifth. For a recent discussion of Ukraine in this context see Roman Olearchyk, "Frozen conflict emerges from heat of war," *The Financial Times*, 2 October 2014.

39 The Internet was supposed to be the great exception to state control of information. In 1999, Putin endorsed the views of economic and social groups opposed to building a "Great Firewall" in Russia. Since returning to the presidency, Putin has increasingly sought to emulate China's effort to con-

NOTES

trol cyberspace.

40 The announced plan to resume broadcasts for thirty minutes each day is hardly a significant alternative.

41 President Putin has consistently put a brave face on the economic impact of the Ukraine invasion. His economic advisers have been less sanguine. Andrew Kramer, "Putin Trumpets Economic Strength, but Advisers Seem Less Certain," *The New York Times*, 3 October 2014. For recent scholarly analysis see Natal'ia Zubarevich, "Prostranstvo Rossii posle Kryma i na fone krizisa (The Russian Space after Crimea and against the background of the crisis)," *Pro et Contra* 18, (May-August 2014): 118-128. *Also* Sergei Aleksashenko, "Ekonomika Rossii k nachalu epokhi 'posle Putina' (The Russian Economy at the Beginning of the Post-Putin Epoch)," *Pro et Contra* 18, (May-August 2014): 104-117. *Also* Nikolai Petrov, "Rossiia v 2014-m: skatyvanie v voronku (Russia in 2014: Sliding Down the Funnel)," *Pro et Contra* 18, (May-August 2014): 57-86.

42 Paul Goble, "Crimea's Consequences for Russia's Non-Russians—A Net Assessment of Long-Term Nationalities Trends Within the Russian Federation Since the Start of 2014," *Eurasia Daily Monitor* 11, no. 182, (15 October 2014). *Also* Paul Goble, "Crimea's Consequences for Russia's Non-Russians—A Net Assessment of Long-Term Nationalities Trends Within the Russian Federation Since the Start of 2014, *Eurasia Daily Monitor* 11.182 (15 October 2014), Internet, http://www.jamestown.org/programs/edm/single/?tx_ttnews[tt_news]=42958&cHash=86f5ac7b58a3b23c3a65f4832357bde6#.VFwoABbwoII (date accessed: 24 November 2014). For excellent coverage of the economic and political impact of the Ukraine invasion on Russian regions, see Paul Goble's blog *Window on Eurasia*, Internet, http://windowoneurasia2.blogspot.com (date accessed: 24 November 2014).

43 For a typical Putin comment, see "Russia could lose over 100 bln rubles from EU-Ukraine association - Putin," INTERFAX, 26 August 2014. For other calculations indicating that the results for the Russian economy would be neutral or positive, see the sources in note 2.

44 Outside of the Middle East, Russia has the largest number of Muslim citizens fighting in ISIS groups in Syria and Iraq. Ceylan Yeginsu, "ISIS Draws Steady Stream of Recruits from Turkey," *The New York Times*, 15 September, 2014: 1. *Also* Vladislav Mal'tsev, "Nezametnaia islamskaia revoliutsiia (The Unnoticed Islamic Revolution)," *Nezavisimaia gazeta*, 6 November 2014, Internet, [English translation unavailable], http://www.ng.ru/columnist/2014%2011%2006/2_dagestan.html (date accessed: 24 November 2014).

45 During a three-week trip to Russia in June, many acquaintances repeated this view. There is a high degree of irony in the incessant labeling of Kiev's leaders as "fascists." The most extreme political group garnered just 1.6 percent of the vote in the November Ukrainian election. Zhirinovskii's Liberal Democratic Party of Russia, Zyuganov's Communists, and Rogozin's Rodina Party all have polled much higher numbers, and all three hold leadership positions in Putin's government.

46 Elizabeth Dunn and Michael Bobik, "The Empire Strikes Back: War without war and occupation without occupation in the Russian sphere of Influence," *American Ethnologist* 41.3(2014): 405-413. *Also* Mary Kaldor, *New and Old Wars: Organized Violence in a Global Era* (Stanford: Stanford University Press, 2012). The frozen conflict in South Ossetia obliterated the tax base. The regime financed operations by printing some $20 billion in counterfeit $100 bills. On Donetsk and Luhansk, see Aleksey Matsuka, "Writing the truth in the People's Republic of Donetsk," OpenDemocracy, 18 July 2014, Internet, www.opendemocracy.net/od-russia/aleksey-matsuka/writing-truth-in-people%E2%80%99s-republic-of-donetsk (date accessed: 24 November 2014). *Also* Tetyana Zarovnaya, "Terrorists are already kidnapping people just for the sake of ransom, but militia is inactive," 28 May 2014, Internet, http://uacrisis.org/activists-of-donetsk-euromaidan/ (date accessed: 24 November 2014). *Also* Pavel Knyagin, "Kidnapped Russian Journalist Pavel Kanygin on his own abduction: 'This is not a ransom, this is your contribution to our war,'" 26 May 2014, Internet, http://maidantranslations.com/2014/05/26/kidnapped-russian-journalist-pavel-kanygin-on-his-own-abduction-this-is-not-a-ransom-this-is-your-contribution-to-our-war/ (date accessed: 24 November 2014).

47 Sergei Baburin, *Krym naveki s Rossiei: istoriko-pravovoe obosnovanie vossoedineniia respubliki Krym i goroda Sevastopol' s Rossiiskoi Federatsei* (Crimea With Russia Forever: The Historical-Legal Basis for Uniting the Crimean Republic and City of Sevastopol with the Russian Federation), (Moscow: knizhnyi mir, 2014). *Also* Ivan Mironov, *Aliaska predannaia i prodannaia: istoriia dvortsovogo zagovora* (Alaska betrayed and sold: The History of a Palace Conspiracy), (Moscow: Knizhnyi mir, 2014).

48 Steven Pifer and Strobe Talbott, "Time to give Ukraine defensive weapons," *Kyiv Post*, 18 September 2014, Internet, http://www.kyivpost.com/opinion/op-ed/steven-pifer-and-strobe-talbott-time-to-give-ukraine-defensive-weapons-365119.html (date accessed: 24 November 2014).

49 Gazeta.ru Commentary, "Odin-za vse: Chem opasna personifikatsiia vlasti (One-for Everything: The Danger in the Personification of Power)," Internet [English translation unavailable], http://www.gazeta.ru/comments/2014/11/07_e_6292885.shtml (date accessed: 24 November 2014). On the damage inflicted by Putin and his cronies see Dawisha, *Putin's Kleptocracy*, Chapter 7. *Also* Jo Becker and Steven Lee

NOTES

Myers, "Putin's Friend Profits in Purge of School-books," *The New York Times*, 2 November 2014. *Also* Harley Balzer, "Authoritarianism and Modernization in Russia: Is Russia Ka-Putin?" *Politics and Economics in Putin's Russia* (Carlisle: U.S. Army War College, December 2013): 125-174. Putin has revised his view of the Molotov-Ribbentrop Pact, the agreement to give the USSR the Baltics and divide Poland with Hitler. Neil MacFarquhar, "Russia: Putin Defends Soivet-Nazi Pact," *The New York Times*, 7 November 2014.

50 For a good recent survey of these issues and the difficulties involved, see Angela Stent, *The Limits of Partnership: U.S.-Russian Relations in the Twenty-first Century* (Princeton and Oxford: Princeton University Press, 2014.) The forthcoming paperback edition is being revised to include a discussion of Ukraine.

51 Echo Moskvy, Interview with Lev Gudkov, note 26.

Politics&Diplomacy

Headwinds

Growth, Democracy, and the Middle Class in Latin America

Margaret Hayes

The decade of the 2000s was generally good for Latin America. Many countries grew robustly, driven by expanding trade relations and China's demand for commodities like agricultural products, minerals, and oil. The economic expansion led to a dramatic growth of the middle class in Mexico, Brazil, Columbia, Peru, and other countries. The 2008 economic crisis and the persisting slow recovery of the developed world, along with China's efforts to control its own growth rate, now weigh heavily on Latin America's return to robust growth. Exports, investments, and growth have slowed dramatically in several key countries. A wide range of recent reports concludes that the region is unlikely to return to the robust growth of the 2000s anytime soon.[1] The "tailwinds" of the past decade "are clearly receding" for Latin America.[2] The region must turn to domestic engines of growth and to growth-enhancing reforms that can drive each country's competitiveness.

Figure 1 depicts world and regional growth since 1999. Global growth has been led by countries of emerging and developing Asia: China, and more recently India, Vietnam, and other countries expanded at record levels, but have begun to slow and control their growth more recently.

Margaret Hayes is an Adjunct Professor at Georgetown University. She is also Vice President of Evidence Based Research, Inc. Dr. Hayes was formerly a founding Director of the Center for Hemispheric Defense Studies at National Defense University, and served as External Relations Advisor at the Inter-American Development Bank.

Advanced economies, the most economically mature, have posted the lowest growth rates. The Western hemisphere falls between these two, posting growth around 6 percent or more year-on-year during the latter half of the decade, and briefly following the crises of 2009 and 2010.

opment Bank, summarized the challenges to the region in a recent speech: "The direction of winds from the global economy impelling the regional economy have shifted, and we have to prepare to navigate with our own efforts and without the tailwinds that we have had in recent years."[3] The need to program

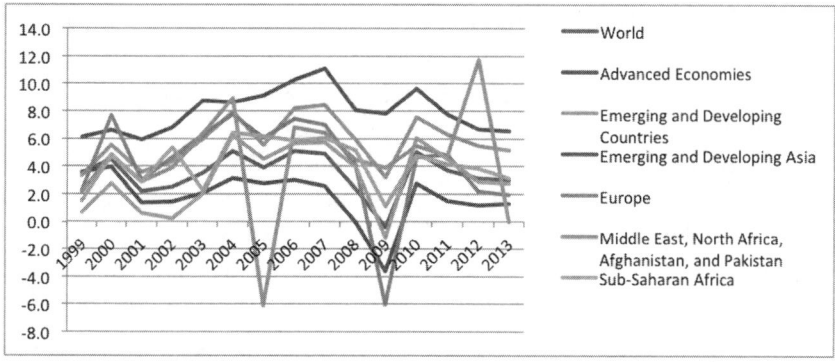

Figure 1 World GDP Growth, Year-on-Year

The challenges for Latin America, and particularly for its largest economies, are to diversify productive sectors, improve labor productivity, and enhance their competitiveness in the global marketplace. The region's middle classes were demanding these changes in their recent street protests calling for better education, better health services, better transportation and infrastructure, better business climates, and more efficient and responsive government. Many of these changes will take time to show results. Governments' responses to the new challenges will have profound influence on Latin America's evolving democracies and their future growth prospects.

Enrique Iglesias, the former Secretary General of the Economic Commission for Latin American and former President of the Inter-American Devel-

economic and social development with greater reliance on internal conditions underscores a fundamental role for economic integration of Latin America in present circumstances.

To address these challenges, Iglesias argues that Latin America should pursue selective regional cooperation, make serious efforts to increase the flexibility of existing integration agreements, and promote greater coordination. Doing so will require progressive cooperation in the areas of infrastructure, production sectors like the auto industry, and coordination of efforts in innovative research and development (R&D). The region also needs to take advantage of the more than 500 "multilatinas" (Latin American multinationals) that are already working and expanding their influence.[4] By creating new spaces for regional cooperation,

Latin America will be able to unlock new frontiers of industrialization that no single country, no matter how big, could accomplish alone.

Latin America's Competitiveness.

The World Economic Forum's (WEF) annual Global Competitiveness Index (GCI) provides insight into the region's challenges. The index is constructed from scoring competitiveness factors on twelve pillars allocated across three clusters: *Basic Requirements, Efficiency Enhancers, and Innovation and Sophistication Factors.*[5] *Basic Requirements* encompasses public and private institutional performance, including evaluations of property rights, ethics and corruption, ciency, financial market development and technological readiness, and size of both domestic and export markets. Lastly, *Innovation and Sophistication Factors* assess the sophistication of businesses and innovative R&D.[6] The *Basic Requirements* sub-index components are critical for factor-driven economies that produce primary products, while *Efficiency*-driven economies rely on combinations of labor, capital, trade, and production. *Innovation*-driven economies combine knowledge, research, and technology to the above mix. Utilizing a wide variety of quantitative data and responses to the WEF's Executive Opinion Survey, these twelve pillars are aggregated and tallied on a seven-point scale, reveal-

	Overall Competitiveness Index		Basic Requirements		Efficiency Enhancers		Innovation and Sophistication Factors	
	Rank	Score	Rank	Score	Rank	Score	Rank	Score
Chile	33	4.6	30	5.25	29	4.68	49	3.88
Panama	48	4.43	53	4.82	55	4.29	46	3.95
Brazil	67	4.34	83	4.4	42	4.46	56	3.82
Mexico	61	4.27	69	4.59	60	4.2	59	3.73
Peru	65	4.24	74	4.52	62	4.19	99	3.34
Argentina	104	3.79	104	4.08	93	3.75	96	3.37
Venezuela	131	3.32	131	3.36	124	3.35	135	2.71

Table 1 Latin American Global Competitiveness Rankings

government efficiency and security, infrastructure availability, the macroeconomic environment, and health and primary education. *Efficiency Enhancers* are comprised of the quantity and quality of secondary and higher education, market efficiency (including both domestic and foreign competition), trade restrictions, labor market effi-

ing the GCI. Table 1 summarizes the GCI performance scores of seven Latin American economies.

Switzerland possesses the top score of 5.7. Chile is the highest-ranked Latin American economy at 33. China precedes Chile at rank 28 and a score of 4.89. Panama is the second highest-ranking Latin American country in the list, and Venezuela, which recently earned the label of "probably the world's worst-managed economy," falls at the bottom of the rankings with only Haiti below it.[7] Most of these Latin American countries are transitioning to *Innovation*-driven economies. Peru and Colombia rank as *Efficiency*-driven but not yet in transition, while Venezuela falls between *Factor* and *Efficiency*-driven.

A closer examination of the three on assessments of higher education and training quality, and several receive a strong score boost from their overall market size. Nevertheless, quite low scores on goods and labor market efficiencies, and on technology readiness, offset the more positive ratings. Brazil, Chile, Colombia, Mexico, and Panama score above the scale's median regarding innovation and business sophistication, but these rankings are driven

By creating new spaces for regional cooperation, Latin America can unlock new frontiers of industrialization that no single country could accomplish alone.

sub-indexes shows that Latin American competitiveness is seriously impacted by shortfalls in *Basic Requirements*. Several countries rank noticeably lower in these requirements than their overall ranking would suggest, while doing much better with respect to *Efficiency Enhancers*. Panama, Brazil, and Mexico rank reasonably well in terms of *Innovation and Sophistication Factors*, even though poor scores on institutional performance and infrastructure adequacy pull the countries down. Chile, Colombia, and Peru all score over 5.0 regarding their macroeconomic environments, and all of the listed countries score over 5.0 in their provision of heath and primary education. Only Mexico and Chile receive scores over 4.0 on infrastructure adequacy. Institutional performance scores range from 2.1 in Venezuela to 4.8 in Chile, with all other nations remaining at 3.5 and below. With respect to *Efficiency Enhancers*, most countries do well

by their business sophistication, while their innovation scores are much lower. More generally, corruption remains a concern in most of these economies, except for Chile. Government inefficiency is also a widely expressed concern that negatively affects the ease of doing business and the viability of business sophistication and growth. In short, Latin America is very inconsistent in its competitiveness indicators, and this impedes the development of reinforcing synergies.

The Importance of Education.

Education is an important component of the GCI. While education is generally available in Latin American countries, the overall quality, particularly at the primary and secondary level, is a subject of much discussion. This is demonstrated by Latin America's performance well below the Organization for Economic Cooperation and Development (OECD) average on the global Program for International Student Assessment (PISA) exam (see Table 2).[8] The OECD argues that "improvements in education have the potential to boost growth more than virtually all other types of structural reform."

A Brazilian study reflected the region's concern with its quality of education: "Brazil's several high-quality, free public universities must teach students arriving from the *notoriously weak system of public education*."[9] In 2011, the country spent on college students almost five times what it spent on stu-

share of top performers in math. Other Latin American countries were well below 1 percent. As a result, businesses in the region often have difficulties finding workers with the necessary skills to meet job requirements.

Criticisms of the education systems in the region are that they are "outdated," "too academic," and do not prepare students to compete in the global marketplace.[11] Curriculum changes are needed to incorporate technology and emphasize greater analytical skills. As one Brazilian commented: "We need to be bolder. We cannot have a school

	Mean Math Score	Share of Top Performers in Math	Mean Reading Score	Mean Science Score
OECD Avg	494	12.6	496	501
Chile	427	1.6	441	445
Mexico	421	0.6	424	415
Brazil	391	0.8	410	405
Argentina	388	0.3	396	406
Colombia	376	0.3	403	399

Table 2 Latin American performance on the OECD PISA Exam 2012

dents in basic education. One result of this distortion is that while some 85 percent of Brazilians from ages fifteen to seventeen are enrolled in school, only half of them are at the appropriate grade level.[10] The minority of high performing students who raise overall national performance scores often attend private schools. Across the spectrum, however, the majority of students perform at the lowest levels. Only 1.6 percent of students who took the PISA exam in Chile, the region's best performer, fell into the OECD average

of the 19th century, with teachers of the 20th century, if we are to interest students of the 21st century."[12] Since most students will end education at the secondary school level, education should require greater access to technology and greater attention to practical skills at earlier ages. Mexico, with one of the most dynamic industrial sectors in the region, has just begun to introduce technology schools into its education system. This kind of skills training is also needed to draw workers into the formal market and out of the low-wage informal market.[13] Brazil launched a National Program for Access to Technical Education and Employment (Pronatec) in 2011. For Pronatec to work, there needs to be much closer collaboration between the private sector and the education community so that the skills being taught meet market requirements.

Resource curse? Growing external demand and rising prices for basic goods like agriculture, minerals and ores, and petroleum drove the past decade of Latin America's economic expansion. Analysts now urge the region to focus on "knowledge, technology and innovation" as a basis for development.[15] According to the U.S.

Businesses in the region often have difficulties finding workers with the necessary skills to meet job requirements.

Teacher qualifications and training must also be better. Mexican President Enrique Peña Nieto bravely took on the entrenched national teachers union as one of his first actions in office. The unions predictably responded by violently protesting and shutting schools down. The teachers unions are a challenge to education reform in other countries as well, resisting any kind of change and any external evaluation of their performance. In many cases, teachers in primary and secondary schools are not licensed, especially in the final years of middle and high school.[14] If "improvements in education have the potential to boost growth more than virtually all other types of structural reform," they are going to have to change, and countries must insist on education that provides greater access to technology, an emphasis on analytical abilities, and improved teaching requirements. The region must begin to compete with countries at the top of the PISA scale.

Energy Information Administration, the Americas in 2013 accounted for one-third of proved world reserves of crude oil, one-tenth of proved natural gas reserves, and enormous amounts of recoverable reservoired resources like tight oil and shale gas.[16] Venezuela, Canada, the United States, and Brazil are the principal sources of these resources, but Argentina, Peru, Ecuador, Colombia, and Mexico are all producers and exporters of petroleum, and oil exports have been an important component of the recent energy expansion. Brazil, Chile, Colombia, and Peru are also major exporters of ores. Brazil's discovery of vast offshore pre-salt petroleum reserves has sparked national excitement, but bringing the reserves to market will be slow, given the challenging market environment, the requirement for advanced petroleum recovery technologies, and a still uncertain regulatory environment that has discouraged some of the most experienced offshore operators from bidding on the reserves' first auction.[17]

While the boom in oil, copper, and

iron-ore exports have captured news headlines in recent years, Latin America possesses a fairly diverse production environment. An examination of the percentage share of total exports for the top ten exports of the region's large economies shows considerable potential for diversification expansion. While several economies are obviously dependent on raw material exports—Chile, Colombia, and especially Venezuela—oil producers like Argentina, Brazil, and Mexico enjoy considerable diversity in their exports. Agriculture remains an important export for most countries, including Argentina, Brazil, and Ecuador. Manufacturing exports, including automobiles, automobile parts, sophisticated aircraft, and other products are important in Mexico, Argentina, and Brazil.[18] Only Venezuela is overwhelm-

ing, expanding the use of information and communication technologies, and promoting and rewarding innovation. It also requires addressing serious infrastructure bottlenecks: road networks, lack of rail communication, ports that are inefficient and inadequate for the volume of goods that already should pass through them, insufficient power supplies in critical urban and industrial areas, and others. Reducing bureaucracy and corruption in decision-making apparatuses is also important to facilitate business expansion and to reduce the "corruption taxes" that affect far too many countries. Finally, countries must make the hard political decision to level taxes on incomes and profits that can generate the revenues needed to address infrastructure shortfalls. Together, these reforms should help

Reducing bureaucracy and corruption in decision-making apparatuses is also important to facilitate business expansion.

ingly dependent on oil for 88 percent of its exports, and that country unfortunately has allowed its non-oil sectors to languish in the past two decades. Most other countries are consciously seeking to diversify exports, but they still lack the regional coordination of efforts that Enrique Iglesias suggests is needed to fully exploit synergies.

What is to be done? Analysts agree that Latin American countries must undertake major efforts to improve productivity and increase economic competitiveness. This requires investments in education and worker train-

countries move into the *Efficiency*-driven phase of competitiveness and acquire more diversified participation in the global value chain.

The OECD, World Bank, and Economic Commission for Latin America have all listed structural and policy changes that need to be implemented. In a new report, the Inter-American Development Bank also argues that these changes will require important adjustments in the public sector policy-making bureaucracy.[19] Governments will have to be more flexible in addressing problems, implementing policy changes, and operating more as "learning organizations" by learning empirically about best practices to address their shortcomings. They will have to work more closely with the private sector while avoiding "capture" by specific sectors and firms. Finally, government agencies must learn to coordinate more effectively with each other to implement solutions in the best possible manner.[20]

Enrique Iglesias also argues that Latin America must make better use of its existing trade agreements, and address trade barriers, like high tariffs, that could enhance the Latin American share in the global value chain. Moreover, Latin America must pursue new agreements with new partners. Chile, Peru, Colombia, and Mexico are actively pursuing the Trans-Pacific Partnership. Greater Latin American integration would very likely draw Brazil and Argentina into that Partnership, furthering regional gains from trade. Brazil is considering negotiating directly and alone with the European Union, despite reluctance on the part of MERCOSUR partners. MERCOSUR and other regional agreements should be streamlined and made more efficient and less bureaucratic.

Implications for Democracy. Public opinion research reports strong support for democracy in most Latin American countries. Even while expressing concerns about different aspects of democratic performance, citizens support the idea that "democracy is the best system"—what the Latinobarometro poll calls the "Churchillian" concept. Nevertheless, protests over the availability and quality of government services have been increasing. The protestors tend to be young, single, and well educat-

ed—the youth of the emerging middle class. From 2011 to 2012, Chilean students marched in the streets protesting against the high cost of secondary and higher education, which are largely private, and demanding more state support for middle schools and colleges. In 2013, demonstrators in Brazil protested against government corruption, low-quality education and insecurity, as well as the large sums of money being spent in preparation for the FIFA World Cup despite the nation's poor healthcare services. Protestors demanded, "We want FIFA-quality healthcare!" In early 2014, Venezuelans protested against the high levels of violence, increasing inflation, and the absence of the most basic goods in stores. Some Venezuelan demonstrators demanded the resignation of President Nicolas Maduro. All too often, protests were met by heavy-handed police responses.[21]

Regional frustrations with government and democracy tend to be focused on the quality and delivery of public goods. Citizens are most supportive of their governments when the economy is growing, insecurity is contained, and corruption is controlled. Support for political parties is low, at 36.8 percent, while support for the Catholic Church and the armed forces is high at 63.1 percent and 62.2 percent, respectively.[22] Survey respondents expressed low levels of confidence in political leaders and political parties, when questioned "Do political parties listen to people like me?" or "Are political leaders interested in what people like me think?" In Mexico, Argentina, Chile, Colombia, and Brazil, fewer than 40 percent of respondents answer affirmatively to these questions.[23]

Conclusion. Latin American governments' abilities to face the challenging "economic headwinds" of the coming years and introduce policies that can contribute to enhanced productivity, increased competitiveness, and greater insertion into the global value chain are particularly important for building the foundations for stable regimes. In addition, the ability to deliver better education and healthcare, while growing the middle class and expanding opportunities for more challenging jobs, is necessary to address the rising expectations of people in the region and build their confidence in governments that serve the public's interest. Ultimately, Latin American governments will need their citizens to share in the reshaping of the region's economic and political development if they are to be successful.

NOTES

1 International Monetary Fund (IMF), "Regional Economic Outlook – Western Hemisphere," (Washington, D.C.: IMF, April 2014). *Also* Organization for Economic Cooperation and Development (OECD), "Latin American Economic Outlook 2014: Logistics and Competitiveness for Development" (Paris: OECD Publishing, 2014). *Also* Economic Commission for Latin America, "Estudio Economico de America Latina y el Caribe: Desafios para la sostenibilidad del credimiento en un Nuevo context externo" (United Nations: Comision Economica para America Latina, 2014). *Also* IMF, "International Financial Statistics Database," Internet, http://elibrary-data.imf.org/FindDataReports.aspx?d=33061&e=169393 (date accessed: 1 October 2014).

2 Agusto de la Torre, "Latin American and the Caribbean as Tailwinds Recede: In Search of Higher Growth" (Washington, D.C.: World Bank, 2013). *Also* IMF, "World Economic Outlook: Recovery Strengthens, Remains Uneven" (Washington, D.C.: IMF, April 2014).

3 Enrique Iglesias, "Speech to the XVIII Annual CAF Conference" (Washington D.C., 4 September 2014), Internet, http://www.thedialogue.org/uploads/Iglesias Keynote2014CAFConf.pdf (date accessed: 1 October 2014).

4 Ibid.

5 World Economic Forum, "The Global Competitiveness Report 2014-2015" (Geneva: World Economic Forum, 2014), Internet, http://www.weforum.org/reports/global-competitiveness-report-2014-2015 (date accessed: 1 October 2014).

6 Ibid., 49-50.

7 "Of oil and coconut water," *The Economist*, 20 September 2014, Caracas, Print Edition.

8 OECD, "PISA 2012 Results in Focus: What 15-years-olds know and what they can do with what they know" (Geneva: OECD, 2014), Internet, http://oecd.org/pisa/keyfindings/pisa-2012-results-overview.pdf (date accessed: 1 October 2014).

9 Fundacão Getulio Vargas (FGV), "Can Brazil Find a Route to Competitiveness?" *The Brazilian Economy*, August 2014, 12-25.

10 Fundacão Getulio Vargas (FGV), "Brazil: Education 2.0," *The Brazilian Economy*, July 2014, 7-14.

11 Ibid.

12 Ibid.

13 OECD Economic Survey (Mexico and Paris: OECD Publishing, May 2013), Internet, http://www.oecd.org/eco/surveys/Overview%20Eng.pdf (date accessed: 1 October 2014).

14 FGV, August 2014.

15 Ibid.

16 Energy Information Administration (EIA), U.S. Department of Energy, "Liquid Fuels and Natural Gas in the Americas," January 2014.

17 "Consortium wins Brazil Deepwater Oilfield Auctions," *Financial Times*, 21 October 2013, Internet, http://www.ft.com/intl/cms/s/0/5ba1e982-3a68-11e3-9243-00144feab7de.html#axzz3EpvJI5vX (date accessed: 1 October 2014).

18 Ricardo Haussman, Cesar Hidalgo et al., "The Atlas of Economic Complexity: Mapping Paths to Prosperity" (Boston Center for International Development: Harvard University and Observatory of Economic Complexity, Media Lab: Massachusetts Institute of Technology, 2014), Internet, http://chidalgo.com/Atlas/HarvarMIT_AtlasOfEconomicComplexity_Preface.pdf (date accessed: 1 October 2014). *Also* Observatory of Economic Complexity, Media Lab, Massachusetts Institute of Technology, Internet, http://atlas.media.mit.edu/ (date accessed: 1 October 2014). *Also*, "Time for Correction," *The Brazilian Economy*, September 2014, 13-33.

19 Gustavo Crespi, Fernandez-Arias and Stein Ernesto (Eds), "Rethinking Productive Development: Sound Policies and Institutions for Economi Transformation" (Palgrave-Macmillan for the Inter-American Development Bank), Internet, http://idbdocs.iadb.org/wsdocs/getdocument.aspx?docnum=39045377 (date accessed: 1 October 2014).

20 Ibid.

21 *The Economist*, 2014.

22 Mitchell Seligson et al., "The Political Culture of Democracy in the Americas, 2012: Towards Equality of Opportunity" (Vanderbilt University: Latin American Public Opinion Project, November 2012), Internet, http://www.vanderbilt.edu/lapop/ab2012/AB2012-comparative-report-v3-PreliminaryVersion.pdf (date accessed: 1 October 2014).

23 Ibid.

Hostage Negotiations and Other Talks with Terrorists

Price vs. Principle

Audrey Kurth Cronin

Should the U.S. government ever negotiate with terrorists? The release of journalist Peter Theo Curtis and Army Sergeant Bowe Bergdahl juxtaposed against the dreadful beheading of journalists James Foley, Steven Sotloff, and others rocketed this question back to the headlines. No one wants to compromise principles or capitulate to terrorists; for most people, the instinctive answer to the question is "No." But when contemplating how best to defeat a terrorist group and to pursue long-term U.S. interests, the issue gains complexity. The U.S., European, and Israeli governments take very different approaches to hostage negotiations, for example, affecting the likelihood of release of their citizens while also shifting the strategic counterterrorism picture for everyone else. Whose interests take priority? As for negotiations over political stakes, an in-depth analysis of hundreds of terrorist campaigns yields complex conclusions. Under certain conditions, with certain types of groups, negotiations can undermine terrorist groups' popular support, alter their ambitions, further the national security interests of the state, and defeat terrorism. The obverse is also true: ruling out negotiations, under any circumstances, can unwittingly help a group survive. The key is to cold-

Audrey Kurth Cronin is a Distinguished Service Professor with tenure at George Mason University's School of Policy, Government and International Affairs. Prior to joining the university, she was a professor and director of the core course on military strategy at the National War College (2007-2011).

ly analyze the stakes, opponents, and conditions under which policymakers are operating, then go from there. Strangely enough, the record indicates that sometimes negotiations with terrorists are the only way to win.

Of course, we must clarify exactly what we mean by "negotiations." The term refers to a range of interactions between governments and terrorist organizations. Many people envisage high-level parleys like the Israeli-Palestinian peace process with Yasser Arafat's Palestinian Liberation Organization (PLO) that led to the 1993 Oslo

they did not. In short, "talks with terrorists" are not simply one-dimensional, but rather cover a wide spectrum of potential interactions.

This article will have three sections, moving from the narrowest to the broadest point on the spectrum of talks. First, we will explore the dynamics and dilemmas of negotiating with terrorist groups holding hostages. For governments, companies, or individuals, the trade-offs in responding to that kind of blackmail are grim. As a result, international approaches to kidnapping for ransom are diverse. Second, we will

Unlike most European governments, the U.S. government has a clear policy that it **will not pay ransoms.**

Accords, or the Northern Ireland peace process involving the Provisional Irish Republican Army (PIRA) that led to the 1998 Good Friday Agreement in Belfast. These are indeed important cases, but high-level deliberations over broad political terms are rare. Instead, talks occur directly or indirectly, at high (public) or low (deniable) levels, very often through third-party intermediaries. Talking with terrorists can cover a range of issues, from the narrowest immediate concerns (like the fate of hostages) to the broadest political disagreements (like the nature of governance). Even the most stalwart regimes engage in some form of "talks" or interactions with their opponents, usually secretly, through intelligence operatives, mediators, proxies, or other associates. They would shirk their responsibility to safeguard citizens if

focus on the tactical reasons to talk with groups over their political aims, even without truly negotiable terms. Negotiations can provide great intelligence, for example, by smoking out terrorist group members or illuminating their organizational dynamics. Third, we will explore strategic considerations, analyzing the conditions under which governments can employ negotiations to defeat terrorist groups over time. Rigorous analysis of the endings of groups demonstrates that talking to terrorists can be critical to effective counterterrorism.

Talks with Groups Holding Hostages.
Beginning with the narrowest interpretation, "talking with terrorists" refers to hostage negotiations, especially kidnapping-for-ransom. An in-depth study by the *New York Times* found

that al-Qaeda and its direct affiliates had gained some $125 million in revenue from kidnappings since 2008, of which some $66 million was paid just in 2013.[1] Unlike most European governments, the U.S. government has a clear policy that it will not pay ransoms. Indeed, the American position is uniquely strong; if a U.S. company or other private entity pays off a designated foreign terrorist organization, the Justice Department may even prosecute it for funding terrorism.[2] On the other hand, clandestine kinetic operations to release U.S. hostages are not uncommon; the logic is that kidnappers should be punished, not rewarded, and that future hostage-takers will be dissuaded by the show of force and the deaths of their predecessors. Of course, the hard part is figuring out where the hostages are actually being held, ensuring they are still there, and then carrying out operations that target kidnappers and spare captives. Whether or not you support this strict U.S. no-negotiations policy probably depends on whether or not you know any current hostages.[3]

Other countries have a range of approaches. Like the United States, the British government refuses to negotiate ransoms; however, if a private company or individual family pays for a British citizen's release, the U.K. government looks the other way.[4] The French, Italian, Spanish, Swiss, and other European governments regularly pay ransoms directly to groups. The Israelis have perhaps the most unusual hybrid policy, combining ransoms or prisoner releases with harsh retribution as a follow-up. Their practice in this regard has evolved: Israeli Prime Minister

Golda Meier was famous for her public refusal to negotiate with the Black September terrorists holding eleven Israeli athletes at the 1972 Munich Olympics, saying: "If we should give in, then no Israeli anywhere in the world shall feel that his life is safe...It's blackmail of the worse kind."[5] In the aftermath of the massacre of the athletes, the Israeli Mossad (intelligence organization) tracked down and killed all of the Palestinians involved (except one), in a global operation made famous by the 2005 movie Munich.

The Israeli government now often negotiates with Palestinian groups who capture Israeli soldiers or civilians, usually swapping large numbers of prisoners from Israeli jails. The first such disproportionate exchange occurred in 1979, when the government released 76 PLO prisoners in exchange for one Israeli hostage. The most lopsided payoff to date was the 2011 ransom for the release of Gilad Shalit, held by Hamas in the Gaza Strip for five years. Shalit was exchanged for the release of 1,027 Palestinian prisoners—although many were subsequently recaptured or killed by the Israelis, including in the 2014 Gaza conflict.[6]

In this way, negotiating for hostage release is in a category of its own. It pits the desire to rescue innocent individuals from captivity or a horrible end against the fear of enriching a group with a ransom or other incentive. The killing of James Foley came after more than a dozen European hostages held with him were reportedly freed in return for ransoms averaging more than $2.5 million per person.[7] Among them were four French, one Danish and two Spanish hostages, released after their governments, their organizations, or their families paid exorbitant sums.[8] No wonder some al-Qaeda affiliates like al-Qaeda in the Islamic Maghreb (AQIM) have had staying power: with a reliable source of income that does

of Europeans taken as hostages by jihadist groups appears to be circumstantial evidence that this long-standing policy has reduced the incentives to snatch U.S. citizens, but it also heightens the likelihood that, if taken, American citi-

With a **reliable source of income** that does not depend on state sponsorship or mobilizing widespread popular support, [al-Qaeda affiliates] can continue operating without the traditional restraints that may moderate terrorist behavior.

not depend on state sponsorship or mobilizing widespread popular support, these groups can continue operating without the traditional restraints that may moderate terrorist behavior. This is hugely damaging to international efforts to fight violent Islamist terrorism.

Despite the appalling killing of American hostages, U.S. officials believe that a no-ransom policy protects other Americans from being targeted, since terrorist groups know hostages cannot be cashed in and that holding them increases the risk of a lethal reaction. The Treasury Department's Under Secretary for Terrorism and Financial Intelligence said in a 2012 London speech that "recent kidnapping-for-ransom trends appear to indicate that hostage-takers prefer not to take U.S. and U.K. hostages—almost certainly because they understand that they will not receive ransoms...and because they fear a kinetic response if they do."[9] He also termed kidnapping-for-ransom "the most significant source of terrorist financing."[10] The much larger number

zens will be murdered.[11] It is also worth noting that we have no way to compare the number of Americans versus Europeans actually taken hostage in places like Syria, Pakistan, and Iraq against the number of opportunities jihadist groups actually have to capture them. In other words, it is possible that for jihadist groups, there are simply more Europeans around to grab.

Another dimension that is often ignored in this debate is the public outrage and media attention following the deaths of much-admired hostages like Daniel Pearl in Pakistan and James Foley in Syria, or even public figures such as Ambassador Christopher Stevens in Libya. Terrorist groups use strategies of provocation to draw states into unwise or emotion-driven responses that work against the state's own interests.[12] A knee-jerk intervention with overwhelming military force in Iraq, for example, could hurt longer-term, regional efforts to divide the Sunni coalition aligned with the Islamic State of Iraq and Syria (ISIS, also known as ISIL or IS) and force the mainly Shiite

Iraqi government to share power. The public murder of James Foley played a direct role in the lionizing of ISIS by senior U.S. leaders such as Secretary of Defense Chuck Hagel, who said two days later that the group is "beyond anything we've seen."[13] A group's despicability drawing media attention can be more valuable than gaining millions of dollars through ransoms. In these circumstances, policymakers must hope that the deep revulsion felt by millions of Muslim onlookers will overpower the macabre fascination by individuals drawn to a group's cause and, in this case especially, that a strong anti-ISIS coalition and backlash will result.

Tactical Reasons to Negotiate.

Negotiations always carry risks, and governments must be mindful of their own coalitions and constituencies in pursuing them. Appearing to capitulate to terrorism can be disastrous for democratic leaders. However, governments often talk to terrorists secretly, undermining public support.

Negotiations can be a great way to collect intelligence unavailable through other means. For all the hype about reconnaissance from the air, drones cannot substitute for human intelligence on the ground.[14] Just seeing who shows up for talks can tell governments a great deal about the structure of a group and the positions of different members—intelligence that might then be exploited by offering specific proposals attractive to one faction but not another. There are famous examples of intelligence operatives who secretly tested opportunities or sowed the seeds for later talks. British intelligence pursued covert channels with Irish republicans starting in the mid-1970s. Niel Barnard and Mike Louw, both part of the South African National Intelligence Service, initiated talks with Nelson Mandela during the 1980s when he was imprisoned as a "terrorist." Israel's Shin Bet built the foundations for the Israeli-Palestinian peace process of the

Negotiations can help to split groups apart by revealing factional differences over ideologies, constituencies, methods, organizational loyalties, or even long-term political goals.

directly, or through others, for pragmatic reasons having nothing to do with concessions. Negotiations are not the obverse of fighting: tactical motives are intertwined, and states simultaneously counter groups in different ways. Over the range of tactical purposes for talks, three are highlighted here: gathering intelligence, disaggregating groups, and

1990s. But short of such broader purposes, talks can also indicate a lot of practical things about shadowy groups and their leaders, including personal habits, dress, accents, and internal decision-making practices.

Negotiations can help to split groups apart by revealing factional differences over ideologies, constituencies, methods, organizational loyalties, or even long-term political goals. In Islamist groups, for example, local nationalist forces may be at odds with foreign fighters. The very act of offering to negotiate with a group can highlight its weaknesses and divisions and force it to splinter, as different tribes, nationalities, or factions turn against each other. For example, the Real Irish Republican Army (RIRA) split off from the IRA, and the Democratic Front for the Liberation of Palestine (DFLP), Popular Front for the Liberation of Palestine (PFLP), and Popular Front for the Liberation of Palestine-General Command (PFLP-GC) all split off from the Palestinian Liberation Organization (PLO). Splintering may not reduce the overall violence of a campaign, especially in the short term, but it can divide constituencies and undermine efforts to marshal financial and political resources.[15]

Finally, a government's willingness to negotiate can sometimes be an effective information strategy that erodes public support for a group. Terrorism is violence intended to influence audiences by intimidating them, inspiring them, or convincing them that killing noncombatants is the only option. Governments must also be mindful of those audiences. Offering to talk can counter the group's narrative. Clearly this does not apply to extremist groups such as al-Qaeda or ISIS; however, it may apply to certain Afghan Taliban factions or Iraqi Sunni tribes instrumentally aligned with them. Negotiations can happen gradually, starting with one part of a group or movement, even as another part is engaged in violence. This is not ideal, however: if a group is growing in size or support, negotiations can help disaggregate the threat and find elements whose supporters want different things. Still, as negotiations may actually increase the violence of a campaign in the short-term, it is crucial to consider a state's long-term strategic goals when deciding whether or not to enter negotiations.

Strategic Reasons to Negotiate.

Although they rarely cause the demise of groups on their own, negotiations can contribute to the decline and death of groups over time as part of a state's comprehensive approach to counterterrorism. A wide range of organizations such as the Provisional IRA in Northern Ireland, the Philippine Moro Islamic Liberation Front (MILF), the 19th of April Movement (M-19) in Colombia, and the Guatemalan National Revolutionary Unity (URNG) have either reduced their violence or ended it altogether in the wake of negotiations. Sometimes governments lose patience and crush terrorist groups with military force after repeated efforts to negotiate, as was the case with the Liberation Tigers of Tamil Eelam (LTTE) in Sri Lanka. Other times, the two sides repeatedly go in and out of talks, as with the Basque group Euskadi Ta Askatasuna (ETA), episodically stopping and restarting its violence and gradually losing support and momentum over time.

From a strategic perspective, the best way to think about negotiations is as a means to shift the violence or energy of an established group into a different channel. In my own research I have comparatively examined hundreds of groups, zeroing in on 457 carefully-defined groups who had engaged in terrorism since 1968.[16] To my surprise, only about 18 percent of those groups had negotiated at all. Those who did enter talks tended to be longer-lived (twenty to twenty-five years) compared

they can contribute to its end.

Conclusion. The next time a government leader asserts that his or her state "never negotiates with terrorists," it is worth thinking through exactly what

---

The most **effective negotiations stop and start**, accompanied by a lower level and lower frequency of violence over time.

---

to the rest (average age about eight years). Only about 10 percent of those who did negotiate gave up the talks altogether and walked away. The predominant pattern was for talks to drag on, neither succeeding brilliantly nor failing completely. From a state's perspective, negotiations are best sought with older groups where governments have prepared their constituencies for a long-term process.

The real question is whether the situation following talks is better or worse than it might have been without the negotiations. Given the small number of individuals needed to carry out terrorist attacks, negotiations do not end violence on their own, and it is foolish to promote the impression that they will. My research indicates that the most effective negotiations stop and start, accompanied by a lower level and lower frequency of violence over time. These talks neither resolve key differences nor fall apart altogether, even as other factors (e.g. loss of popular support, infighting, better intelligence gathering, police work, transition to legitimate activities) enter the picture. Negotiations do not instantly lead to the end of terrorism; however, if wisely handled,

he or she means. The choices are grim and complex. Depending on the country, the statement may mean that the government never negotiates ransoms for kidnapped hostages. If so, that is a judgment about short-term versus longer-term stakes in counterterrorism, and it may also be a gamble over secret kinetic operations versus contemptible media attention. Regarding tactical "talks," states are mainly public, terrorist groups mainly clandestine. It should not be surprising that public and private counterterrorism policy often differs. The government may be engaged in outreach through third parties or secret probings by intelligence operatives for indispensable information or advantage. Finally, from the broadest strategic perspective, the record indicates that over time wisely handled negotiations—especially with older groups that have strong constituencies and realistic negotiable terms—may ultimately help states win.

What are the implications specifically for the United States? In recent years, the U.S. government has relied very heavily upon military responses to terrorist attacks, in effect trying to separate politics from military force.

Its kinetic reactions have been far better funded and more well-developed than its political strategy has been. The United States has answered the 9/11 attacks primarily with military operations in Iraq, Afghanistan, and Iraq again in 2014. But terrorism is a primarily political strategy. It uses shocking illegitimate violence against innocents to gain leverage from a position of military weakness, so as to strengthen the political position of the group using it. Overwhelming military responses cannot "kill" a terrorist group's political power.

Thus negotiations are not the opposite of using military force; they are an integral part of a political strategy against terrorism. Indeed, sometimes they are the only way to ensure that government counterterrorism policy can be effective. Regarding hostage policy, for example, the enormous political attention ISIS drew by publicly killing U.S. hostages James Foley and Steven Sotloff sadly outweighed the benefits gained from the strict U.S. no-ransom-may-be-paid-by-anyone approach. In the future, when every other option has been exhausted, it is time to consider looking the other way if nongovernmental actors can arrange deals for the release of U.S. hostages. Prosecuting them afterwards punishes the wrong people.

As for larger questions of tactics and strategies of negotiation, the dangerous transnational Islamist movement threatening the United States and its allies is not a monolith and should not be approached as if it were. For example, there is ample in-fighting and disagreement about al-Qaeda's agenda and aims that are readily apparent in the split between al-Qaeda and its affiliates on the one hand, and ISIS on the other. Many long-standing groups now loosely aligned with "al-Qaeda" are more interested in local nationalist aims than they are in establishing a caliphate led by Iraqis or Saudis. The United States and its allies should clarify and exploit these differences, gleaned through sophisticated analysis on a case-by-case basis, in places such as Morocco, Tunisia, Indonesia, Afghanistan, Kashmir, and Turkey. Sometimes that may mean negotiating with local groups or supporting local governments as they do so. A strict no-negotiations policy helps unite disparate factions and is not a viable political strategy over the long run.

NOTES

1 Rukmini Callimachi, "Paying Ransoms, Europe Bankrolls Qaeda Terror," *The New York Times*, 29 July 2013, Internet, http://www.nytimes.com/2014/07/30/world/africa/ransoming-citizens-europe-becomes-al-qaedas-patron.html?_r=0 (date accessed: 25 November 2014).

2 U.S. designation of foreign terrorist organizations is a formal legal process that triggers sanctions. *See* Audrey Kurth Cronin, *The 'FTO List' and Congress: Sanctioning Designated Foreign Terrorism Organizations*, Congressional Research Service #RL32120 (2003), Internet, http://fas.org/irp/crs/RL32120.pdf (date accessed: 25 November 2014).

3 In another widely publicized case, Raymond Davis, who was a U.S. contractor with the CIA in Lahore, Pakistan, shot and killed two Pakistanis as they tried to rob him in January 2011. Pakistani authorities then jailed him. Two months later the United States freed Davis by paying "blood money" to the surviving relatives. Strictly speaking, this was not kidnapping for ransom. *See* Mark Mazetti, "How a Single Spy Helped Turn Pakistan Against the United States," *The New York Times*, 9 April 2013, Internet, http://www.nytimes.com/2013/04/14/magazine/raymond-davis-pakistan.html?pagewanted=all (date accessed: 25 November 2014).

4 David Blair, "Should governments pay a ransom for hostages? How the US, Britain and Europe are split over ransom payments," *The Telegraph*, 21 August 2014.

5 Simon Reeve, *One Day in September* (New York: Arcade Publishing, 2000).

6 Ronen Bergman, "Gilad Shalit and the Rising Price of an Israeli Life," *The New York Times*, 9 November 2011. *Also* Orlando Crowcroft, "Palestinians freed in 2011 Gilad Shalit Prisoner-Swap back in Custody," *The Guardian*, 18 June 2014, Internet, http://www.theguardian.com/world/2014/jun/18/palestinians-freed-2001-gilad-shalit-custody (date accessed: 25 November 2014).

7 Rukmini Callimachi, "U.S. Writer Held by Al Qaeda Affiliate in Syria Is Freed After Nearly 2 Years," *The New York Times*, 24 August 2014.

8 Ibid. *Also* Justin Huggler, "Freed Islamic State hostage 'may have been held with James Foley,'" *The Telegraph*, 25 August 2014, Internet, http://www.telegraph.co.uk/news/worldnews/middleeast/syria/11054917/Freed-Islamic-State-hostage-may-have-been-held-with-James-Foley.html (date accessed: 25 November 2014). *Also* David Gauthier-Villars, "French Journalists Told U.S. About Time in Captivity With James Foley," *The Wall Street Journal*, 21 August 2014, Internet, http://online.wsj.com/articles/french-journalists-told-u-s-about-time-in-captivity-with-james-foley-1408634007 (date accessed: 25 November 2014).

9 Remarks of Under Secretary David Cohen at Chatham House on "Kidnapping for Ransom: The Growing Terrorist Financing Challenge," 5 October 2012, Internet, http://www.treasury.gov/press-center/press-releases/Pages/tg1726.aspx (date accessed: 25 November 2014). *Also* Howard LaFranchi, "Why did the US refuse Islamic State Ransom Demand for James Foley?" *Christian Science Monitor*, 21 August 2014, Internet, http://www.csmonitor.com/USA/Foreign-Policy/2014/0821/Why-did-US-refuse-Islamic-State-ransom-demand-for-James-Foley-video (date accessed: 25 November 2014).

10 Cohen.

11 Callimachi.

12 For more on strategies of terrorism, see Audrey Kurth Cronin, *How Terrorism Ends: Understanding the Decline and Demise of Terrorist Campaigns* (Princeton: Princeton University Press, 2009), especially Chapter 5. *Also* Cronin, *Ending Terrorism: A Strategy for Defeating al-Qaeda* (London: Routledge, 2008).

13 "ISIS is 'beyond anything we have ever seen': Chuck Hagel warns terror network is an 'imminent threat to every interest we have,'" *Daily Mail*, 21 August 2014, Internet, http://www.dailymail.co.uk/news/article-2731289/ISIS-seen-says-Chuck-Hagel-details-emerge-failed-rescue-attempt-aimed-reclaiming-James-Foley.html (date accessed: 25 November 2014).

14 *See* Audrey Kurth Cronin, "Why Drones Fail: When Tactics Drive Strategy," *Foreign Affairs*, July/August 2013, Internet, http://www.foreignaffairs.com/articles/139454/audrey-kurth-cronin/why-drones-fail.

15 Splintering can also occur on the government side, as with the Ulster Volunteer Force in Northern Ireland, for example.

16 How I reached these conclusions, including the strengths and weaknesses of the data, are explained in *How Terrorism Ends*, especially the statistical Appendix.

Diagnosing the Health of Russia's Third Sector

Putin, Women's Health, and Foreign NGOs

Lena Surzhko-Harned

In early 2014, Russian president Vladimir Putin introduced several amendments to an already controversial law regulating the work of foreign-sponsored non-governmental organizations (NGOs) in Russia. Several high profile organizations, such as Agora and Memorial, were labeled as "foreign agents," and concerns over the Russian government's grip on civil society grew precipitously.

A vibrant and independent civil society has long been symptomatic of a healthy democracy. Concerns over the regulations that the Russian state imposes on the so-called third sector, which consists of the nongovernmental noncommercial organizations, seem to be connected to overall concerns for the viability of Russian democracy. However, these concerns are misguided. In light of Russia's recent restrictions— including but not limited to the aforementioned laws on foreign NGOs, laws forbidding "gay propaganda," and the deepening rift between the West and Russia regarding Russia's "near abroad" reaching the highest point since the end of the Cold War—questions about the viability of a Russian democratic transition have seemed irrelevant, with numerous authors questioning the academic approach to studying post-Soviet Russia as a transitioning state. These latest events

Lena Surzhko-Harned is an Assistant Professor of Political Science at Mercyhurst University. She is an author of a number of papers dealing with issues of nationalism and ethnic conflict, identity politics, electoral politics, comparative democratization, and political behavior in post-communist states.

have solidified this attitude. As Lilia Shevtsova wrote in an August op-ed in the *American Interest*: "[j]ust think how many analytical publications, speeches, and dissertations have now been rendered superfluous."[1]

Since 2004, Vladimir Putin has made a pointed effort to subvert the actions of the foreign-sponsored NGOs in Russia. Such actions are based on the Russian government's distrust of these organizations' practices, their donors, and their overall goals in Russia. Like the 2004 administration, the 2012 Putin administration is very concerned about the destabilizing effects that these organizations might have on Russian citizens. In the state's view, NGOs promote ideologies, views, and practices that might corrupt Russian minds and bodies—and by extension, corrupt Russian society as a whole. The latest policy has been widely perceived as yet another step in Putin's administrative tradition—particularly evidence since the passage of the 2006 NGOs law—to curtail and monitor the work of foreign NGOs, which Putin suspects as conspiring against his regime.

Putin's policies have certainly restricted the work of NGOs in Russia. However, it can be argued that their success in promoting civil society and democratization was narrow even prior to Putin's reforms. Several important studies have pointed out NGOs' limitations in building civic engagement in Russian society due to a number of interrelated issues. To elucidate such limitations, this paper draws on the impressive body of literature pioneered by Julie Hemment and Michele Rivkin Fish and focuses on the work of non-governmental organizations con-

cerned with women's health. Women's rights and women's healthcare have an important connection to the development of a healthy democracy and society, as well as the protection of human rights.

I begin with a brief overview of Russia's civil society and its perceived importance in democratic consolidation. I then turn to examine the work of foreign NGOs in Russia prior to Putin's reforms in the mid-2000s. I pay special attention to the connection between women's health and democratization in Russia and then conclude with a brief rejoinder.

Civil Society and Democratization Theory.
Civil society has long been considered an essential ingredient for a healthy democracy. From Alexis de Tocqueville's 1835 study of "Democracy in America" to recent, ongoing studies on democratization, the term "civil society" has figured prominently in our understanding of a democratic public.[2] Linz and Stepan famously argue that civil society is an inherent part of democratic consolidation.[3]

Despite the prominence of the term, its conceptualization and precise meaning are less than clear. There are two interrelated approaches to understanding civil society that are widely used in literature. The first involves a narrow view of civil society as an abundance of nongovernmental organizations, which bring together the citizenry in the pursuit of various interests and goals.[4] The second views civil society as the capacity of citizens to value cooperation, civic mindedness, tolerance, and mutual respect.[5] These two approaches are interconnected and arguably mutually reinforcing, as membership and work in NGOs contribute to the development of civic mindedness and cooperation. Furthermore, this strengthens social capital, which the World Bank defines as the "institutions, relationships, and norms that shape the quality and quantity of a society's social interactions," influences public participation in NGOs, and strengthens commitment to democratic processes.[6]

collapse. President Boris Yeltsin's liberalization and democratization policies seemed to signify a new era for the Russian political system; in conjunction, it was indeed necessary to assess the viability of civil society in Russia and help promote the healthy growth of social capital by supporting the non-governmental and noncommercial "third sector" in Russian polity.

The promotion of NGOs in newly democratizing states has been one of the pillars of the democratic promotion policies of the United States.

While it has been recognized that not all nongovernmental organizations seek to promote civic mindedness and tolerance, democratization policies still tend to place a high value on promoting NGO activity in emerging democracies.[7] NGOs can advance democratization in transitioning societies in a number of ways: by providing for additional services in sectors where governmental institutions fail, by facilitating the communication between public and private sectors, and by increasing transparency and trust between various sectors of society, among other functions. As such, promotion of NGOs in newly democratizing states has been one of the pillars of the democratic promotion policies of the United States, other countries, and developmental agencies within the United Nations and the World Bank.

This practice was particularly prominent with regard to the former republics of the Soviet Union, especially the Russian Federation after the Union's

Foreign Donors, Domestic Challenges, and Civil Society During the 1990s. The euphoria that followed the USSR's collapse seemed to imply that real democratic development in Russia was possible, if not inevitable. Studies of Russian public opinion showed reason for optimism.[8] The principles of democratic civil society appeared to be present in Russian society, even if their effects were, in the words of James Gibson, "a mile wide and an inch deep."[9] Scholars were hopeful, arguing that with proper political reforms, a vibrant civil society in Russia was possible. Thus, the United States Agency for International Development (USAID), among others, contributed millions of dollars to the propagation of international, professionally organized NGOs in Russia.

Yet as the decade progressed, scholars and donors started to question the viability and utility of the "third sector" in Russia. A number of studies pointed out that foreign aid for Russian NGOs did not always produce its desired results, such as promotion of the genuine domestic grassroots activism.[10] Foreign donors' often shortsighted optimism, domestic challenges in their host countries (such as resource distribution and societal limitation), and ideological disparities between Western and local participants contributed to the challenges faced by NGOs in Russia.

In her trailblazing 2002 study of western NGOs in Russia, Sara Henderson points out that despite their well-intentioned aspirations, the relationship that developed between foreign donors and their local affiliates failed to foster horizontal networks of grassroots activism.[11] Instead, Henderson finds that an NGO's home office abroad and local office in Russia develop a very structured, institutionalized, and bureaucratic vertical relationship that incentivizes both offices to focus on the short-term goals of institutional survival over the long-term goal of democratization. Jule Hemment's research also supports this finding, and she explains that employment opportunities are important inducements for the Russian NGO participants.[12] Local activists seem to be less "activists" in the idealistic sense of an independent civic-minded individual; rather, they tend to be employees concerned with their organization's institutional survival, the continual flow of funding, and their own job security. These opportunistic tendencies stem in many ways from the lack of job opportunities during the societal and economic crises following the USSR's collapse.

One significant challenge is that the success of NGOs in Russia depends largely on the perception of Russian audiences. Hemment argues that the Russian population in the 1990s seemed to have a very conflicting view of foreign NGOs.[13] On one hand, citizens saw the development of "third sector" activism as a blessing and salvation from the previous regime's corrupt bureaucracy. On the other hand, some were very suspicious of foreign organizations like the Soros Foundation, which some Russians saw as agents of Western neo-colonialism.[14]

The ideological differences—whether real or perceived—between Western donors and local activists thus proved to be very important. In her compelling study, Lisa McIntosh Sundstrom argues that the ideological focus and issue framing of an NGO's activism plays an important role in the NGO's success or failure.[15] Using survey data, she shows that an NGO's focus on universal principles—such as prevention of bodily harm—in framing the support for soldiers and victims of domestic violence proved successful in galvanizing grassroots activism on that issue. On the other hand, campaigns that focus on Western-style principles of gender equality fail to raise the necessary support. These ideological issues seem to be predominantly pronounced in connection to women's rights groups.

Healthcare, Women's Health, and the "Third Sector." Michele Rivkin Fish observed the attitudes of Western healthcare professionals who arrived in Russia to promote change in women's health practices, such as those related to birth control, pregnancy, and childbirth. Western specialists have utilized the language of democratization to urge

reform, emphasizing the individual rights of women and women-centered practices that do not violate the human dignity of women during any of the procedures.[16]

Feminist literature has long stressed the link between the protection of women's individual rights and democracy. Creating a woman-centric approach to women's healthcare was indeed a democratizing task in Russia. By the early 1990s, women's healthcare in Russia was an embodiment of paternalistic and dehumanizing practices, and shifting its focus to take into account the individual patient was an example of a shift to democratic principles in healthcare and the society at large. For decades, for instance, abortion remained the main form of birth control, and prenatal care birthing practices focused less on the well-being and comfort of the mother but rather on the expertise of the medical staff.[17] Birthing rooms often housed more than one woman giving birth at the same time, newborn infants were not permitted to stay with the mothers after birth, and family visits were not permitted during the birth or at any point in time while the mother and a newborn remained at the hospital. These were just a few of the practices that Western activists sought to transform in the new Russia.

Yet these practices were not limited entirely to women's healthcare alone. The Russian healthcare system in the 1990s carried legacies of the Soviet regime in many ways. While the quality of healthcare increased dramatically during the 1960s due to the general increase in education, infrastructure, and focus on vaccination, the USSR saw stagnation in healthcare services and

a decline in the general welfare by the 1980s. Urbanization, pollution, environmental degradation, poor nutrition, and a rise in alcoholism contributed to the overall decline in health. As Dov Chernichovsky and his colleagues argue, the pitfalls of the Soviet health system were not due entirely to the fact that it was controlled by the state, but rather that it was not a priority.[18]

Instead, the socialist state prioritized social healthcare. More emphasis was placed on infections and societal diseases, rather than individual, chronic ailments like cardiovascular and neurological diseases. Moreover, higher priority was given to the healthcare of the productive members of the society, such as working age and able-bodied persons. The socialized healthcare did not place any value in patient-centered care because, as Chernichovsky and his colleagues argue, healthcare services were viewed as consumption—a bourgeoisie concept antithetical to Marxist notions.[19]

Women's health, however, faced a double burden of dehumanization. Women's reproduction was seen as a part of state goods and was therefore placed in the hands of capable and trained medical professionals who treated women's reproductive functions as a factory assembly line. Women also received less attention and priority from the state healthcare system than their able-bodied male counterparts. The deeply conservative and patriarchal Soviet society preferred to keep the issues of women's health compartmentalized and tucked away from the public realm.

In 1993, President Yeltsin introduced reforms that allowed Russian healthcare to open up to private and third-sector organizations. This was done to improve the healthcare system, introduce better service practices, and increase transparency in a highly corrupt sector of post-Soviet Russia. Under the initiatives of the World Health Organization (WHO) and the World Bank, numerous NGOs concerned with reforming women's health

ditional morality.

These continued practices and attitudes, however, are at odds with the liberal agenda of Western NGOs. As Rivkin Fish highlights, Western liberal feminists see the decline in fertility as a positive attribute of female equality, because lower birth rates are positively and highly correlated with an increase in education, professional opportu-

Creating a woman-centric approach to women's healthcare was indeed a democratizing task in Russia.

came to Russia.

However, Western NGOs faced a myriad of challenges in Russia. While Western activists mobilized around liberal and feminist ideas of gender equality, Russian women did not perceive their lot in these terms. Socialism nominally encouraged the social and political equality of women in the pubic realm, and post-Soviet Russian women already felt sufficiently emancipated in that sense.[20] Additionally, the dissolution of the Soviet state did not eradicate the parochial attitude of the state as a protector of the nation. The revival of new national identities in the post-Soviet decade also meant strengthening the notion that reproduction was an important state issue.[21] Consequently, women's health yet again fell into a compartmentalized category placed firmly under state-control and hidden from the public view. Faced with the tremendous decrease in fertility rates, the Russian state's new priority was to raise birth rates by reinforcing the concept of the nuclear family and tra-

nities, and income parity for women.[22] As a result, the Russian state and some members of Russian society have blamed foreign NGOs for the decline in Russian birthrates.[23] Some have gone further in suggesting that it was the West's malicious attempt to de-populate and destroy Russia.[24] Very similar logic was applied to NGOs that worked on other human rights issues, such as the rights of homosexuals.

Putin's administrations from 2000 to the present have continued to voice support for traditional views of the nuclear family.[25] Putin-era reforms to the Russian welfare system, such as the 2006 Maternity Capital program, encourage and monetarily incentivize married couples to have children—thus promoting traditional morality at the state level. As part of the effort to increase fertility, the Putin administration has not only been suspicious of birth control practices, but has also imposed numerous restrictions on abortion, such as a 2003 law outlawing abortions after the first trimester. The majority of women continue to rely on traditional forms of contraception such as male condoms and withdrawal rather than hormonal pills. This is particularly true of the women in the Russian countryside.

The government's new focus on increased fertility does not necessarily mean that it will emphasize the reproductive health of women. To the contrary, this might lead to a shift in priorities which places a greater emphasis on the quantity of births rather than the quality of child-bearing and birthing care, not to mention other important aspects of women's health like sexual education, prevention of sexually transmitted diseases, and preventative screening for breast and ovarian cancers. Thus, Russia's societal challenges are further exacerbated by the state's policies. Russia's focus on increasing fertility has put the state at odds with the work of many Western NGOs, creating a rift between the state's goals for national health and the principles of individual-centered healthcare espoused by foreign activists.

Projects like the Women's Wellness Center in St. Petersburg, where international efforts to transform Russian women's health care toward a patient-friendly focus, have arguably been beacons of hope. Yet these triumphs are limited. Moreover, the Russian state's fertility-based approach to women's reproductive health combined with a new set of laws further restricting the work of foreign NGOs may jeopardize future successes. Russia's increased hostility toward the West, and in particular the United States, places a greater burden on its domestic efforts—rather than foreign influences—in the area of

Russian healthcare reform.

Conclusion. Although there was hope in the 1990s that Russia might sincerely democratize, possibly with the assistance of foreign NGOs, subsequent state policies severely restricted the space for civil society in Russia to operate. The Putin administrations in particular have consistently suspected that foreign NGOs pose a threat to the Russian state and society. Building a sovereign democracy, in Putin's mind, requires controlling civil society growth in order to minimize anti-regime protests by the "brainwashed" members of the "fifth column."

This paper sought to highlight how Putin's laws regulating foreign NGO activity in Russia have put a considerable strain on the functions of these organizations. However, even during the relatively liberal 1990s, when Russia made its largest strides in civil society development, NGOs faced serious limitations. The liberal democratic ideals that inform and inspire the work of many NGOs can place them at odds with the goals of the Russian state and sometimes the goals of local activists who do not share these ideals. Overall, socioeconomic and structural challenges have limited foreign NGOs' capacity to translate their goals into mobilized large-scale grassroots activism among Russians.

At this point in the current political climate, the work of foreign NGOs in Russia is going to be rather limited. Yet it is absolutely necessary that in the field of women's healthcare, projects such as the Women's Wellness Center continue to operate in order to create incremental change in domestic audiences' perspectives on healthcare. However, the work of domestic activists also remains uncertain until the Russian govern- ment takes steps toward democratization and decentralization.

NOTES

1 Lilia Shevtsova, "Putin Ends the Interregnum," American Interest, Internet, http://www.the-american-interest.com/2014/08/28/putin-ends-the-interregnum/ (date accessed: 29 November 2014).

2 G.A. Almond and S. Verba, *The Civic Culture: Political Attitudes and Democracy in Five Nations* (Princeton: Princeton University Press, 1963), 562. Also L.J. Diamond, *The Spirit Of Democracy: The Struggle to Build Free Societies Throughout the World* (New York: Times Books/Henry Holt and Company, 2008), 448. Also S.P. Huntington, *The Third Wave: Democratization in the Late Twentieth Century (The Julian J. Rothbaum Distinguished Lecture Series)* (Norman: University of Oklahoma Press, 1991), 366. Also R.D. Putnam, R. Leonardi, and R. Nanetti, *Making Democracy Work: Civic Traditions in Modern Italy* (Princeton: Princeton University Press, 1993), 258. Also P. Norris, *Critical Citizens: Global Support for Democratic Government* (New York: Oxford University Press, 1999), 303. Also P. Norris, *Democratic Phoenix: Reinventing Political Activism* (New York: Cambridge University Press, 2002), 290.

3 J.J. Linz and A.C. Stepan, *Problems of Democratic Transition and Consolidaton: Southern Europe, South America, and Post-Communist Europe* (Baltimore: Johns Hopkins University Press, 1996).

4 Ibid.

5 J.L. Gibson, R.M. Duch, and K.L. Tedin, "Democratic Values and the Transformation of the Soviet Union," *Journal of Politics* 54, no. 2 (1992): 329-371. Also J. Gibson, "Putting Up With Fellow Russians: An Analysis of Political Tolerance in the Fledgling Russian Democracy," *Political Research Quarterly* 51, no. 1 (1998): 37-68. Also J. Gibson, "The Structure of Attitudinal Tolerance," *British Journal of Political Science* 19, no. 4 (1989): 562-570. Also R.J. Dalton, "Citizen Attitudes and Political Behavior," *Comparative Political Studies* 33, no. 6-7 (2000): 912-940. Also R.J. Dalton, *The Good Citizen: How a Younger Generation is Reshaping American Politics* (Washington, D.C.: CQ Press, 2009), 230.

6 R.D. Putnam, R. Leonardi, and R. Nanetti, *Making Democracy Work: Civic Traditions in Modern Italy* (Princeton: Princeton University Press, 1993), 258. Also R.D. Putnam, *Bowling Alone: The Collapse and Revival of American Community* (New York: Simon & Schuster, 2000), 541. Also World Bank, "Social Capital," Internet, http://web.worldbank.org/ (date accessed: 29 November 2014).

7 D.S. Brown, J.C. Brown, and S.W. Desposato, "Who Gives, Who Receives, and Who Wins: Transforming Capital Into Political Change Through Nongovernmental Organizations," *Comparative Political Studies* 41, no. 1 (2008): 24-47. Also C. Ruzza, "Populism and Euroscepticism: Towards Uncivil Society?" *Policy and Society Associates* 28, no. 1 (2009): 87-98. Also P. Kopecký and C. Mudde, "Rethinking Civil Society," *Democratizatsiya* 10, no. 3 (2003): 1-14. Also J.L. Snyder, *From Voting to Violence: Democratization and Nationalist Conflict* (New York: Norton, 2000).

8 J.L. Gibson, R.M. Duch, and K.L. Tedin, "Democratic Values and the Transformation of the Soviet Union," *Journal of Politics* 54, no. 2 (1992): 329-371. Also

J. Gibson, "Mass Opposition to the Soviet Putsch of August 1991: Collective Action, Rational Choice, and Democratic Values in the Former Soviet Union," *The American Political Science Review* 91, no. 3 (1997).

9 Ibid. Also J.L. Gibson, "A Mile Wide But an Inch Deep(?): The Structure of Democratic Commitments in the Former USSR," *American Journal of Political Science* 40, no. 2 (1996): 396-420.

10 S.L. Henderson, "Selling Civil Society: Western Aid and the Nongovernmental Organization Sector in Russia," *Comparative Political Studies* 35, no. 2 (2002): 139-167. Also J. Hemment, "The Riddle of the Third Sector: Civil Society, International Aid, and NGOs in Russia," *Anthropological Quarterly* 77, no. 2 (2004): 215-241. Also V. Petukhov, "Political Participation and Civic Self-Organization in Russia," *Russian Social Science Review* 47, (2006): 4-22. Also M. M. Howard, "The Weakness of Postcommunist Civil Society," *Journal of Democracy* 13, no. 1 (2002): 157-169. Also J. Crotty, "Making a Difference? NGOs and Civil Society Development in Russia," *Europe-Asia Studies* 61, (2009): 85-108. Also A. Evans, L. Henry, and L. M. Sundstrom, eds., *Russian Civil Society: A Critical Assessment* (London: M.E. Sharpe, 2005), 305-322.

11 S.L. Henderson, "Selling Civil Society: Western Aid and the Nongovernmental Organization Sector in Russia," *Comparative Political Studies* 35, no. 2 (2002): 139-167.

12 J. Hemment, "The Riddle of the Third Sector: Civil Society, International Aid, and NGOs in Russia," *Anthropological Quarterly* 77, no. 2 (2004): 215-241.

13 J. Hemment, "Colonization or Liberation: The Paradox of NGOs in Postsocialist States," *The Anthropology of East Europe Review* 16, no. 1 (1998): 31-39.

14 Ibid.

15 L. McIntosh Sundstrom, "Foreign Assistance, International Norms, and Civil Society Development: Lessons from the Russian Campaign," *International Organization* 59, no. 2 (2005): 419-49.

16 M. Rivkin-Fish, *Women's Health in Post-Soviet Russia: The Politics of Intervention* (New Anthropologies of Europe) (Bloomington: Indiana University Press, 2005).

17 M. Rivkin-Fish, "Health Development Meets the End of State Socialism: Visions of Democratization, Women's Health, and Social Well-Being for Contemporary Russia," *Culture, Medicine and Psychiatry* 24, (2000): 77-100.

18 D. Chernichovsky, G. Ofer, and E. Potapchik, "Health Sector Reform in Russia: The Heritage and the Private/Public Mix," *MOCT-MOST* 6, (1996): 125-152.

19 Ibid.

20 J. Hemment, *Empowering Women in Russia: Activism, Aid, and NGOs* (New Anthropologies of Europe) (Bloomington: Indiana University Press, 2007). Also L. McIntosh Sundstrom, "Women's NGOs in Russia Struggling from the Margins," *Democratizatsiya* 10, no. 2 (2002).

NOTES

21 M. Rivkin-Fish, "Change Yourself and the Whole World Will Become Kinder: Russian Activists for Reproductive Health and the Limits of Claims Making for Women," *Medical Anthropology Quarterly* 18, no. 3 (2004): 281-304. *Also* M. Rivkin-Fish, "Pronatalism, Gender Politics, and the Renewal of Family Support in Russia: Toward a Feminist Anthropology of 'Maternity Capital,'" *Slavic Review* 69, no. 3 (2010): 701-724.

22 M. Rivkin-Fish, "Anthropology, Demography, and the Search for a Critical Analysis of Fertility: Insights from Russia," *American Anthropologist* 105, no. 2 (2003): 289-301. *Also* R. Inglehart and P. Norris, *Rising Tide: Gender Equality and Cultural Change Around the World* (New York: Cambridge University Press, 2003), 226.

23 M. Rivkin-Fish, "Pronatalism, Gender Politics, and the Renewal of Family Support in Russia: Toward a Feminist Anthropology of 'Maternity Capital,'" *Slavic Review* 69, no. 3 (2010): 701-724.

24 Mehriban Nasibova, "Diminishing Fertility Rates: Response of Russia and Azerbaijan" (Columbia University: Columbia University Partnership for International Development, September 2013).

25 M. Rivkin-Fish, "Pronatalism, Gender Politics, and the Renewal of Family Support in Russia: Toward a Feminist Anthropology of 'Maternity Capital,'" *Slavic Review* 69, no. 3 (2010): 701-724.

Culture&Society

Believable Victims

Asylum Credibility and the Struggle for Objectivity

Michael Kagan

In April 2002, the United Kingdom government issued a report about human rights violations in Sudan. It contained exactly three sentences about problems in Darfur, referencing vague "claims" of "inter-ethnic" fighting. It concluded that "there is no evidence" of systematic persecution in Darfur.[1] A year later, Darfur would become one of the world's most well known cases of systematic persecution, to the extent that many considered it genocide. While the situation in Darfur certainly worsened from 2002 to 2003, the more dramatic change may have been the way in which the world suddenly became aware of a long-brewing crisis.

Asylum adjudication is often the invisible frontline in the struggle by oppressed groups to gain recognition for their plights. Through this process, individual people must tell their stories and try to show that they are genuine victims of persecution rather than simply illegal immigrants attempting to slip through the system. In 2002, because the world had not yet acknowledged the nature of the calamity from which they were escaping, many Darfurian asylum cases would have relied on the ability of each individual to convince government offices to believe their stories. They would have had to be deemed "credible," or they would be in danger

Michael Kagan is the co-director of the Immigration Clinic at the University of Nevada-Las Vegas, where he is also an Associate Professor at the William S. Boyd School of Law. Kagan is currently leading a major empirical study about how the federal courts adjudicate immigration appeals.

of being sent home. Today, a similar process is playing out for youths fleeing gang violence in Central America. The 2014 State Department Human Rights Report on Guatemala, for instance, includes three sentences about gangs recruiting "street children."[2] But recent arrivals pleading to stay in the U.S. have described a far direr situation.[3]

Credibility is not an explicit legal requirement for being recognized as a refugee, or for winning asylum. The legal criteria derive from the United Nations' 1951 Convention relating to the Status of Refugees, which requires an asylum-seeker to show a "well-founded fear of being persecuted" for reason of race, religion, nationality, membership in a political social group, or political opinion. In theory, if independent evidence showed that a person was in clear danger of persecution, it might not be necessary for the asylum-seeker to even testify. Imagine, for instance, if a three-year-old Jewish child arrived from Germany in 1941, and either gave completely arbitrary information or none at all. It would clearly violate the Refugee Convention to refuse her asylum simply because her testimony was not credible in a strict sense. But such scenarios are extraordinarily rare.

Asylum-seekers typically arrive with no independent evidence that they really face such a danger. As a result, it is a practical necessity for asylum-seekers to be believed, as they usually cannot prove their cases except through their own testimony. For the current cases of Central American youths, even if the government were to accept that gang violence in general might be grounds for asylum, it would be left to individual applicants to explain how such

violence places them in personal and immediate danger. Previous research has shown that individual credibility assessment determines the fates of more asylum applications than do the technical legal criteria.[4] Yet this is a fraught process. The fact that genuine refugees cannot conclusively prove their persecution has led the United Nations to call for asylum-seekers to be granted the "benefit of the doubt."[5]

However, this very same reality has led to doubts about asylum-seekers' veracity. William Hague, the British Foreign Secretary until 2014, once made a major political speech complaining that "bogus claimants" were flooding the United Kingdom.[6] In 2014, American law enforcement arrested around thirty individuals for running an asylum fraud ring, which the *New York Times* dubbed "an industry of lies."[7] In 2014, one can see doubts about the veracity of asylum-seekers as mapped onto political reactions to the influx of Central American youth. New Mexico Congressman Steve Pearce, who made a brief visit to Guatemala and Honduras, publicly disputed whether the children are really fleeing from violence.[8] *Investor's Business Daily* claimed that the children prey on American "gullibility."[9]

One by one and case by case, asylum-seekers must navigate the tension between refugee protection and migration control as they struggle to be deemed "credible." In this process, asylum-seekers face a paradox created by our modern media environment. Today, there is more information readily available about other countries than ever before. Reports that were once published annually and available only in a government library are now a click away and updated throughout the year. But this does not mean that every human rights abuse is immediately reported, even if we have created the impression of a culture of access to complete information. And just as more information is available more quickly, public opinion can also be aroused quickly, creating the potential for political pressure on an asylum system before there has been sufficient time to consider each claim carefully.

Images of Genuine Victims.

Asylum is hardly the only field in which an adjudicator must decide whether a particular witness should be believed. But it is unique in that the stakes are unusually high, and there is typically little or no independent evidence to corroborate an applicant's account. Asylum adjudication is also an intensely personal process, involving lengthy interviews about painful subjects, often in private rooms where the adjudicator and the applicant are the only people present. Subjectivity and inconsistency remain inherent in asylum adjudica-

genuine victim is likely to look and talk can be unusually important. Consider, as an example, the potential role that gender might play in this process. In other legal contexts, social scientists have detected a tendency for adjudicators in particular to be especially protective of female victims and especially punitive both toward men who abuse women and toward women who do not adhere to conventional images of femininity.[12] Professor Jacqueline Bhabha has warned that asylum cases often turn on "simplistic, even derogatory, characterizations of asylum seekers' countries of origin as areas of barbarism or which lack civility."[13] Post-9/11 studies have shown a tendency for Western politicians and media to portray Muslim men as dangerous, while Muslim women are seen as victims.[14] Such images of victims and perpetrators can help or hinder an asylum-seeker's quest to be believed, especially given court culture. Immigration judges work in a setting in which implicit bias is especially likely to influence decision making because they are systemically overworked and have

---

Not every human rights abuse is immediately reported, even if we have created the impression of a culture of access to complete information.

---

tions.[10] More specifically, governments and the United Nations High Commissioner for Refugees (UNHCR) remain divided on whether it is appropriate for adjudicators to consider an applicant's demeanor in determining credibility.[11]

In a context where unstructured subjectivity can play such a pivotal role, unarticulated assumptions about how a

little time for deliberate decision making or analysis.[15]

The tendency for adjudicators to import preconceptions into asylum cases can often be vividly seen with asylum claims based on religion. When asylum-seekers flee persecution in countries like Iran or Eritrea because they converted from one religion or another, their cases often turn on whether they are seen as genuine in their faith. This can lead government officials to harshly interrogate asylum-seekers on matters of religion. This has led to many a contentious situation. In one notable case, an American appeals court complained that an immigration judge had administered "a mini-catechism."[16] In an Australian case, a judge suggested that it is a contradiction to claim to be both gay and Catholic.[17] An American court once doubted whether an Iranian had actually converted from Islam to Christianity because he continued to eat pork-free meals in prison.[18] Taking even another step further, in Europe, some governments have been accused of trying to test the truthfulness of gay asylum-seekers by measuring their sexual arousal while forcing them to watch pornography.[19]

Studies have found that asylum adjudicators also make assumptions about how a person fleeing persecution and persecutory governments should behave. Adjudicators base decisions on assumptions about how people would behave in the face of persecution, as well as about how persecutory governments would act. A study in Britain found that asylum adjudicators disbelieved applicants' accounts of persecution because, among other things, they assumed a foreign government would "make discrete inquiries" rather than arrest a dissident. In another case, adjudicators doubted that a government prosecutor in another country might swear or use ethnic slurs.[20] Moreover, a Canadian study found that asylum adjudicators made assumptions about how people would behave in the face of danger, with the assumptions often

contradicting social science literature about how people actually behave in such circumstances.[21]

Accepting a Level of Doubt. One
of the challenges facing asylum adjudicators is that it is rare to ever learn with certainty whether an individual is actually telling the truth, much less how high the risk of persecution really is. In some cases, this only becomes clear in retrospect. For example, we now know the scale of government-sponsored ethnic violence in Darfur, and that an asylum-seeker who reported escalating attacks in late 2002 would have been telling the truth. An asylum adjudicator, though, would not have been able to see this so clearly based on the information that was available at the time.

In common law legal traditions, different types of cases call for different levels of proof. Convictions in a criminal trial require proof beyond a reasonable doubt, while civil cases typically require a mere probability or preponderance of the evidence. These differences approximate the different stakes in different cases, and may be best understood by the legal system's willingness to accept occasional errors. In criminal cases, the danger of convicting an innocent person of a serious crime calls for the most stringent burden of proof possible so as to make errors as rare as possible. In civil cases, the system is willing to accept a higher degree of error, and thus sets a lower standard of proof. In all areas of law, adjudicators must constantly adjust their willingness to accept doubt, balancing against the harms that would result from an incorrect decision.

The balance in refugee cases is

unique, and calls for a particularly low standard of proof. If a genuine refugee is errantly rejected, the harm is immediate and severe. A person will be deported to a place where he or she is in danger of persecution. But the harm from a fraudulent applicant slipping through the system is more diffuse. While a single high profile case may create a strong public impression about the whole system, the vast majority of asylum claims remain anonymous and confidential. The true danger of false claims slipping through is that, cumulatively, they may produce a public sense that the asylum system lacks integrity. This, in turn, would then fuel more draconian measures against all asylum claims. In theory, fraudulent asylum claims might be analogous to counterfeit money. A single fake bill does not have any significant macroeconomic impact, but if too many enter circulation, the results could be disastrous.

Asylum law has tried to accommodate this delicate balance by establishing a fairly low, yet certainly more nuanced,

argues that an asylum-seeker should be considered credible if his or her account is "capable of being believed."[22] This does not require that an adjudicator be entirely free of doubt. It also does not require the level of certainty that might be demanded in a criminal case. It is not, however, such a low standard that even a story no reasonable person could believe would be accepted. Instead, it creates a middle ground protecting the lives of those who, if not for the lower threshold, might be sent back to a country where they could face certain persecution and perhaps even death.

Moving Toward Objectivity. In
1989, UNHCR advised that refugee credibility assessment "be a matter of personal judgment."[23] This was typical of early approaches to credibility assessment. This subjective approach is closely tied to two related ideas that have long legal roots, but may empirically be quite questionable. The first idea is that directly observing the way

If a genuine refugee is errantly rejected, **the harm is immediate and severe...**but the harm of a fraudulent applicant slipping through the system is more diffuse.

threshold of proof in asylum cases. An asylum claim may be based solely on the applicant's own testimony if no other evidence is reasonably available. More to the point, UNHCR has tried to steer credibility assessment away from a search for truth, given that doubts nearly always remain. Instead, UNHCR

a person talks will reveal their level of honesty, as lying will be indicated by the way they talk or by their demeanor. Yet, social scientists have not found much evidence that demeanor actually assists much in detecting falsehood.[24] The second idea that supports the subjective approach is the rule in many legal systems that appellate courts should defer to first instance adjudicators on credibility precisely because they listened to and watched the testimony directly. The result of such rules is that high courts are often reluctant to step in to offer clear guidance on credibility questions the way they might on questions of law.

In addition to the limited usefulness of demeanor, a significant difficulty with asylum credibility is that adjudicators may not learn to be better at interpreting it through experience. The reason for this is that we rarely find out whether an asylum decision was right or wrong. As a result, an adjudicator cannot learn easily from experience. This problem is compounded when the adjudicators are not fully independent, as is often the case in administrative immigration procedures.[25] In a highly politicized environment, where adjudicators are under pressure to decide asylum cases in a particular way, there is a danger that adjudicators will be implicitly rewarded for confirming preconceptions about asylum claims rather than for objective analysis.

Because of these concerns, the state of the art in credibility assessment is to move toward a more objective analytical approach. In a comprehensive 2013 report on credibility assessment in Europe, UNHCR advocated a structured analysis in which adjudicators should specifically note positive and negative factors, isolate areas of testimony where credibility problems appear to exist, and clearly articulate their reasoning.[26] This newer approach has been captured in a training manual financed by the European Commission, and is promoted by a new UNHCR/European Commission project known as the CREDO Initiative.[27]

Regrettably for asylum-seekers in the United States, American asylum law is in danger of being left behind by these developments. In 2005, Congress enacted the REAL ID Act, which states that immigration judges may base credibility assessments on, among other things, "the demeanor, candor, or responsiveness of the applicant or witness, the inherent plausibility of the applicant's or witness's account," and may reject a claim in its entirety because of any apparent inconsistency or minor inaccuracy "without regard to whether an inconsistency, inaccuracy, or falsehood goes to the heart of the applicant's claim."[28] This law effectively enshrines an unstructured approach to credibility that invites judges to rely on methods that have largely been rejected by empirical science. Its biggest impact may be to further limit the role of appellate courts in refining the standards that should be used to assess credibility. As a result, as Central American children begin to make asylum claims based on fear of gang violence, their fates depend largely on the approach taken by individual judges. Somehow, even though we live in an age of information, credibility assessment still seems to be rooted in an older era based on instinct and unarticulated assumptions.

A careful, structured analysis of asylum claims requires training, time, and resources. Deciding refugee credibility subjectively is much faster, even if it is less likely to be reliable. Time is regrettably something that many asylum systems simply do not have. Analysis of data published by UNHCR indicates that in 2013, at least 902,756 people submitted individual refugee claims around the world, but only 555,827 of them had their cases decided.[29] This imbalance creates the significant danger that adjudicators in many systems will face pressure to simply decide cases as fast as possible, rather than to analyze each application carefully and articulate their reasoning in writing. To safeguard against this tendency, appellate courts need to vigilantly scrutinize asylum adjudication for procedural short cuts that impair applicants' opportunities to a full airing of their cases.

Conclusion. Human rights problems are often sources of public controversy because it is often debatable—at least at first—whether claims of persecution are real or if they are exaggerated to serve a particular agenda. But while these debates play out in the media and in official statements, they also play out with individual lives on the line. Implicit assumptions about how foreign countries work and, most importantly, how a genuine victim would act or talk can lead to inconsistent, unreliable decisions with grave consequences for people in danger.

The experience of the UNHCR in deciding refugee cases in the Middle East, Africa, and Asia offers an encouraging example of the potential to improve the system by establishing a more structured approach to refugee status determination. In 2003, UNHCR published for the first time a comprehensive set of standard for its offices in these cases, in addition to new training programs. The new standards were aimed at all aspects of the process, but their general goal was to force adjudicators to articulate a clear logical base for each step of their decision making. In the context of credibility assessment—which previously had accounted for the majority of UNHCR rejections—this forces adjudicators toward a more objective approach. Afterward, UNHCR's recognition rate climbed from below fifty percent to above eighty percent.[30] The UNHCR standards are not meant to be applied to governments and need not be replicated precisely, but they illustrate the impact of moving toward a more structured approach.

The difficulty with reality is that the information culture in which we live does not accept doubt easily. Our growing access to information creates an impression that all claims should be immediately verifiable, and it creates an outlet by which strong opinions may be expressed far more quickly than ever before. Asylum cases are defined by uncertainty, and to be decided effectively they need to be analyzed methodically and slowly. This is a challenge when systemic pressures push adjudicators to make decisions quickly, and public opinion expects certainty where none can be had. The battle to preserve asylum requires protecting a system that is rigorous and objective, but in which we must grow comfortable knowing no one is ever sure in advance of the results.

NOTES

1 UK Home Office Immigration & Nationality Directorate, "Country Assessment: Sudan," Internet, refworld.org (date accessed: 1 April 2002): 5.60.

2 U.S. Department of State, *Country Reports on Human Rights Practices for 2013: Guatemala* (2014).

3 United Nations High Commissioner for Refugees, *Children on the Run*, Internet, http://www.unhcrwashington.org/sites/default/files/1_UAC_Children%20on%20the%20UAC_Full%20Report.pdf (date accessed: 1 December 2014). *Also* Jill Replogle, "Violence Fuels Dramatic Rise in Central American Asylum-Seekers," KPBS, Internet, http:// www.kpbs.org/news/2014/feb/25/violence-fuels-dra¬matic-rise-central-american-asyl/ (date accessed: 25 February 2014). *Also* Jill Replogle, "For Central Americans, fear is increasingly the reason for entering the U.S.," Public Radio International, Internet, http://www.pri.org/stories/2014-03-11/central-americans-fear-increasingly-reason-entering-us (date accessed: 11 March 2014).

4 Michael Kagan, "Is Truth In the Eye of the Beholder? Objective Credibility Assessment in Refugee Status Determination," *Georgetown Immigration Law Journal* 17 (2003): 368-369.

5 Ibid., 371-374.

6 William Hague, "William Hague's full speech," *The Guardian*, 18 April 2000, Internet, http://www.theguardian.com/uk/2000/apr/18/immigration. Immigrationandpublicservices (date accessed: 1 December 2014).

7 Kirk Semple et al., "Asylum Fraud in Chinatown: An Industry of Lies," *The New York Times*, 22 February 2014.

8 Milan Simonich, "Rep. Pearce: Most fled Central America for economic reasons," *Santa Fe New Mexican*, 16 July 2014.

9 "Editorial: Border Surge is About Magnets, Not Gangs," *Investors Business Daily*, 4 August 2014.

10 Jaya Ramji-Nogales and others, "Refugee Roulette: Disparities in Asylum Adjudication," *Stanford Law Review* 60 (2007): 295-412.

11 United Nations High Commissioner for Refugees, *Beyond Proof: Credibility Assessment in EU Asylum Systems* (2013): 189-190.

12 Margaret Farnsworth and Raymond H.C. Teske, Jr., "Gender Differences in Felony Court Processing: Three Hypothesis of Disparity," *Women & Criminal Justice* 6 (1995): 23. *Also* Steven F. Shatz and Naomi R. Shatz, "Chivalry Is Not Dead: Murder, Gender and the Death Penalty," *Berkeley Journal of Gender, Law & Justice* 27 (2012): 64. *Also* Chimene I. Keitner, "Victim or Vamp? Images of Violent Women in the Criminal Jus¬tice System," *Columbia Journal of Gender & Law* 11 (2002): 38. *Also* Margareth Etienne, "Sentencing Women: Reas¬sessing the Claims of Disparity," *Journal of Gender, Race & Justice* 14 (2011): 73. *Also* S. Fernando Rodriguez and others, "Gender Differences in Clinical Sentencing: Do Effects Vary Across Violent, Property, and Drug Offenses?" *Social Science Quarterly* 87 (2006).

13 Jacqueline Bhabha, "Internationalist Gatekeepers? The Tension Between Asylum Advocacy and Human Rights," *Harvard Human Rights Journal* 15 (2002): 162.

14 Smeetra Mishra, "'Saving' Muslim women and fighting Muslim men: Analysis of representations," *The New York Times*, Global Media Journal 6.

15 Jayashri Srikantiah, "Perfect Victims and Real Survivors: The Iconic Victim in Domestic Human Trafficking Law," *Boston University Law Review* 87, no. 157 (2007): 201-202.

16 Fatma E. Marouf, "Implicit Bias and Immigration Courts," *New England Law Review* 45 (2011): 429-432. *Also* Yan v. Gonzales, 438 F.3d 1249, 1252 (10th Cir. 2006).

17 SZAKD v. Minister for Immigration (2004), FMCA 78, 2004 WL 723864 (19 March 2004) (Austl.).

18 United States v. Bastanipour, 980 F.2d 1129, 1131 (7th Cir. 1992).

19 Dan Bilefsky, "Gays Seeking Asylum in U.S. Encounter a New Hurdle," *The New York Times*, 28 January 2011.

20 Jane Herlihy et al., "What assumptions about Human Behaviour Underlie Asylum Judgments?" *International Journal of Refugee Law* 22 (2010): 351-366.

21 Hilary Evans Cameron, "Risk Theory and 'Subjective Fear': The Role of Risk Perception, Assessment, and Management in Refugee Status Determination," *International Journal of Refugee Law* 32 (2008): 568.

22 United Nations High Commissioner for Refugees, *Note on Burden and Standard of Proof in Refugee Claims* (1988): Paragraph 11.

23 United Nations High Commissioner for Refugees, *Determination of Refugee Status* (1989): Chapter 1, RLD 2.

24 Charles F. Bond, Jr. and Bella M. DePaulo, "Accuracy of Deception Judgments," *Personality & Social Psychoogy Review* 10 (2006): 214, 231.

25 Marouf, "Implicit Bias and Immigration Courts," 429.

26 United Nations High Commissioner for Refugees, *Beyond Proof: Credibility Assessment in EU Asylum Systems* (May 2013): 246-246.

27 Gabor Gyulai, ed., *Credibility Assessment in Asylum Procedures*, 2013, Internet, http://helsinki.hu/wp-content/uploads/Credibility-Assessment-in-Asylum-Proce-dures-CREDO-manual.pdf (date accessed: 1 December 2014).

28 REAL ID Act § 101(a)(3) (codified at 8 U.S.C. § 1158(b)(1)(B)(iii) (2006)).

29 United Nations High Commissioner for Refu¬gees, *Global Trends* 2013, Internet, http://www.unhcr. org/5399a14f9.html (date accessed: 1 December 2014).

30 Michael Kagan, "Is Truth In the Eye of the Beholder? Objective Credibility Assessment in Refu¬gee Status Determination," *Georgetown Immigration Law Journal* 17 (2003): 369. *Also* Asylum Access, "UNHCR recognition rates rise in the wake of new

NOTES

standards," *Asylum Access*, 24 July 2008, Internet, http://rsdwatch.wordpress. com/2008/07/24/unhcr-recognition-rates-rise-in-the-wake-of-new-standards (date accessed: 1 December 2014). *Also* Asylum Access, "UNHCR recognition rates rise in the wake of new standards," *Asylum Access*, 24 July 2008, Internet, http://rsdwatch.wordpress.com/2008/07/24/unhcr-recognition-rates-rise-in-the-wake-of-new-standards (date accessed: 1 December 2014).

Eroding Cultures and Environments
What a Rapidly Changing Earth Means for the Richness of Human Experience

Paul Robbins

The ice that has covered the Arctic for millennia is now melt-ing at a remarkable rate. Summer Arctic sea ice has declined a stunning 13.7 percent per decade since 1979, according to the National Oceanic and Atmospheric Administration's 2013 Arctic Report Card.[1] Unsurprisingly, the concomitant collapse in local ecosystems, fisheries, and landscapes has had a devastating impact on local communities and cultures. The Inuit cultures of the Arctic have evolved and adapted under specific regimes of temperature and precipitation and have developed sophisticated strategies for making a living. Inuit knowledge and identity are rooted in a world domi-nated by ice, permafrost, and the companionship of the niche species that thrive in cold weather. Loss of key hunting and fishing species, changes in modes of transportation, and the declining availability of resources make it harder to be Inuit in any recognizable way, never mind to pass along Inuit traditions and knowledge from one generation to the next.[2] As the land and sea change, so too does an entire way of life.

Cultures like those of the Inuit arguably include some of the most sophisticated and venerable of the world's tradi-tions. For those interested in preserving these ways of life, as well as for those concerned about rapidly changing environ-

Paul Robbins is the director of the Nelson Institute for Environ-mental Studies at the University of Wiscon-sin-Madison, where his research focuses on human interac-tions with nature and the politics of resource management and wild-life conservation.

ments across the planet, it has grown clear that cultures and environments are inseparably intertwined. Amidst global change, the need for policies that address both peoples and landscapes has become increasingly obvious.

Culture in its environmental context.

The need for new policies is not confined to the Arctic by any means. For an entirely different landscape, consider the Raika of northwestern India. A remarkable pastoral community at the edges of the Thar Desert region of Rajasthan, the Raika are culturally distinctive and well known for their rich ethno-veterinary and ecological knowledge, as well as their unique form of renunciant Hindu religious practice. Most famous is their long-range migratory strategy wherein combined herds of thousands of animals leave the desert for the central states of India and return on a sophisticated annual schedule.[3]

The Raika have, however, faced significant challenges in recent years. The introduction of high capacity wells has resulted in intensified agricultural production, a decline in fallow lands, and a loss of land for grazing. Thousands of square kilometers of grasslands, historically the key landscape for pastoral livelihoods, have been put under the plow. Long-range migration has been made far more difficult by the enclosure of forest common lands. On top of this, invasive species and prolonged drought present additional stresses on the region. These environmental shifts mean changes in livelihoods, settlement patterns, and cultural practices. Many Raika have abandoned livestock raising altogether (camel raising is in

especially steep decline), as well as many traditions linked to this way of life.[4] In this case, the culprit is the fundamental re-working of the agroecology and land economy of India. Agrarian policy in India, notably, has relegated many community lands to the legal status of "revenue waste land," a category that allows their expropriation. Water policy in the thirsty state of Rajasthan has also encouraged irrationally over-intensive cultivation by undervaluing water and encouraging irrigation. Herders have been exclosed from traditional grazing lands in the name of conservation. These policies mean declining grazing resources for Raika herders—resources that represent the backbone of Raika livelihood and culture.[5]

In the Arctic as in every region, changes in the land mean changes in the world's cultures; environmental change impinges on the richness of human experience. This is because cultures—understood as unique systems of meaning and practice shared by a group of people—create, operate in, and emerge from unique environmental conditions. Cultures include beliefs and worldviews, livelihoods and practices, knowledge bases and languages, and norms and institutions, all of which people have adopted and adapted across the countless diverse environments of the world.[6] Shaping and being reshaped by the environments around them, humans have created unique livelihoods and concomitant patterns of thought, language, expression, dress, worship, manners, and cosmology.

Decline of cultures is hard to measure in any rigorous way, but the decline of languages around the world provides a pretty good index. A unique way of understanding the world lies within each language; each vocabulary has its own ontology and every form of grammar contains a model of causes and effects. Lost languages are lost cultures even if every lost culture is not reflected by its own lost language. And the numbers are not encouraging: By the year 2100, between 50 and 90 percent of the languages spoken today will likely have no remaining speakers. A language vanishes roughly every two weeks.[7]

assimilate with non-native cultures. Anthropologist Stephen Pax Leonard lives and works with the Inughuit community. He has stressed that their unique dialect, *Inuktun*, which is spoken by fewer than one thousand speakers, has never been documented and is at risk of extinction alongside the unique landscapes and species of the northern Arctic.[9]

Treating cultures as endangered species follows a highly colonial logic: a vision of subject peoples stewarded by imperial masters.

Moreover, the geography of these simultaneous cultural and ecological declines is remarkably matched. One recent study demonstrates that those areas with relatively high remaining linguistic diversity (a good but imperfect index of cultural diversity) are also those that contain the highest remaining biodiversity. The countries with some of the highest numbers of endemic vertebrae species notably including Mexico, Australia, India, Indonesia, and Papua New Guinea, are also among the countries with the highest number of endemic vertebrate species.[8]

The Inuit communities of the far north fall outside this biodiverse tropical belt, but they too are experiencing linguistic and biodiversity challenges. The Inughuit in northwest Greenland, the world's northernmost people, are faced with the dwindling hunting resources and conditions which result from climate change alongside concomitant pressures to move south and

In part, this parallel decline between language/culture and biodiversity occurs because the places where many minority languages and cultures persist are also those where there is some autonomy or distance from otherwise invasive centralized state control, and where large-scale land conversion, which typically follows integration into the global commodity economy, has made fewer inroads. Such conditions are also good, as it turns out, for the conservation of species.

Eroding landscapes, eroding cultures.
As a result, places where biodiversity is on the decline, where large-scale environmental upheavals have occurred, and where ecosystems have been transformed (which is in fact virtually everywhere), are places where many traditional and indigenous cultures have been imperiled or eliminated. This is no coincidence, since the forces that erode the diversity of life on earth are the very same ones that imperil cultural diversity.

These linked forces include direct declines, driven by climate change, in the environments in which minority communities live. Examples abound: Farmers in Malawi face rainfall-stress while the Eeyouch (Cree) of Quebec face perilous warming trends; cattle and goat herders in the Kalahari face rising temperatures and dune expansion; and Saami reindeer herding communities in Finland, Norway, and Sweden slog through rainy winters and declining herds.[10]

Climate is not the only driver; cultural-ecological stress also follows direct losses of productive local resources. Violent examples of this kind of resource loss include the aggressive appropriation of resources for mining, dam-building or other large-scale, land-transforming industrialized forms of production. In Sarawak, Malaysia, plans to build twelve large dams on the island of Borneo threaten rainforest landscapes along with the thousands of endemic species and forty indigenous groups that dwell there.

Is such cultural decline a problem? In many ways, yes, and in others, no; the distinction rests on how, why, and under what conditions local communities face, and adapt to, modernization.

Certainly each culture, and its associated systems of meaning, local forms of knowledge, and unique ways of knowing and understanding the world, is an inherited treasure in and of itself. Like a species, in this sense, the death of a culture or a language represents an irreplaceable loss in the creative cultural patrimony of humanity. Inuit culture is a remarkable treasure, unique in the world owing to its vibrant and thriving way of living in a singular ecological and geographic context. Its disappearance lessens us as people.

So too does each such culture contain unique forms of knowledge of potentially enormous value. A decline in cultural practices arguably makes humanity, as a whole, less adaptive in the face of change. Every culture carries with it strategies for facing complex ecological conditions, such as intimate knowledge of landscapes, crops, and soils. Each possesses unique philosophies and social capacities for coping with change. As linguist Nicholas Evans put it: "Variety is the reservoir of adaptability."[11] The old anthropological chestnut that claims that Northern Arctic people have hundreds of words for ice or snow is problematically hyperbolic. Nonetheless, as anthropologist Fikret Berkes has noted, the subtle and changing conditions of snow and ice are indeed reflected in a diverse, supple, and complex taxonomy of indigenous northern cultures.[12] In a world that is experiencing environmental change, it seems as though having more ways of seeing, doing, and understanding the world would make humanity more resilient.

Nature, Culture, and Policy: Avoiding a Colonial Trap.
On the other hand, viewing cultural decline as a problem in and of itself is surely misleading. Approached this way, we might imagine cultural preservation as identical in a policy perspective to nature conservation—a problem that might be solved territorially, perhaps with a park. Writing in nature in 2011, Kelly Swing captured this approach boldly. Swing, the director of the Tiputini Biodiversity Station in Ecuador, argued by direct

analogy: Groups like the Taromenane clans of the lowland rainforests of Yasuní should be treated like intact ecosystems, "through hands-off policies that are akin to those used for endangered species."[13]

However, treating the problem of cultural decline as one of "protecting" indigenous cultures from "outside" interactions adopts a dangerously imperialist approach. It treats the people who make up these cultures as specimens or zoo animals. Treating cultures as endangered species, an act of power, follows a problematic and highly colonial logic since it imposes a singular vision of culture onto living and sovereign people, a vision of subject peoples stewarded by imperial masters.

People abandon old ways of doing and seeing things for plenty of good reasons. Urbanization offers opportunities for liberation and allows thriving cultural cosmopolitanism. Modernization and the availability of new technologies from cell phones and computers to tractors and solar panels certainly mean changes in language, livelihoods, and practices for people, but can also represent a welcome trade-off for people embracing new ways of life. The rate of urbanization in places like India and China is at an unprecedented high; some 250 million people in China alone will move to urban environments in the next decade, with most of them seeking greater opportunities, better infrastructure, and improved living conditions. The cultural change that comes with this great upheaval is one that migrants either tolerate or embrace.

So, too, is culture always in a state of change. As ethnographer Jarich Oosten

and his colleagues have observed for the Inuit, it is typically only *Qallunaat* ("white people") who observe and bemoan the decline of Inuit culture, including shamanic religious traditions. Inuit themselves, by contrast, often tell stories that valorize the adaptive and changing nature of their cultural traditions, interacting with a changing world around them.[14] Working to preserve cultures "in amber," in a "pristine" or "primitive" condition, is folly in this sense. It represents a paternalistic urge, one not typically shared by the members of cultures in transformation or decline.

Nevertheless, there are a good many peoples who would like to retain their historical languages, livelihoods, and modes of cultural expression even while advancing their own modern development agendas. Hopi tribal members strive to reproduce their native culture through the use of mentoring by elders and innovative radio stations, maintaining their identity amidst dramatic challenges by embracing technology, not rejecting it.[15] Mayan land movements collide with the government of Belize over logging concessions, but do so by asserting their rights to develop the forest, rather than simply leaving it a wilderness.[16]

More often than not, the environmental forces driving the lifestyles of people to extinction are violent, unwelcome, and part of larger and dismal historical trend where the strong (or lucky) eliminate the weak. Certain peoples resist cultural erosion with good reason.

Embalming local cultures or forbidding cultural change (if such a thing were even possible) cannot be the core for any policy addressing environmental and cultural change. Instead, policy must directly address the more fundamental problem of galvanizing and defending the rights of local communities to the resources, landscapes, places, and ecosystems that allow their cultures to thrive. This is the approach taken by organizations such as Cultural Survival, whose goal is not to preserve indigenous and traditional cultures in a museum or archive but instead to defend the use of traditional territories and resources, the right to informed consent before being "developed" by any outside project, and the rights to maintain languages, cultural practices, and sacred places.[17] Hewing closely to the United Nations Declaration on the Rights of Indigenous Peoples, updated most recently at the 2014 World Conference on Indigenous Peoples, Cultural Sur-

languages, metaphors, and complex systems of meaning that are bound up with this way of life. Instead, the Inuit are confronting all these issues simultaneously.

On top of all of this, they face a new and growing onslaught of people. As the climate changes, a host of newly interested actors and agents have entered the Arctic, from environmentalists pushing to halt native hunting to oil and gas wildcat prospectors seeking resource claims and state bureaucrats carving up the new land and seascapes revealed by the retreating ice. With the multiplication of claims on this vast landscape, the Inuit and their culture become simply one of many "interested stakeholder communities" where once they were sovereign. This loss of sovereignty (over and above the terrible losses of the nineteenth and twentieth centuries),

To ignore cultures while seeking to conserve environments would relegate to extinction some of the most invaluable bodies of knowledge.

vival partners with local communities for *self-determination*.[18]

Conclusion: Policy, nature, and culture beyond colonial conservation. This returns us to the Arctic. Here, Inuit communities are not facing only a perilous loss of sea ice and the closely linked resources upon which they depend. They are neither solely confronting the decline of traditional hunting and fishing practices rooted in those resources, nor are they merely coming to terms with the loss of native

coupled with the catastrophic decline in rare ecosystems and ways of life during this "Great Thaw," is devastating to the Inuit. As such, any effort to address Inuit cultural loss must necessarily be one that addresses Inuit political sovereignty, Inuit claims on natural resources, and Inuit power.

Some form of adaptation, which honors and preserves Inuit livelihoods and systems of meaning while simultaneously adapting to a quickly-changing situation, is essential. Here, some communities have linked up with academics to advance their interests. Following precisely the approach advocated by Cultural Survival, Professor Nancy Doubleday, Hope Chair in Peace and Health at McMaster University in Canada, has been working to connect Inuit people to the science that monitors arctic environmental change while securing them the kind of decision-making authority that can help aid them in maintaining their culture. Such responsible, community-based participatory research marks the frontier in working with threatened cultures, in a context that is inevitably politically fraught.[19]

Policies that follow from this kind of research also honor and support self-determination while still taking seriously the protection of ecosystems. Such policies stress political empowerment, especially of historically marginalized communities. They also entail principles of self-governance and territorial control where the fate of landscapes targeted for conservation lies within the control and consultation of the people who have lived in, and very often created, these same environments.[20] Such rights are recognized in International Labour Organization Convention 169 and the United Nations Subcommittee on the Elimination of Discrimination and Protection of Minorities, as well as the United Nations Human Rights Committee.[21] The implication of such rights is demonstrated by ongoing efforts to evolve national and regional conservation policies that tolerate and embrace the rights of communities living in and around protected areas, areas slated for restoration, and areas targeted for development.

The alternatives to such policies are grim. Practically, any effort to protect the environment that does not come to terms with the diversity of human cultures and the sovereignty of the communities inexorably linked with them is likely to fail. The absence of local cooperation has time and again spelled the doom of the best-laid plans of environmentalists.[22] On the other hand, efforts to protect languages, beliefs, values, and practices that do not attend to the material resources and ecologies on which they depend do little but postpone the inevitable. To ignore cultures and communities while seeking to conserve or develop environments would relegate to extinction some of the most important and invaluable bodies of knowledge and practice alongside the people who create, nurture, and possess them. It would do so in a fashion tantamount to a new form of colonialism.

It must finally be added that efforts to implement such policies inevitably face opposition. Policies supporting native sovereignty over their lands most obviously limit the freedom of action of some forestry and mining interests. Such policies also impinge on the urges of some kinds of environmentalists, who might otherwise attempt to constrain the actions of indigenous peoples and limit or direct their use or development of the land. As differing outside interests tug policy in both directions, struggles to maintain cultures in the face of environmental upheaval will remain just that—struggles. Rapid environmental change has surely revealed not only the close linkages between people and the environment, but also those between nature, culture, and power.

NOTES

1 NOAA, "Arctic Report Card: Update for 2013," Internet, http://www.arctic.noaa.gov/reportcard (date accessed: 1 December 2014).

2 Igor Krupnik and Dyanna Jolly, eds., *The Earth is Faster Now: Indigenous Observations of Arctic Environmental Change* (Fairbanks: Arctic Research Consortium of the United States, 2002).

3 Arun Agrawal, "Mobility and Control Among Nomadic Shepherds: The Case of the Raikas II," *Human Ecology* 22, no. 2 (1994), 131-144. *Also* Ilse Kohler-Rollefson, "From Royal Camel Tenders to Dairymen: Occupational Changes within the Raikas," R. Hooja and R. Joshi, eds., *Desert, Drought, and Development* (1999), 305-315. *Also* Paul Robbins, "Pastoralism Inside-Out: The Contradictory Conceptual Geography of Rajasthan's Raika," *Nomadic Peoples* 8, no. 2 (December 2004), 136-149.

4 A recent and highly accessible survey of the history of the Raika as well as their current challenges can be found: Ilse Kohler-Rollefson, *Camel Karma: Twenty years among India's camel nomads* (New Delhi: Tranquebar Press, 2014).

5 Paul Robbins, "Nomadism Now: Cultural Survival in a Changing Desert Environment," *Annals of Arid Zone*, vol. 43 (2005), 1-19.

6 A recent and highly accessible survey of the history of the Raika as well as their current challenges can be found here: Ilse Kohler-Rollefson, *Camel Karma: Twenty years among India's camel nomads* (New Delhi: Tranquebar Press, 2014).

7 Nicholas Evans, *Dying Words: Endangered Languages and What They Have to Tell Us* (Chichester: Wiley-Blackwell, 2010), 18.

8 L.J. Gorenflo et al., "Co-occurrence of linguistic and biological diversity in biodiversity hotspots and high biodiversity wilderness areas," *Proceedings of the National Academy of Sciences of the United States of America* 109, no. 21 (2012), 8032-8037. *Also* David Harmon and Luisa Maffi, "Are linguistic and biological diversity linked?" Conservation Biology in Practice 3, no. 1 (2002), 26-27.

9 Nicholas Evans, Dying Words: *Endangered Lan¬guages and What They Have to Tell Us* (Chichester: Wiley-Blackwell, 2010), 18.

10 A. Peter Castro, Dan Taylor, and David W. Brokensha, eds., *Climate Change and Threatened Communities: Vulnerability, capacity and action* (Warwickshire: Practical Action, 2012).

11 Nicholas Evans, *Dying words: Endangered languages and What They Have to Tell Us* (Chichester: Wiley-Blackwell, 2010).

12 Fikret Berkes, *Sacred Ecology: Traditional Ecological Knowledge and Resource Management* (Philadelphia: Taylor and Francis, 1999).

13 Kelly Swing, "Developing world: Endangered cultures need protection too," *Nature* vol. 476 (2011), 283.

14 Jarich Oosten, Frédéric Laugrand, and Cornelius Remie, "Perceptions of Decline: Inuit Shamanism in the Canadian Arctic," *Ethnohistory* 53, no. 3 (2006) 445-477.

15 Hopi radio, including Hopi language programing, live streaming from KUYI 88.1FM: http://www.kuyi.net/listen-online (date accessed: October 2014).

16 Joel Wainwright, *Decolonizing Development: Colonial power and the Maya* (New York: Wiley-Blackwell, 2008).

17 Cultural Survival, Internet, https://www.culturalsurvival.org/what-we-do (date accessed: 1 December 2014).

18 Hopi radio, including Hopi language programing, live streaming from KUYI 88.1FM: http://www.kuyi.net/listen-online (date accessed: October 2014).

19 Bryan S.R. Grimwood et al., "Engaged acclimatization: Towards responsible community-based participatory research in Nunavut," *Canadian Geographer-Geographe Canadien* 56, no. 2 (April 2012), 211-230.

20 Cultural Survival, Internet, https://www.cul¬turalsurvival.org/what-we-do (date accessed: 1 December 2014).

21 Indigenous Global Coordinating Group of the World Conference on Indigenous Peoples, Internet, http://wcip2014.org (date accessed: 1 December 2014).

22 Paul Robbins, *Political Ecology: A Critical Introduction*, 2nd ed. (New York: Wiley-Blackwell, 2012).

Law&Ethic

Sex-Selective Abortion Bans

Anti-Immigration or Anti-Abortion?

Sital Kalantry

A new wave of legislation is sweeping state legislatures across the United States: laws prohibiting health professionals from providing an abortion if they believe a woman is seeking one because she does not want to have a child of a certain sex. Eight states have enacted such laws, and twenty-one other state legislatures in the country have considered them since 2009. Although the texts of the laws do not refer specifically to Asian Americans, supporters argue that these restrictions are needed to curb the trend among Asian-American women to abort female fetuses. This article first describes the narrative that proponents use to justify these laws—namely, that immigrants from countries where women abort female fetuses in favor of male children are coming to the United States and replicating those patterns. The emergence of these bills targeting Asian immigrants occurs at a time when Asian Americans are the fastest growing racial group in the United States. As a result, it is natural to question whether abortion bans are being adopted in response to the growing Asian population in the United States. To test the hypothesis, I determined whether there is an association between whether a state considers and/or passes a ban on sex-selective abortion and the growth rate of Asian immigrants by

Sital Kalantry is a Clinical Professor of Law at the Cornell Law School and co-director of the Immigration Appellate Law and Advocacy Clinic. She was a project director and co-author of an inter-disciplinary study and report on sex-selective abortion laws in the United States.

state. Indeed, I found that nearly 70 percent of the states with growth rates of the Asian population in excess of 70 percent between 2000 and 2010 considered and/or adopted laws to ban abortions, whereas only 51 percent of the states with low Asian population growth rates (i.e., below 70 percent) considered and/or adopted sex selective abortion bans.

Asian immigrant growth rates are only part of the explanation for why sex-selective bans are booming in state legislatures, particularly given the fact that there is scant empirical support for the notion that Asians in the United States prefer to have boys and abort girls. Indeed, the strong anti-abortion movement and anti-abortion sentiments in the United States also provide impetus for these bills to emerge. I also found an association between states' consideration of sex-selective abortion bans and other anti-abortion legislation in general. Of the states that had adopted other anti-abortion laws as of 2012, nearly 70 percent of those states also passed and/or considered bills on sex-selective abortion since 2009. On the other hand, only 44 percent of the states that had not adopted other anti-abortion laws as of 2012 considered and/or adopted sex selective abortion bans.

Additionally, according to a logit regression analysis for the binary outcome of passage or consideration of anti-abortion legislation, the passage of other anti-abortion legislation is significantly associated with consideration of sex-selective abortion bans, whereas the growth in Asian immigration is not. Thus, anti-abortion sentiments appear to be driving these bans more

than the rate of Asian immigration. American lawmakers should be careful not to base laws in reaction to practices that occur in other countries assuming that because people in China and India engage in certain practices, Asians in the United States from those countries will also engage in those same practices.

Bans on Sex-Selective Abortion Are Being Enacted to Prevent Asian Americans from Aborting Female Fetuses.

State legislatures are increasingly passing laws to regulate immigration. A well-known example is from Arizona, which enacted a law in 2010 that required state and local law enforcement officials to detain people who they reasonably believed were unlawfully present in the United States.[1] Parts of the law were later declared unconstitutional.[2] The other well-known example is the ordinance adopted by Hazelton, a city in Pennsylvania, which sanctioned employers for hiring undocumented workers and landlords who rented to undocumented people.[3] An appellate court found this to be an improper intrusion on federal government authority and overturned the ordinances.[4]

A new wave of legislation, aimed at Asian immigrants, has hit state legislatures: bans on sex-selective abortions. Eight states have enacted laws prohibiting sex-selective abortion (see Table 1) and twenty-one other state legislatures in the country have considered such bans since 2009 (see Table 2). In 2010, a majority of the U.S. House of Representatives voted in favor of such bans.[5] Unlike the Arizona law and the Hazelton ordinance, sex-selective abortion bans do not attempt to regulate illegal immigration, but rather address what is (incorrectly) assumed to be the behavior of Asian immigrants. These laws prohibit medical professionals from performing an abortion if they believe that a woman is seeking to obtain one because of the sex of

A common line of reasoning can be seen in legislative discussions surrounding bills under consideration in the U.S. Congress as well as state legislatures across the United States. First, some argue that a preference for boys in India and China causes women to

There is **scant empirical support** for the notion that Asians in the United States prefer to have boys.

the fetus. Providers in South Dakota for example, the most recent state to pass such a law, are obliged to inquire whether a woman knows the sex of the fetus and whether she is seeking an abortion on that basis.[6]

These laws prohibit using abortion as a method for sex selection, but they do not ban other increasingly common methods of sex selection. Families can sex-select through artificial insemination, whereby only sperm that will produce the desired sex are allowed to fertilize the egg. In-vitro fertilization can also allow for sex selection by removing eggs from a woman and fertilizing them outside of the body. Three days after fertilization, one or two cells are removed from the embryo and the sex of the embryo is determined through chromosomal analysis of the removed cells such that only the embryos of the desired sex are implanted in the uterus. These sex-selection procedures are legally available in the United States and, indeed, fertility clinics actively promote their availability. Notwithstanding this, none of the laws that ban sex-selective abortion in the United States prohibit sex selection prior to conception or implantation.

abort female fetuses to avoid having a female child. For example, a report by the Judiciary Committee of the House of Representatives, undertaken in connection with the federal legislative ban on sex-selection, states that "the selective abortion of females is . . . the intentional killing of unborn females, due to the preference for male offspring or 'son preference.'"[7] The report explains why "son preference" exists in other countries: girls are a financial burden and do not carry the family name.[8]

It is true that sex selection in favor of boys is well documented in places like India. Several studies have shown that the ratio of girls to boys has drastically decreased in India. The normal at-birth ratio for boys to girls is 1000 boys to 952 girls. Yet the overall ratio across the country is 1000 boys to 943 girls, according to the 2011 census.[9] Many assume that these women used ultrasound technology (which became increasingly available since the mid-1980s) to detect the sex of the fetus and abort it if it was female.[10]

The second step in the argument supporting sex-selective abortion bans in the United States is the claim that people from India and China are coming to the United States and aborting female fetuses consistent with practices in their countries of origin. For example, Don Hagger, a Republican state representative in South Dakota, stated:

> Let me tell you, our population in South Dakota is a lot more diverse than it ever was. There are cultures that look at a sex-selection abortion as being culturally okay. And I will suggest to you that we are embracing individuals from some of those cultures in this country, or in this state. And I think that's a good thing that we invite them to come, but I think it's also important that we send a message that this is a state that values life, regardless of its sex.[11]

Additionally, the federal bill that would ban sex-selective abortion in the United States asserts: "Evidence strongly suggests that some Americans are exercising sex-selection abortion practices within the United States con-

to ban sex-selective abortion also notes that it is needed to promote equality.[14]

Interestingly, this common narrative that has emerged in state legislatures since 2009 was not present in the discussions of bans in the 1980s, possibly reflecting the fact that there were fewer Asian immigrants in the United States at that time. But the wave of legislation can also be attributed to an influential article released in 2008 that claimed to provide empirical evidence of sex selection in favor of boys among Asian Americans. Historically, Illinois was the first state in the United States to ban sex-selective abortion. In 1984, Illinois adopted a bill that modified its abortion law in light of certain rulings by courts, but then also added a provision relating to sex-selective abortion.[15] I found neither discussion nor trends of the global sex ratio or practices of female infanticide or feticide in the transcripts of the Illinois Senate and

A new wave of legislation, aimed at Asian immigrants, has hit state legislatures: bans on sex-selective abortions.

sistent with discriminatory practices common to their country of origin, or the country to which they trace their ancestry."[12]

The third part of the narrative is that sex-selective abortion bans are needed to promote equality for women and girls. In his submission to a House committee, United States Representative Lamar Smith states: "The reason for opposing sex-selection is uniform: the desire to combat discrimination."[13] The preamble to the Congressional bill

House of Representatives.[16]

The second state to ban sex selection was Pennsylvania in 1989. During the deliberations on this bill, no supporters of the bill mentioned the situation in other countries or the global sex ratio. The geographical focus of the discussion was the United States. For example, the main sponsor of the bill, Representative Stephen Friend, cited a *New York Times* poll, which indicated that 20 percent of the medical geneticists interviewed for the poll counseled for sex-selective abortions. He further admitted that even if no sex-selective abortions "are performed [in the United States] and that poll is wrong, then this legislation prohibiting it does no harm whatsoever."[17] Senator Karen Ritter, an opponent of the bill, was the only person to mention sex selection in other countries, saying: "This is a terrible practice in other countries like India and China, but we do not do it here."[18]

Growth of Asian Immigration in the United States.

The view that Asian immigrants are performing sex-selective abortions in the United States emerged with the growth of Asian immigration in the United States. The number of Asian Americans has nearly doubled every decade since 1970 (see Graph 1). At this moment, the Asian-American population is the fastest-growing racial group in the country.[19] Indeed, as of July 2013, the U.S. Hispanic population grew by 2.1 percent over 2012, whereas the Asian population grew by 2.9 percent.[20] Among the 17,329,586 Asian Americans in the United States, 3,183,063 are of Indian descent and 4,010,114 are from Chinese descent.[21] In other words, nearly 42 percent of all Asian Americans trace their heritage (through one or both parents) to India or China.

The growth rate of Asian Americans has varied dramatically by state. From 2000 to 2010, the Asian population in Nevada grew over 116 percent whereas it grew by only 30 percent in Rhode Island (see Graph 2).[22] Given that sex-selective abortion bans target the (assumed) practices of Asians in the United States, we would expect that states with the highest Asian population growth rates would be more likely to consider such laws than states with lower growth rates of Asian Americans.

Indeed, nearly 70 percent of the states where the Asian population grew by more than 70 percent from 2000 to 2010 considered and/or adopted laws to ban abortions since 2009 (see Table 3). On the other hand, 51 percent of the states where the Asian population grew less than 70 percent considered and/or adopted the laws (p=.337).[23] Pennsylvania and Illinois were not included in this analysis because they adopted the bans in the 1980s. In thirteen of the forty-eight states studied in this analysis, 35 had growth rates below 70 percent and 13 had growth rates of Asian immigration above 70 percent (see Table 7).

Empirical Data on Sex-Selection Abortions in the United States Among Asians.

Illinois banned sex-selective abortion in 1984, followed by Pennsylvania four years later. Thereafter, for a period of 20 years, no states introduced bills prohibiting sex-selective abortions until 2009, when five state legislatures considered banning sex-selective abortions. Since then, 21 states have considered adopting such bans, and six have passed them (see Table 2).

This new legislative interest in sex selection bans came immediately after the 2008 publication of an article in the influential journal, the *Proceedings of National Academy of Sciences*, which suggested that sex selection in favor of boys was occurring among certain Asian communities in the United States. Douglas Almond and Lena Edlund calculated sex ratios at birth, broken down by ethnic groups from the 2000 U.S. Census. Sex ratios at birth are calculated by dividing the number of boys born in a given population at any given time by the number of girls born. They found male-biased sex ratios at birth for the second and third children of foreign-born Chinese, Indian and Korean families after the birth of one and two girls.[24] In other words, these three groups were more likely than European Americans to have a boy as their third child when they had two girls.

Policymakers assume from this analysis of birth records that abortion (rather than pre-implantation means of sex selection) is what accounts for the fact that a small number of Asian families are more likely to have a boy as their third child when they already have two girls than European Americans. A number of other studies thereafter confirmed the findings.[25]

Almond and Edlund's study made very narrow findings about national level data; nonetheless, it has been used extensively to support laws banning sex-selective abortion bills.[26] First, a male-biased sex ratio was found only in three very specific foreign-born Asian communities: Indians, Chinese, and Koreans. Within this group, a statistically significant trend was found only in families that had girls as their first two children. Second, the number of families in the study that were foreign-born Chinese, Indian, and Korean that had three children (with the first two being girls) was 324. It should be noted that this data represented only 5 percent of the U.S. census data in a 10-year period. Third, by studying only sex ratios at birth, we cannot be certain of the method being used to sex-select abortion or pre-implantation reproductive technologies. However, this study (and other studies confirming it) is the entire empirical basis to support this wave of legislation sweeping the states.

Policymakers are thus basing laws on the behavior of a very small group of Asian families. Moreover, this trend is very different from what is happening in their countries of origin. Graph 3 below depicts the sex ratios at birth of foreign-born Chinese and Indian families in the United States and people in India and China. When comparing these groups, we see that the sex ratios at birth of people living in India and China are very male-biased (sex ratios above 1.07 are considered to be male-biased), but they are not male-biased for Asians in the United States (when all of their births are taken into account).

In other work, my co-author analyzed more recent data from 2007 to 2011 from the American Community Survey, using the same methodology used by Almond and Edlund, and confirmed that a very small group of Asian families in the United States are more likely to have a boy in their third birth when they have two girls than white Americans. We also found, however, that when foreign-born Indian, Chinese, and Korean families have two girls, they are more likely to have boys than are white Americans after having two girls. Thus, what more recent U.S. census data suggests is that Asian Americans do not seem to have an aversion to daughters; they want both boys and girls.[27] Indeed, certain economic and social factors that drive people in India to prefer sons over daughters are not present in the United States.[28]

Sex-Selective Abortion Bans and the Anti-Abortion Movement.

Anti-abortion groups in the United States have pushed for federal and state bans on sex-selective abortion. Steven Mosher for example, the head of leading anti-abortion group Population Research Institute, wrote in 2008:

> I propose that we—the pro-life movement—adopt as our next goal the banning of sex-selective abortion. . . . By formally protecting all female fetuses from abortion on ground of their sex, we would plant in the law the proposition that the developing child is a being whose claims on us should not depend on their sex.[29]

In furtherance of this strategy, Americans United for Life have developed a legislative toolkit to help promote state-wide legislative bans on sex-selective abortion.[30] A ban on sex-selective abortion is seen as one more restriction on access to abortion, which (for example) requires an inquiry into

(1) those that as of 2012 had passed laws either (a) requiring women seeking abortions to submit to ultrasounds, (b) allowing health care providers to refuse to perform abortions and other medical procedures they may find morally objectionable, (c) declaring that life begins "at the moment of conception," (d) defunding Planned Parenthood by limiting funds to the organization, and/or (e) outlawing abortions after 20 weeks gestation; and (2) states which had not passed such laws as of 2012.[31] Twenty-four states were included in category (1) and twenty-four states were included in category (2) (see Table 7). I use the state's passage of anti-abortion laws as a proxy for the general climate in the state legislatures towards abortion rights. It should be noted that I have not identified whether there was a change in elected members of state legislatures from the time that the sex-selective abortion ban was introduced and the other anti-abortion measures was introduced, but I assume that the general climate towards abortion has remained the same in state legislatures

More recent U.S. census data suggests that Asian Americans do not seem to have an aversion to daughters.

the reasons of every woman seeking an abortion (not just Asian-American women).

To determine whether there is an association between a state's general climate towards abortion restrictions and whether or not sex-selective bans are introduced in state legislatures, I categorized states into two categories:

between 2009 to 2014 (the time period within which the sex-selective abortion bills that are part of this study were considered and/or adopted).

Of the states that had adopted other anti-abortion laws as of 2012, nearly 70 percent of those states also passed and/or considered bills on sex-selective abortion since 2009. On the other hand, only 44 percent of the states that had not adopted other anti-abortion laws as of 2012 considered and/or adopted sex-selective abortion bans. This suggests that the decision among states to adopt other abortion restrictions is associated with the adoption of sex-selective abortion bans (p=.089).[32] Indeed, an analysis of the voting states considered and/or passed the bans (Table 6). This suggests that in-state legislatures that passed other anti-abortion laws, the level of Asian immigration into the state does not seem to impact whether or not they considered the bans (p=.449).[35]

Indeed, according to a logit regression analysis for the binary outcome

Laws that purport to address immigration face the risk of being based on **stereotypes rather than reality.**

records of the six states also suggests a strong connection to abortion politics in the United States. Over 90 percent of Republican representatives (who I assume are more likely to be anti-abortion) in the six states that enacted bans in the last four years voted for the bans. In contrast, less than 10 percent of Democrats voted for the bans in four of the six states.[33]

In further examining the states that did not have other anti-abortion laws, only 37 percent of the low Asian immigration growth rate states considered and/or passed the law and 67 percent of high Asian immigration growth rate states considered and/or passed the laws (Table 5). This suggests that high Asian growth rate is associated with consideration of the bans in state legislatures that do not have a record for passing anti-abortion laws (p=.098).[34] On the other hand, in states that had other anti-abortion laws in place by 2012, 68 percent of the states that had low Asian immigration growth considered and/or passed the bans, while 71 percent of high Asian immigration growth

of passage or consideration of anti-abortion legislation (Table 8), the passage of other anti-abortion legislation is significantly associated with consideration of sex-selective abortion bans (p=.88), whereas the growth in Asian immigration is not (p=.315). Thus, it appears that anti-abortion sentiments are more likely driving consideration of sex-selective abortion bans rather than Asian immigration growth. Conversely, supporters of these bills argue that the laws must be passed to stop the (assumed) practices of Asian immigrants.

Conclusion. In the last five years, over half of the state legislatures in the United States have considered banning sex-selective abortion because of the (false) belief that Asian Americans are disproportionately giving birth to more boys than are European Americans. Supported by the data that applies to a very small subset of Asian Americans, proponents of the law stereotype Asian Americans by assuming that their birthing patterns are the same as those of people in India and China.

One might assume that the rapidly growing Asian immigrant community in the United States provides impetus for states to adopt these bans. Indeed, I found an association between the growth rate of Asian immigration in U.S. states and the decision to consider and/or adopt legislation prohibiting sex-selective abortion in those states. Bills were introduced (and in some cases garnered enough votes to pass) in 70 percent of state legislatures that had high growth rates (over 70 percent) of Asian immigrants from 2000 to 2010.

While there does seem to be some association with immigration, there is also another story behind these laws: a strong anti-abortion movement and anti-abortion sentiments are encouraging these laws in the United States. I found a strong association between a state's adoption of other anti-abortion laws and its adoption of sex-selective abortion bans. Of the states that had adopted other anti-abortion laws since 2012, nearly 70 percent of those states also passed and/or considered bills on sex-selective abortion since 2009. On the other hand, only 44 percent of the states that had not adopted other anti-abortion laws as of 2012 considered and/or adopted sex-selective abortion bans.

Upon further analysis, I also found that high Asian immigrant growth rates are associated with consideration of the bans in state legislatures that do not have a record for passing anti-abortion laws, but in state legislatures that passed other anti-abortion laws, the level of Asian immigration into the state does not seem to impact whether or not they considered the bans. It should be noted that we are not able to determine whether the growth of Asian immigration and/or the general climate towards abortion in the state legislatures causes them to consider and/or pass bans on sex-selective abortion, but there appears to be a stronger association with anti-abortion sentiments than with Asian immigration growth. Indeed, according to a logit regression analysis for the binary outcome of passage or consideration of anti-abortion legislation, the passage of other anti-abortion legislation is significantly associated with consideration of sex-selective abortion bans, whereas the growth in Asian immigration is not.

Laws such as sex selective abortion bans that purport to address immigration face the risk of being based on stereotypes rather than reality. The aforementioned Arizona laws allow police to detain people who they suspect are undocumented based on their looks alone. Sex-selection laws are based on the (inaccurate) stereotype that Asian immigrants into the United States (particularly those from China and India) favor boys and abort girls at the same rates as people in India and China. As previously discussed, this is clearly not the case. As a result of anti sex-selection bans, Asian women who desire to obtain reproductive services could be profiled by medical professionals and denied services even when they are not attempting to sex-select.

Because of the undue focus on Asian immigrants in the discussions of sex-selection bans, the real conversation that should occur in the American democratic system is short-circuited. States legislators and voters fail to discuss whether or not sex selection is a gateway to eugenics concerns, whether or not sex selection perpetuates gender stereotypes, and whether or not sex selection should be used for family balancing. Any bans on sex-selective abortion should take these issues into account and should not be based on misinformed views about the practices of Asian immigrants in the United States.

Graphs and Tables.

Table 1: States That Have Passed Anti Sex-Selection Abortion Laws

State	Year of Enactment
Illinois	1984
Pennsylvania	1989
Oklahoma	2010
Arizona	2011
Kansas	2013
North Carolina	2013
North Dakota	2013
South Dakota	2014

Table 2: States That Have Considered But Not Passed Anti Sex-Selection Abortion Laws

State	Year(s) Considered by State Legislature
California	2014
Colorado	2013
Florida	2012, 2013
Georgia	2010
Iowa	2013, 2014
Idaho	2010
Indiana	2013
Massachusetts	2012, 2013
Michigan	2009, 2010, 2012
Minnesota	2009, 2010
Missouri	2012, 2013, 2014
Mississippi	2009, 2010, 2014
New Jersey	2009, 2010, 2011, 2012
New York	2011, 2012, 2013, 2014
Ohio	2012
Oregon	2013, 2014
Rhode Island	2011, 2012, 2013, 2014
Texas	2013
Virginia	2013, 2014
Wisconsin	2013, 2014
West Virginia	2009, 2010, 2011, 2012, 2013, 2014

Table 3: Sex-Selective Abortion Laws and Growth Rate of Asian Population

	Asian Growth Rate Below 70%	Asian Growth Rate Above 70%
States that did not Consider or Pass Sex-Selective Abortion Bans	17 (48.57%)	4 (30.77%)
States that Considered and/or Passed Sex-Selective Abortion Bans	18 (51.43%)	9 (69.23%)
Total	35 (100%)	13 (100%)

Table 4: States that Considered and Passed Sex-Selective Abortion Bans and Other Anti-Abortion Laws

	States that Did not Adopt Other Anti-Abortion Bills	States that Adopted Other Anti-Abortion Bills
States that did not Consider or Pass Sex-Selective Abortion Bans	14 (56%)	7 (30.43%)
States that Considered and/or Passed Sex-Selective Abortion Bans	11 (44%)	16 (69.57%)
Total	25	23

Table 5: States That Have Considered But Not Passed Anti Sex-Selection Abortion Laws and Asian Immigration Growth

States that Considered and/or Passed Sex Selective Abortion Bans	Asian Immigration Growth Below 70%	Asian Immigration Growth 70% or more
No	12 (63.15%)	2 (33.33%)
Yes	7 (36.84%)	4 (66.66%)
Total	19	6

Table 6: States That Adopted Other Anti-Abortion Laws and Asian Immigration Growth

States that Considered and/or Passed Sex Selective Abortion Bans	Asian Immigration Growth Below 70%	Asian Immigration Growth 70% or more
No	5 (31.25%)	2 (28.57%)
Yes	11 (68.75%)	5 (71.42%)
Total	16	7

Table 7: Sex-Selective Abortion Laws and Growth Rate of Asian Population by State

States	Considered (But Did not Pass) Ban	Passed Ban	% Change in Asian Population From 2000 to 2010	States that Passed Other Anti-Abortion Laws as of 2012
Alabama	No	No	69.9	Yes
Alaska	No	No	54.2	Yes
Arizona	**	Yes	94.6	Yes
Arkansas	No	No	76.9	No
California	Yes	No	33.7	No
Colorado	Yes	No	53.7	Yes
Connecticut	No	No	64.7	No
Delaware	No	No	77.9	No
Florida	Yes	No	72.1	Yes
Georgia	Yes	No	82.9	Yes
Hawaii	No	No	11.1	No
Idaho	Yes	No	70.8	Yes
Indiana	Yes	No	74.0	No
Iowa	Yes	No	49.6	Yes
Kansas	**	Yes	49.7	Yes
Kentucky	No	No	67.4	Yes
Louisiana	No	No	31.1	No
Maine	No	No	55.0	No
Maryland	No	No	55.2	No
Massachusetts	Yes	No	48.9	No
Michigan	Yes	No	39.0	Yes
Minnesota	Yes	No	52.2	No
Mississippi	Yes	No	39.9	Yes
Missouri	Yes	No	62.1	Yes

Montana	No	No	47.6	No
Nebraska	No	No	51.3	Yes
Nevada	No	No	116.0	Yes
New Hamp-shire	No	No	79.6	Yes
New Jersey	Yes	No	51.6	Yes
New Mexico	No	No	52.0	No
New York	Yes	No	35.1	No
North Caro-lina	**	Yes	85.4	No
North Dakota	**	Yes	85.1	No
Ohio	Yes	No	49.1	Yes
Oklahoma	**	Yes	43.3	Yes
Oregon	Yes	No	46.3	No
Rhode Island	Yes	No	30.0	Yes
South Caro-lina	No	No	68.4	Yes
South Dakota	**	Yes	70.0	No
Tennessee	No	No	64.5	No
Texas	Yes	No	72.4	No
Utah	No	No	59.7	No
Vermont	No	No	58.0	No
Virginia	Yes	No	71.5	Yes
Washington	No	No	52.7	No
West Virginia	Yes	No	38.7	Yes
Wisconsin	Yes	No	47.4	No
Wyoming	No	No	63.8	No

**States that passed the laws

Note: Pennsylvania and Illinois are not included because they adopted the bans in the 1980s, whereas all of the other states that have considered and/or adopted the laws have done so after 2009.

Table 8: Logistic regression relating the passage or consideration of anti-abortion legislation with the passage of other anti-abortion legislation (OTHER LEGIS) and growth in Asian immigration over 70% (ASIAN GROWTH). Standard error are in parenthesis, "*" indicates p < .10, n=48, and c-statistic = 0.725.

	Odds Ratio
Other Legis	2.85* (1.75)
Asian Growth	2.04 (1.45)
Constant	.0.66 (.29)

Graph 1: Growth of Asian Population in the United States

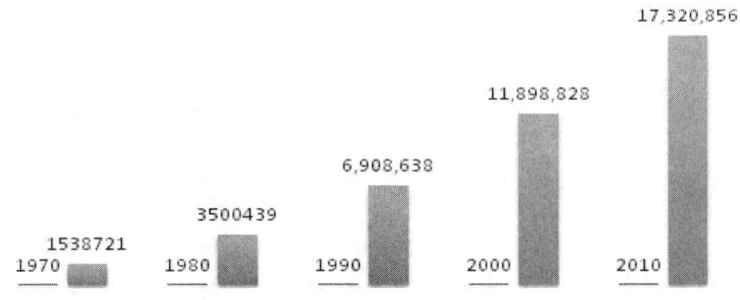

Source: U.S. Census (1970, 1980, 1990, 2000, 2010)

Graph 2: Histogram of Growth in Asian Immigration Population in U.S. States

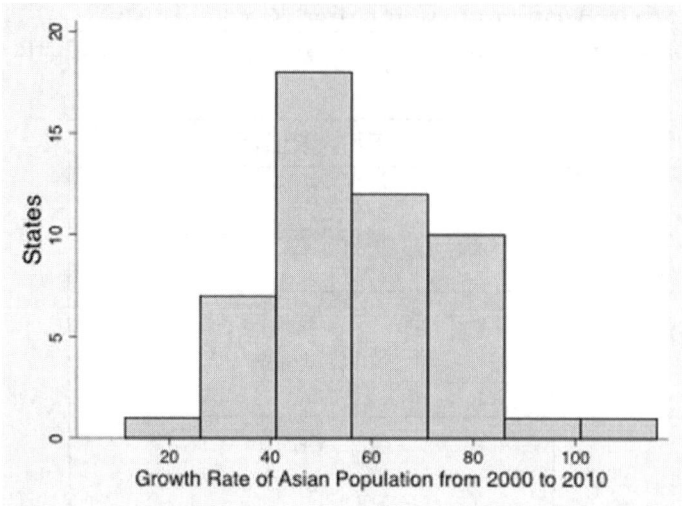

Source: U.S. Census 2010

Graph 3: Comparison of the at birth sex ratios (boys to girls) of various groups

Comparison of Sex Ratios at Birth in Inida and China with Foreign-Born Indian and Chinese Americans and US-Born White Americans

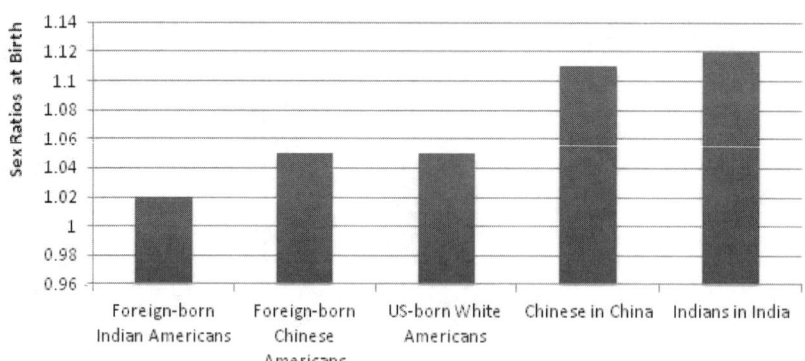

Source: For sex ratios in India and China, the CIA World Factbook. For sex ratios of foreign-born Indian and Chinese Americans and US-born whites, the American Community Survey from 2007 to 2011.

NOTES

I would like to thank Marty Wells, the Charles A. Alexander Professor of Statistical Sciences at Cornell University for his generous help in the statistical analysis, Sidney Tarrow, Emeritus Maxwell M. Upson Professor of Government at Cornell University for his review and comments, and Dawn Chutkow, Executive Director of the *Journal of Empirical Legal Studies*, for helpful discussions, and Angela Ribuado, Managing Editor of the *Georgetown Journal of International Affairs*. This project grows from work I have done with Miriam Yeung, Executive Director of the National Asian Pacific Women's Forum, Shivana Jorawar, Reproductive Justice Program Director, National Asian Pacific Women's Forum, Sujatha Jesudason, Director of CoreAlign at the University of California, San Francisco, and Brian Citro, Clinical Lecturer in Law, University of Chicago Law School.

1 S. 1070, 49th Legislature of Arizona (2010), Internet, http://www.azleg.gov/legtext/49leg/2r/bills/sb1070s.pdf (date accessed: 1 November 2014).

2 *Arizona v. United States*, 567 U.S. (2012).

3 Illegal Immigration Relief Act Ordinance, *Hazleton, Pa., Ordinance 2006-18* (21 September 2006).

4 *Lozano, et al., v. City of Hazleton* (3rd Cir., 26 July 2013).

5 Ed O'Keefe, "Bill Banning 'Sex-selection Abortions' Fails in the House," *Washington Post*, 31 May 2012.

6 H.B. 1162, 89th Leg. Reg. Sess. (S.D 2014) (enacted).

7 House Subcommittee on the Constitution of the House Committee on the Judiciary *Susan B. Anthony and Frederick Douglass Prenatal Nondiscrimination Act of 2011: Hearing on H.R. 3541*, 112th Congress 7 (2011).

8 Ibid.

9 Census Organization of India, "Sex Ratio of India," Internet, http:// www.census2011.co.in/sexratio.php (date accessed: 1 November 2014).

10 Mara Hvistendahl, *Unnatural Selection: Choosing Boys Over Girls, and the Consequences of A World Full of Men*, (New York: Public Affairs, 2011), 49. *Also* Christophe Z. Guilmoto, *Characteristics of Sex-Ratio Imbalance in India, and Future Scenarios* (4th Asia Pacific Conference on Reproductive and Sexual Health and Rights, Hyderabad, India, 29-31 October 2007), 4-8, Internet, http://www.unfpa.org/gender/docs/studies/india.pdf (date accessed: 1 November 2014).

11 Molly Redden, "GOP Lawmaker: We Need to Ban Sex-Selective Abortions Because of Asian Immigrants," *Mother Jones*, 27 March 2014, Internet http://www.motherjones.com/politics/2014/02/south-dakota-stace-nelson-ban-sex-based-abortions-because-asian-immigrants (date accessed: 1 November 2014).

12 Prenatal Nondiscrimination Act of 2013, H.R. 447, 113th Cong. § 2(a)(1)(J) (2013).

13 Submission of United States Representative Lamar Smith (R-TX) to the Committee of the Whole House on the State of the Union, H.R. Rep. No. 112-496, (2012) 15.

14 *See* Prenatal Nondiscrimination Act of 2013, H.R. 447, 113th Cong. (2013) ("To prohibit discrimination against the unborn on the basis of sex or race, and for other purposes.")

15 Phillip Lentz and Michael Lang, "Abortion Foes Push Bill Through House," *Chicago Tribune*, 27 April 1984, A1.

16 State of Ill. Gen. Assemb., S. Transcripts Discussing H.B. 1399, 83d Gen. Assemb., at 36-38 (June 25, 1983). *Also* State of Ill. Gen. Assemb., S. Transcripts Discussing H.B. 1399, 83d Gen. Assemb., at 222-23 (June 29, 1983). *Also* State of Ill. Gen. Assemb., S. Transcripts Discussing H.B. 1399, 83d Gen. Assemb., at 17-33 (Apr. 30, 1984). *Also* State of Ill. Gen. Assemb., S. Transcripts Discussing H.B. 1399, 83d Gen. Assemb., at 142-51 (June 30, 1984). *Also* State of Ill. Gen. Assemb., H. Transcripts Discussing H.B. 1399, 83d Gen. Assemb., at 175-79 (May 27, 1983). *Also* State of Ill. Gen. Assemb., H. Transcripts Discussing H.B. 1399, 83d Gen. Assemb., at 81-86 (Apr. 26, 1984). *Also* State of Ill. Gen. Assemb., H. Transcripts Discussing H.B. 1399, 83d Gen. Assemb., at 50-64 (June 29, 1984).

17 H.R. 173-65, 1989 Sess., at 1743-44 (Pa. 1989), Internet, http:// www.legis.state.pa.us/WU01/LI/HJ/1989/0/19891024.pdf (date accessed: 1 November 2014).

18 Ibid.

19 U.S. Census Data available at http://www.census.gov/newsroom/releases/archives/population/cb14-118.html (date accessed: 1 November 2014).

20 Ibid.

21 U.S. Bureau of the Census, *The Asian Population: 2010*. Prepared by Elizabeth M. Hoeffel et al., March 2012, Internet, http://www.census.gov/prod/cen2010/briefs/c2010br-11.pdf (date accessed: 1 November 2014).

22 U.S. Bureau of the Census, *The Asian Population: 2010*. Prepared by Elizabeth M. Hoeffel et al., March 2012, Internet, http://www.census.gov/prod/cen2010/briefs/c2010br-11.pdf (date accessed: 1 November 2014).

23 The p-value was obtained using the Fisher's exact two-tailed test. In small data sets such as in Tables 3, 4, 5 and 6, p values that are below .1 are considered to be statistically significant. In exact small sample tests it is typical to see p-values that are not below the standard .05 significance level, the marginal significance is considered sufficient evidence of an effect. *See* B. Burt Gerstman, *Basic Biostatistics: Statistics for Public Health Practice* (Boston: Jones and Bartlett Publishing, 2008).

24 Douglas Almond and Lena Edlund, "Son-biased sex ratios in the 2000 United States Census," *PNAS* 105, no. 15 (2008): 5681–5682.

25 *See* Jason Abrevaya, "Are There Missing Girls In the United States? Evidence From Birth Data," *American Economic Journal* 1, no. 2 (April 2009): 1-34, Internet, http://www.aeaweb.org/articles.php?doi=10.1257/app.1.2.1 (date accessed: 1 Novem-

NOTES

ber 2014). *Also* Egan JF et al., "Distortions of Sex Ratios at Birth in the United States." *Also* Evidence for Prenatal Gender Selection," *Prenat Diagn* 31, no. 6 (June 2011): 560-565, Internet, http://www.ncbi. nlm.nih. gov/pubmed/21442626 (date accessed: 1 November 2014).

26 *See* H.R. 447 at § 2(a)(1)(F) (citing the Almond and Edlund study as showing an "obvious 'son preference' in the form of unnatural sex-ratio imbalances within certain segments of the United States population, primarily those segments tracing their origins to countries where sex-selection abortion is prevalent"). *Also* New Jersey, A.B. 2157(1)(f), 215th Leg., Reg. Sess. (N.J. 2013) ("[I]n a March 2008 report published in the Proceedings of the National Academy of Sciences, two economists from Columbia University examined the sex ratio of children born in the United States and found 'evidence of sex-selection, most likely at the prenatal stage'"). *Also* Florida, H.B. 845, 115th Leg., Reg. Sess. (Fla. 2013) ("In a March 2008 report published in the Proceedings of the National Academy of Sciences, Columbia University economists Douglas Almond and Lena Edlund examined the sex ratio of United States born children and found 'evidence of sex-selection, most likely at the prenatal stage.' The data revealed obvious 'son preference' in the form of unnatural sex-ratio imbalances within certain segments of the United States population, primarily those segments tracing their ethnic or cultural origins to countries where sex-selection abortion is prevalent.").

27 Sital Kalantry and Miriam Yeung, "Replacing Myths with Facts: Sex-selective Abortion Laws in the United States - A Project of University of Chicago Law School's International Human Rights Clinic, National Asian Pacific Women's Forum, Advancing New Standards for Reproductive Justice," Internet, https://ihrclinic.uchicago.edu/sites/ihrclinic.

uchicago.edu/files/uploads/Replacing%20Myths%20 with%20Facts%20-%20Sex-Selective%20Abortion%20Laws%20in%20the%20United%20States. pdf (date accessed: 1 November 2014).

28 Ibid.

29 Mara Hvistendahl, *Unnatural Selection* (2011), 240.

30 Americans United for Life, "Ban on Abortions for Sex Selection and Genetic Abnormalities: Model Legislation and Policy Guide For the 2012 Legislative Year," Internet, http://www.aul.org/wp-content/uploads/2012/01/Sex-Selective-and-Genetic-Abnormality-Ban-2012-LG.pdf (date accessed: 1 November 2014).

31 Igor Volsky, "Interactive Map: The Most Restrictive Abortion Measures in the States," Internet, http://thinkprogress.org/health/2012/03/07/439383/interactive-map-abortion/ (date accessed: 1 November 2014).

32 The p-value was obtained using Fisher's exact two-tailed test.

33 Sital Kalantry and Miriam Yeung, "Replacing Myths with Facts: Sex-selective Abortion Laws in the United States - A Project of University of Chicago Law School's International Human Rights Clinic, National Asian Pacific Women's Forum, Advancing New Standards for Reproductive Justice," Internet, https://ihrclinic.uchicago.edu/sites/ihrclinic. uchicago.edu/files/uploads/Replacing%20Myths%20 with%20Facts%20-%20Sex-Selective%20Abortion%20Laws%20in%20the%20United%20States. pdf (date accessed: 1 November 2014).

34 The p-value was obtained from exact two sample proportion tests. *See* Alan Agresti, *Categorical Data Analysis* (Hoboken: John Wiley & Sons, Inc., 2002).

35 The p-value was obtained from exact two sample proportion tests.

The Role of Religion in Constitutions Emerging from Arab Spring Revolutions

Evelyn Mary Aswad

Of the four Arab Spring countries that toppled dictators in 2011, only two have adopted new constitutions: Egypt and Tunisia. While these constitutions contain numerous interesting features, a particularly useful lens for analyzing these social contracts is the evolving role of religion. Understanding the constitutional treatment of religion may help shed light on some frequently asked questions: Were the Arab Spring revolutions about seeking adherence to more conservative interpretations of Islamic law after the reign of strongmen with ties to the West? Were these revolutions expressions of longing for universal human rights regardless of religious affiliations? What role will religion ultimately play in the legal regimes of these countries?

Examining the evolving treatment of religion in these constitutions displays that, while there may have been a common cause for toppling dictators, various constituencies lacked common ground on what the "day after" would look like on issues of religion. Though Western governments praised these new constitutions for protecting human rights, this essay maintains that the key provisions involving religion reveal significant human rights problems.[1] This essay argues that such issues must be acknowledged and that the inter-

Evelyn Mary Aswad is the Herman G. Kaiser Chair in International Law and Professor of Law at the University of Oklahoma College of Law. She is also the U.S. Substitute Member on the Council of Europe's Commission for Democracy through Law, better known as the Venice Commission.

national community should encourage these countries to interpret their constitutions consistently with their international obligations. Both Egypt and

tion and lavish lifestyles existed among Egypt's elites, about 40 percent of the society lived on less than two dollars per day.[5] While liberals and the Muslim

Various constituencies lacked common ground on what the "day after" would look like on issues of religion.

Tunisia have extensive international obligations as parties to the International Covenant on Civil and Political Rights (ICCPR), which prohibits religious discrimination in the provision of treaty rights and guarantees equal protection of the law.[2] The pact also provides for freedom of expression and religious freedom (which includes the freedom to adopt or change one's faith or belief—as well as the freedom to manifest religion or belief in worship, observance, practice, and teaching—subject only to narrowly tailored limitations).

Egypt. As the Arab region's most populous nation (with population estimates ranging from 81-100 million), Egypt commanded the world's attention in February 2011 when President Hosni Mubarak left office after eighteen days of mass protests, ending his thirty-year reign as Egypt's third president since 1952 and "tasking" the military (which had refused to use force against protesters) with the state's affairs.[3] Like his two predecessors, Mubarak came from the military, which was his power base and played many political and economic roles, and his autocratic rule was secured by an oppressive security apparatus.[4] Though rampant corrup-

Brotherhood (banned under Mubarak) had worked to topple Mubarak, they would encounter difficulties afterwards.[6]

Since 2011, Egyptians have been subject to three constitutions. The Muslim Brotherhood's Mohammed Morsi was elected president in 2011, and a new constitution was adopted in a December 2012 referendum. Professor Ann Lesch of the American University in Cairo notes that during this period, political discussions were "dominated by Islamist politicians, with liberal and Christian citizens marginalized and alienated."[7] When the military removed Morsi from office following mass protests in 2013, a new drafting process culminated in the adoption of the current constitution in a January 2014 referendum. Unlike the earlier discussions that sidelined liberals and Christians, these talks were marked by a suppression of the Brotherhood.[8] Overall, scholars have found that the process reflected polarization among opposing groups, rather than dialogue and consensus building.[9]

Given a track record of mistreatment against, among others, Egypt's Christian minority, persons of non-Abrahamic faiths, and atheists, many in the international community viewed the constitution's treatment of religious issues as crucial to democratic development. This segment seeks to illuminate what changed, what did not, and what is problematic with respect to key provisions involving religion in Egypt's constitution.

Egypt's Pre-Arab Spring Consitution.

While many articles involving religion were altered with the adoption of the 2012 constitution and again in the 2014 constitution, one provision proved in effect untouchable: Article 2. It provides that Islam is the religion of the state (Egypt is 90 percent Muslim, predominantly Sunni, and the rest of the population is primarily Christian, mostly Coptic Orthodox) and that the principles of *Sharia* are the principal source of legislation.[10] The Supreme Constitutional Court (SCC) interpreted this article as authorization to conduct an Islamic judicial review of Egyptian laws. Given the extensive research by Professors Clark Lombardi and Nathan Brown, there is significant literature arguing that the SCC engaged in comparatively progressive interpretations under Article 2 that permitted various legal reforms to occur while infrequently overturning laws as "un-Islamic."[11] The professors argue the SCC "interpreted Islamic law *de novo* using its own distinctive, somewhat idiosyncratic, version of modernist reasoning."[12]

The SCC developed a test under Article 2 that required a law: (1) be consistent with authentic, clear, and universal rules of *Sharia* (the SCC found that few rules met this high standard), and (2) promote the goals of *Sharia*.[13] Using this test, the SCC struck down challenges to a variety of laws alleged to be "un-Islamic" in violation of Article 2, including laws banning the veil in school.[14] Such SCC jurisprudence was not popular in quarters that believed the laws did violate *Sharia* principles, raising concerns that the SCC was not utilizing an appropriate methodology.[15]

Other articles in Egypt's pre-Arab Spring constitution also addressed religion. For example, Article 46 guaranteed freedom of belief and the freedom of practice of religious rites, but was silent on other aspects of religious freedom. Article 40 prohibited discrimination based on, among other things, religion, but Article 5 banned any political activity or political party based on religion. This thereby barred the Muslim Brotherhood from playing an active role in politics. Interestingly, the Article 1 "identity clause" stated Egypt was a democratic state based on citizenship and that it was part of the "Arab Nation;" it did not mention religion.

Egypt's 2012 Consitution.

Egypt's revised constitution removed the ban on religious political parties and included a number of new provisions involving religion.[16] For instance, the Article 1 identity clause stated that the Egyptian people were part of the "Islamic nations" and no longer provided that the state was based on citizenship. Moreover, while Article 2 remained the same, two new provisions would greatly impact it. First, Article 4 provided an explicit consultative role for Al-Azhar (Egypt's premier center of Islamic learning) on *Sharia* issues. Second, Article 219 was added, defining how the principles of *Sharia* were to be discerned in a manner that seemed to "tie Egypt's constitution to traditional Islamic jurisprudence," in contrast to the more progressive SCC methods.[17]

Additional new articles involving religion included Article 3, which mentioned Christians and Jews, and which provided that their own religious laws apply to their personal status (e.g., family law) and religious affairs. By specifying members of Judaism and Christianity, and given Article 2's focus on Islam, this new Article 3 seemed to enshrine the view that adherents of other religions or adherents of no religion were not recognized or entitled to equal protections. Religious freedom was purportedly guaranteed in Article 43 but was explicitly limited to "divine religions" (which was used in this context to encompass Judaism, Christianity, and Islam). Furthermore, Article 43 only guaranteed the freedom to practice rites and establish places of worship, and was silent with respect to other aspects of religious freedom such as professing or changing one's faith. It also made all guarantees subject to future laws, essentially undermining any constitutional protections. While Article 81 specified that no laws may constrain the origin or essence of any rights, such text is ambiguous, easily misused, and departs significantly from existing ICCPR safeguards on limiting rights that could easily have been referenced.[18]

Though some constitutional provisions favored only members of "divine religions," Article 33 provided that all citizens were equal before the law. However, unlike the prior constitution, it did not explicitly list any particular grounds of impermissible discrimination such as religion, thereby creating

a risk of weakening of this protection. Another article that attracted significant international attention was Article 44, which banned blasphemy by prohibiting the defamation of all religious messengers and prophets. The U.S. government and others criticized Egypt for essentially elevating its existing ban on blasphemy to its constitution and for the high number of blasphemy prosecutions under Morsi's regime.[19]

Egypt's 2014 Consitution.

The European Union announced that Egypt's 2014 constitution enshrined "fundamental rights and freedoms" and noted that all laws would need to comply with the new constitution.[20] This was an overly-rosy assessment given the complexities of the 2014 constitution: some provisions revert to features from the Mubarak era, other provisions reflect 2012 text, while still others are completely new and could prove helpful in protecting human rights.[21]

While Article 2 (providing that Islam is the religion of the state and that the principles of *Sharia* serve as the principal source of legislation) remained unchanged, several other provisions impacting it changed significantly. In many ways, such changes take the constitution back to the Mubarak era in terms of Article 2, the SCC's role, and the SCC's precedents. For example, Article 219, which seemed to require conservative Islamic jurisprudence and methodologies when applying Article 2, was dropped altogether. Moreover, a new preambular paragraph reaffirms the SCC precedents as the relevant jurisprudence for interpreting Article 2. In addition, Al-Azhar's "consultation" role was removed (though it is mentioned as the main authority for religious sciences and Islamic affairs). Another return to the Mubarak era is Article 74, which bans religious political parties.

Other articles reflect phrasing that is somewhere on the spectrum between the Mubarak and Morsi constitutions. For example, the Article 1 identity clause returns to the Mubarak-era affirmation that the republic is based on citizenship, but it also specifies that Egypt is part of the "Muslim world." While the new Article 50 affirms Egypt's diverse cultural heritage, Article 3 retains the 2012 distinction for "divinely revealed religions," again describing the treatment of personal and religious affairs for only Christians and Jews.

Other articles inherited some problematic features from the Morsi-era constitution. For example, Article 64 continues to limit freedom of religion to followers of "revealed religions," limits this right to the extent of the "law," and describes the scope of the right so narrowly that it focuses solely on rituals and places of worship.[22] Article 92 also continues with an improved, but still ambiguous and easily misused, "general limitations clause" on all rights.

Conversely, the Morsi-era blasphemy ban was dropped (though Article 53 criminalizes "incitement to hate," which is another broad and ambiguous phrase at odds with human rights law protections for freedom of expression).[23] In addition, Article 53 returns to an equal protection clause that is reminiscent of the Mubarak-era constitution specifying that all citizens are equal before the law and sets forth a number of prohibited grounds for dis-

crimination, including religion.

Perhaps the most interesting 2014 additions regard the treatment of international commitments and obligations. For example, a new preambular paragraph states the constitution "is in line with the Universal Declaration of Human Rights (UDHR), which we took part in the drafting of and approved." This is an extraordinary statement of ownership of the UDHR as opposed to often-heard claims that human rights should be disregarded as Western concepts. Furthermore, this paragraph could be used to argue that any textual ambiguities or other problems must be resolved in favor of interpretations that are consistent with the UDHR, as that is the stated overarching intent of the document. Moreover, Article 93 states that Egypt is committed to international human rights treaties it has ratified and that these treaties have the force of law. This article may prove to be an important "catch all" hook for interpreting constitutional protections for fundamental freedoms, including religious freedom, in line with treaty obligations (though Article 151 provides that no treaty can be concluded that is contrary to the constitution).

On balance, compared to the pre-Arab Spring constitution, Egypt's current constitution seems to take a step backward on issues of religious freedom. For example, the constitution recognizes this freedom only for members of the "divine religions." It remains to be seen whether constitutional practice and interpretations can effectively reverse this by relying upon the non-discrimination, the UDHR, and international human rights treaty provisions to protect persons of all faiths or beliefs. Hopefully, the UDHR and treaty clauses can also be used to temper two other new features: the ambiguous and easily misused general limitations clause and the fact that Article 64 ties the constitutional scope of religious freedom to future laws.

Tunisia. Within weeks of the self-immolation of a young vendor protesting injustice and corruption that sparked widespread and popular uprisings and given the military's refusal Ali, Tunisia already had a reputation as a progressive country with significant achievements in women's rights. When its first democratically elected leader came from the Islamist party *Ennahda*, the international community followed with interest, *inter alia*, the role religion would play in the constitution.

While Islamists, secularists, and others debated topics similar to those discussed in Egypt, Tunisia ultimately resolved these tensions through compromises (rather than intervention by

Egypt's current constitution seems to take a step backward on issues of religious freedom.

to support him, President Zine Abidine Ben Ali escaped from Tunisia on 14 January 2011, ending his 23-year reign as Tunisia's second president since 1957.[24] Unlike Egypt, Tunisia's population was small (approximately 10.5 million), primarily urban, and generally better off than Egyptians.[25] As was the case with Mubarak, Ben Ali maintained his power through an oppressive security apparatus, banned Islamist parties, and was responsible for immense corruption.[26] Though Ben Ali had served in the military, Tunisia's military (unlike Egypt) was not an all-powerful force and would play a much lower-key role in the transition politics.[27]

About three years after Ben Ali's departure, Tunisia adopted its new constitution. Unlike Egypt, which relied on a popular referendum, the elected Tunisian National Constituent Assembly approved the text of the new constitution. Before toppling Ben its military).[28] At the conclusion of the process, the U.S. State Department pronounced that the 2014 constitution "respects and guarantees the rights of all Tunisians."[29] This section seeks to illuminate the legal landscape regarding what changed, what did not, and what is problematic about key provisions involving religion in Tunisia's constitutions.

Tunisia's Pre-Arab Spring Constitution.
Though Tunisia is 98 percent Sunni Muslim, Tunisia's constitution under Ben Ali contained only a handful of references to religion.[30] For example, while the preamble noted the people's will to remain faithful to Islamic teachings, *Sharia* was not established as "the" source of law (or mentioned at all). The constitution provided that Islam was Tunisia's religion, but banned religious parties, similar to Mubarak's constitution. It also required the president be Muslim.

Regarding religious freedom, the constitution's protections encompassed some contradictions. For example, Article 5 stated Tunisia guaranteed human rights in their "universal" meaning, but then only protected "the free exercise of religious beliefs, under reserve that it does not disturb the public order." Moreover, Article 7, a general provision regarding all rights, stated citizens could exercise rights "as

this explicit criminalization of blasphemy, though references to protecting religion remained in drafts.[35] In the final phase of the process, one Assembly member accused—or at least was understood as accusing—another member of apostasy (*takfir*), resulting in demands to prohibit accusations of *takfir*, which can expose the accused to violence.[36] This high profile event triggered changes to Article 6, which now provides that

Tunisia's post-Arab Spring constitution risks taking the country in **a regressive direction.**

specified by law" and did not encompass internationally recognized safeguards when limiting rights. Article 6, however, provided that all citizens are equal before the law, without listing any bases of impermissible discrimination.

Tunisia's 2014 Constitution.

Various debates involving religion occurred during the drafting process, two of which are highlighted here.[31] The first involved the role *Sharia* would play in the constitution. Some *Ennahda* members proposed a provision designating *Sharia* a source of legislation.[32] Secularists and others opposed this as improperly Islamizing the legal regime. After significant discussions within the party and with others about the provision's utility, *Ennahda* announced it would not seek a *Sharia* reference.[33]

Another debate involved a blasphemy ban, which *Ennahda* members initially proposed as a criminal prohibition applying to Abrahamic faiths.[34] After debates within the party and with others, *Ennahda* withdrew the demand for

the State is the "guardian of religion," protects "the sacred" and prohibits "any offenses thereto," and prohibits *takfir* (as well as incitement to hatred). Civil society groups criticized this article as vague and easily misused to stifle freedoms of speech and religion, including by prohibiting blasphemy.[37]

The 2014 constitution contains other provisions involving religion. For example, Article 1 continues to state Tunisia's religion is Islam, but Article 2 and the fourth preambular paragraph make clear that Tunisia is a civil state. The constitution provides Articles 1 and 2 cannot be amended. Other clauses highlighting Islam include preambular paragraph 3, which notes Tunisia is committed to Islamic teachings and reform based on Islamic identity, and the fifth paragraph, stating the desire to consolidate affiliation to the "Muslim nation" and towards complementarity with Muslim peoples. Unlike Egypt, Tunisia removed the ban on religious parties in its 2014 Constitution.

In terms of religious freedom, Article 6 states Tunisia guarantees freedom of conscience and the free exercise of religious practices, but is silent on certain other aspects of religious freedom. Moreover, Article 49, the clause allowing for limitations on rights, is narrower than its predecessor. All citizens are equal before the law in Article 21 (again without listing prohibited bases for discrimination), but Article 74 limits the presidency to Muslims.

Compared to its pre-Arab Spring constitution, Tunisia's new constitution risks taking the country in a regressive direction because of the new provision involving issues of blasphemy and *takfir*. Its religious freedom provisions remain too narrow, though at least the general limitations clause on rights has improved (but continues to apply to rights that cannot be limited under the ICCPR). Much will depend on how constitutional practice and interpretations evolve with respect to such provisions.

Some Concluding Observations.

Given very different histories, pre-Arab Spring constitutions, and post-revolution political struggles, it may not be surprising that Egypt and Tunisia adopted constitutions that treat religion quite differently on key points.

against the sacred and *takfir* (Egypt no, Tunisia yes), barring religious parties (Egypt yes, Tunisia no), and reserving the presidency for Muslims (Egypt no, Tunisia yes). And yet on other matters of religion, the constitutions share some measure of similarity: Islam as the religion of both countries, references to Islamic heritage, prohibitions on discrimination, and provisions for some (but incomplete) protection for religious freedom.[38]

Comparing this constitutional landscape of provisions involving religion with the ICCPR, shortfalls are evident. Without discussing all the problems, it is worthy of note that Egypt's new constitutional provisions that privilege "divine religions" while excluding others is a regressive development inconsistent with ICCPR obligations prohibiting religious discrimination. In addition, its narrow protections for religious freedom (which are further jeopardized by being subjected to future laws and an ambiguous "catch all" limitations clause that applies to all rights) are not consistent with the ICCPR's broad religious freedom protections. Tunisia's constitutional provision calling on the state to "protect the sacred" and "prohibit offenses thereto" seems to encompass blasphemy bans that are

Sweeping shortfalls under diplomatic rugs is not a strategy for promoting the long-term democratic development of these countries.

In particular, they differ in: designating *Sharia* principles as the principal source of legislation (Egypt yes, Tunisia no), explicitly banning offenses

not only inconsistent with ICCPR protections for speech and religious freedom but also with the international community's recent consensus to tackle religious intolerance through practical, time-proven steps (like hate crimes laws and inter-faith dialogues) rather than blasphemy bans.[39] Egypt's and Tunisia's new ambiguous constitutional bans on "incitement to hatred" may similarly be invoked to violate rights. While having a state religion is not prohibited by the ICCPR, discrimination based on religion—such as Tunisia's provision that only Muslims can be president—is inconsistent with the treaty.

Given constituencies with different views on the role of religion, and given the product of contentious negotiations is often ambiguous and contradictory text, constitutional shortfalls in such transitions are perhaps inevitable. That said, it is imperative that the international community acknowledge and proactively address these issues (through training programs, diplo-

matic engagement, etc.). This would enhance the likelihood that future Egyptian and Tunisian constitutional practice and jurisprudence will evolve in line with ICCPR obligations. The protection of core liberties and the treatment of citizens as equals before the law are key pillars of the rule of law. These religious freedom problems may indicate larger rule of law issues that could emerge from the constitutions. Sweeping shortfalls under diplomatic rugs is not a strategy for promoting the long-term democratic development of these countries, or other countries with similar constitutional problems. While appropriate constitutional provisions are not a guarantee that human rights will be protected in practice, the absence of such provisions is a good indicator that some fundamental freedoms may be in jeopardy.

NOTES

1 This essay does not discuss all constitutional provisions that are relevant to issues of religion or that are inconsistent with the international human rights obligations of Egypt and Tunisia. Given space limitations, it also does not discuss implementation issues arising under each of the various constitutions.

2 Egypt became a party to the ICCPR in 1982 and Tunisia did so in 1969. *See* https://treaties.un.org/pages/ViewDetails.aspx?src=TREATY&mtdsg_no=IV-4&chapter=4&lang=en (date accessed: 24 August 2014).

3 James L. Gelvin, *The Arab Uprisings: What Everyone Needs to Know* (Oxford: Oxford University Press, 2012) 34, 47.

4 Ibid. at 37-39; 61-62. *Also* Ann M. Lesch, "Troubled Political Transitions: Tunisia, Egypt, and Libya," *Middle East Policy* 21, no. 1 (Spring 2014): 65.

5 Gelvin, 34, 40-41; Lesch, 66.

6 Gelvin, 52-53.

7 Lesch, 68.

8 Ibid.

9 *See*, e.g., ibid.

10 This essay uses a translation of Egypt's pre-Arab Spring Constitution that can be found here: http://www.constitutionnet.org/files/Egypt%20Constitution.pdf (date accessed: 30 October 2014).

11 *See*, e.g., Clark Lombardi and Nathan Brown, "Do Constitutions Requiring Adherence to Shari'a Threaten Human Rights? How Egypt's Constitutional Court Reconciles Islamic Law with the Liberal Rule of Law," *American University International Law Review* 21, no. 3 (2006): 379-435.

12 Nathan Brown and Clark Lombardi, "Islam in Egypt's New Constitution," Internet, http://carnegieendowment.org/2012/12/13/islam-in-egypt-s-new-constitution/etph (date accessed: 30 October 2014).

13 *See* Lombardi and Brown, 418.

14 Ibid., 426.

15 *See* Brown and Lombardi.

16 This essay uses a translation of the 2012 Constitution that can be found here: http://www.constitutionnet.org/vl/item/new-constitution-arab-republic-egypt-approved-30-nov-2012 (date accessed: 30 October 2014).

17 *See* Brown and Lombardi.

18 Under the ICCPR, some rights may not be limited (e.g., freedom from torture) and other rights may be limited but only in very narrowly specified circumstances (e.g., freedom to manifest one's religion).

19 *See*, e.g., U.S. Department of State, "Country Reports on Human Rights Practices for 2012: Egypt (2013)," Internet, http://www.state.gov/documents/organization/204569.pdf (date accessed: 30 October 2014). *Also* U.S. Department of State, "International Religious Freedom Report for 2012: Egypt (2013)," Internet, http://www.state.gov/documents/organization/208598.pdf (date accessed: 30 October 2014).

20 European Union, "Statement by EU High Representative Catherine Ashton on the Constitutional Referendum in Egypt," Internet, http://eeas.europa.eu/statements/docs/2014/140119_02_en.pdf (date accessed: 30 October 2014).

21 This essay uses a translation of the 2014 Constitution that can be found here: http://www.atlanticcouncil.org/blogs/egyptsource/english-translation-of-egypt-s-2013-draft-constitution (date accessed: 30 October 2014).

22 However, new Article 235 does require the passage of a law to organize building and renovating of churches, which many viewed as a welcome addition given the challenges the Christian community has faced.

23 NGOs have expressed concerns about the blasphemy prosecutions, which have continued after the adoption of the most recent constitution. See, e.g., Egyptian Initiative for Personal Rights, "After Luxor Appellate Misdemeanor Court Gives Teacher Six Months for Defamation of Religion," Internet, http://eipr.org/en/pressrelease/2014/06/19/2127 (date accessed: 30 October 2014).

24 Lesch, 62.

25 Gelvin, 34.

26 Ibid., 39-41; 57-58. *Also* Lesch, 64.

27 Lesch, 67.

28 Ibid., 68.

29 U.S. Department of State, "Ratification of the New Tunisian Constitution," Internet, http://www.state.gov/r/pa/prs/ps/2014/01/220658.htm (date accessed: 30 October 2014).

30 This essay uses the following English translation of the Ben Ali era constitution: William S. Hein & Co., trans., Law No. 59-57 (June 1, 1959) (Tunisia) (HeinOnline World Constitutions Illustrated library 2010).

31 This essay uses the English translation of the current constitution that can be found here: http://www.constitutionnet.org/vl/item/tunisia-constitution-2014 (date accessed: 30 October 2014).

32 Duncan Pickard, "The Current Status of Constitution Making in Tunisia," Internet, http://m.ceip.org/2012/04/19/current-status-of-constitution-making-in-tunisia/ah2f&lang=en (date accessed: 30 October 2014).

33 Ibid. *Also* Monica Marks, "Convince, Coerce or Compromise? *Ennahda*'s Approach to Tunisia's Constitution," *Brookings Doha Center Analysis Paper* (February 2014), Internet, http://www.brookings.edu/research/papers/2014/02/10-ennahda-tunisia-constitution-marks (date accessed: 30 October 2014) : 20-22.

34 Marks, 24.

35 Ibid., 24-26. *Also* Amna Guellali, "The Problem with Tunisia's New Constitution," Internet, http://www.hrw.org/news/2014/02/03/problem-tunisia-s-new-constitution (date accessed: 30 October 2014).

36 *See* e.g., Guellali,; "Carter Center Welcomes

NOTES

Human Rights Provisions in Tunisia's Constitution; Calls for Immediate Steps to Implement," at footnote 44, Internet, http://www.cartercenter.org/resources/pdfs/news/pr/tunisia-full-statement-041014.pdf (date accessed: 30 October 2014).

37 Guellali, Carter Center.

38 Egypt's constitution provides that Islam is the religion of the state whereas Tunisia's formulation— "its religion is Islam"—is considered by some to contain some measure of ambiguity about whether Islam is the state religion. *See*, e.g., Carter Center, 14; Marks, footnote 63, but the U.S. Department of State seems to have interpreted this language in the past as meaning Tunisia has a state religion. See U.S. Department of State, "2013 International Religious Freedom Report," Internet, http://www.state.gov/j/drl/rls/irf/religiousfreedom/index.htm#wrapper (date accessed: 30 October 2014). Indeed, in Tunisia's 2007 periodic report to the UN Human Rights Committee, it self-described this phrasing—"its religion is Islam"—in the Ben Ali-era constitution to mean "Islam is the State religion in Tunisia. However, the State is not religious since it is organized in accordance with the Constitution…" International Covenant on Civil and Political Rights Human Rights Committee, "Consideration of Reports Submitted by States Parties under Article 40 of the Covenant Fifth Periodic Report: Tunisia," para 241 (25 April 2007), Internet, http://tbinternet.ohchr.org/_layouts/treatybodyexternal/Download.aspx?symbolno=CCPR%2fC%2fTUN%2f5&Lang=en (date accessed: 30 October 2014).

39 For more on the consensus on UN Human Rights Council Resolution 16/18, see Elizabeth Cassidy, "Fighting Religious Hatred While Protecting Free Speech," Internet, http://journal.georgetown.edu/fighting-religious-hatred-while-protecting-free-speech-by-elizabeth-cassidy/ (date accessed: 30 October 2014).

Madeleine *Albright*
Noam *Chomsky*
Mikhail *Gorbachev*
Richard *Holbrooke*
John *Kerry*
Sergei *Khrushchev*
Ricardo *Lagos*
John *McCain*
Jeffrey *Sachs*
Joseph *Stiglitz*
Stephen *Walt*
Martin *Wolf*
Paul *Wolfowitz*
Fareed *Zakaria*

And more. WA

WATSON INSTITUTE
FOR INTERNATIONAL STUDIES
BROWN UNIVERSITY

W THE BROWN JOURNAL
WORLD AFFAIRS

Georgetown University
School *of* Foreign Service

Bachelor of Science
Foreign Service
bsfs.georgetown.edu

Master of Arts
Arab Studies
ccas.georgetown.edu

Master of Arts
Asian Studies
asianstudies.georgetown.edu

Master of Arts
Eurasian, Russian and East European Studies
ceres.georgetown.edu

Master of Arts
German and European Studies
cges.georgetown.edu

Master of
Global Human Development
ghd.georgetown.edu

Master of Arts
Latin American Studies
clas.georgetown.edu

Master of Arts
Security Studies
css.georgetown.edu

Master of Science
Foreign Service
msfs.georgetown.edu

AN EDUCATION
UNLIKE ANY OTHER

Edmund A. Walsh School *of* Foreign Service | sfs.georgetown.edu

The Rise of Chinese Multinationals

A Strategic Threat or an Economic Opportunity?

Christoph Lattemann & Ilan Alon

The questions of how and why Chinese firms globalize have captured the attention of scholars in recent years and have become a hotly debated topic. The expansion of Chinese multinational enterprises (MNEs) is often perceived to be a threat to global security, and China's current strategy to encourage its enterprises to invest overseas (called a going-out policy) raises serious concerns about geopolitical issues.[1] However, the motivations behind the globalization of Chinese MNEs are largely misunderstood because of the unusual way in which they globalize. Their goals are not to destabilize global security or geopolitics; rather, economic motives drive Chinese outward foreign direct investment (OFDI). This article will explore the how and why of Chinese MNE expansionism, as well as the current relevance and scope of the internationalization of Chinese firms. By comparing the latest theories with the existing realities, this article will expose the singularity of the globalization of Chinese MNEs.

The Rise of Chinese Multinationals and Their Motives. According to International Monetary Fund data, China surpassed the United States in terms of GDP based on purchasing power parity (PPP) in October 2014, mak-

Christoph Lattemann is Professor for Business Administration and Information Management at the Jacobs University Bremen. He is also an international business consultant and a member of the executive board of the Chinese Globalization Association, among others.

Ilan Alon is Cornell Chair of International Business. He has taught courses in top Chinese MBA programs and is also an international business consultant as well as a featured speaker in many professional associations.

ing China the leading global economy in almost every important sector.[2] But how and why Chinese firms go abroad is still a mystery to many casual observers. Recent growth of Chinese OFDI has been nothing less than remarkable.

America, $56.4 billion in Sub-Saharan Africa, $43.7 billion in the Arab countries, and $38.4 billion in Australia. Each region has attracted Chinese investments for different reasons. Australia, Latin America, and Africa,

The financial crisis of 2008 was a strategic opportunity for China to go on an acquisition spree throughout the world.

OFDI was a central component of China's going-out (*zou chuqu*) policy in its Tenth and Eleventh Five-Year Plans for National Economy and Social Development (2001–2010). Since then, Chinese OFDI has reached historic heights. FDI inflows to China reached $124 billion last year, whereas outflows rose to $101 billion, making China the second largest FDI host and the third largest home of FDI outflows after the United States and Japan.[3] The UN's World Investment Report anticipates that OFDI will surpass FDI inflows within the next several years, shifting China's role from a net recipient of FDI to a net supplier.[4]

The financial crisis of 2008 was a strategic opportunity for China—armed with its abundant hard currency—to go on an acquisition spree throughout the world to achieve a more substantial global footprint and to acquire new technologies, brands, and access to natural resources. China has generally spread its OFDI equally around the world.[5] Between 2005 and 2011, it invested $30.5 billion in the United States, $43.2 billion in Europe, $51.7 billion in West Asia, $42.6 billion in East Asia, $72.3 billion in South

for example, provide natural resources to fuel Chinese economic growth and modernization efforts. In contrast, Chinese investments in Europe and North America focus on the acquisition of knowledge, capabilities, and new markets and customers. For market-seeking investments, China has primarily invested in its Asian backyard. However, to date, the majority of China's international sales have still been intra-regional rather than global.[6]

Despite these economic drivers, critics of China suspect its motivations. Is the Chinese government behind all of these acquisitions? Will China overpower and simultaneously undermine the United States and other Western powers? Are there military intentions behind these investments? In fact, many of these worries have little factual base.

A recent survey of the largest state-owned enterprises (SOEs) in China reveals that the country's primary motives are economic.[7] Most companies contemplate overseas investments for their market opportunities, or because of the importance of the target country in terms of competitiveness. SOEs are looking for new customers and markets, not for global domination. They are also seeking strategic resources, such as specific technological know-how. Famous examples include Zoomlion's acquisition of Italy's CIFA and Lenovo's acquisition of IBM's notebook section. The large Chinese SOEs, such as Chinalco, are simply seeking natural resources. Even in the much-discussed energy sector, Chinese OFDI is generally not regarded as a threat to global security.[8]

The outreach to Europe and North America, in particular, is often misunderstood as an internationalization strategy, when, in reality, it is a chance for Chinese companies to build up competitive advantages for their home markets.[9] One example is the acquisition of Volvo by Geely. The motivation behind this acquisition was, among others, to have access to Volvo's expertise and brand name to attract Chinese customers. This shows that geopolitical power games are not the basis for Chinese MNE decision-making. However, the speed and scale of Chinese MNE development remain causes of concern among government officials and business leaders.

Problems with Traditional Explanations of OFDI.

Explaining the emergence of Chinese MNEs is challenging because the existing tools and theories used to explain internationalization were built for a different set of countries during a different period of time. As such, they do not fit the Chinese case. China-specific or, more broadly, emerging market-specific theories, may provide better guidance for understanding the challenges posed by an internationalizing China.[10]

Because of cultural, economic, and environmental differences between China and Western countries, traditional internationalization theories fall short in explaining the way Chinese MNEs globalize. For example, the Uppsala Model and the Product Life-Cycle Theory suggest that companies internationalize incrementally, seeking a low-risk strategy by first externalizing their operations in similar countries and then, over time and as they gain experience, internalizing their foreign operations and venturing to more remote and culturally different regions.[11] But, such explanations do not fit the well-known cases such as Lenovo's acquisition of IBM or Geely's acquisition of Volvo. Instead of beginning their international ventures by exporting products to nearby and culturally close countries, Geely and Lenovo jumped directly into culturally distant countries and engaged in high-risk investment strategies (i.e., FDI). These examples and recent research reveal that emerging-market firms, in particular Chinese ones, internationalize at a much faster pace than traditional internationalization theories would predict.[12] Hence, to fully comprehend the motives behind Chinese MNE expansions, the "how" question of expansion by Chinese MNEs must be answered in a new way. The recent emergence of emerging-market MNEs (EMNEs) is indicative of the need for a refinement and extension of theories on OFDI.

New Business Ecosystems.

The Internet and the WTO. A key difference between China and developed Western countries is that Chinese companies work in an environment with local protectionism, inefficient domestic logistics, and relation-based governance systems that increase the costs of doing business domestically. In China, entrepreneurs may experience lower costs outside their home markets due to, for example, high overland transportation costs in China that might easily exceed transportation costs to other countries.[13] The latest development in information and communication technology—as well as globalization initiatives, such as through the World Trade Organization—are lowering the costs of moving and operating abroad. As such, companies in China and other parts of the developing world are now able to expand at earlier stages and with increasing speed.[14] Thus, a conclusion that is paradoxical to the traditional transaction cost approach can be drawn: in order to achieve competitiveness in the domestic market, firms will first have to move abroad.[15]

Different Firm-Specific Competitive Advantages. Traditional internationalization theories further predict that firms require preexisting competitive advantages in order to be able to expand their business abroad. In general, however, Chinese firms have inferior technologies and production processes, and they have no global brands.[16] The first question, given Chinese firms' economic and technological disadvantages, is then why are emerging economies able to produce MNEs at all?[17]

There are three ways to answer this "why" question. First, as Chinese firms seem to lack ownership advantages (advanced technologies, brands, or management advantages), their internationalization may be a strategy to exploit home country compara-tive advantages, such as cheap labor or natural resources, rather than firm-specific ownership advantages.[18] Second, EMNEs internationalize to obtain the ownership advantages they lack.[19] A third explanation is that Chinese firms do possess ownership advantages that are *different* from the ownership advantages of the developed-market MNEs.[20] Chinese firms' advantages may be more rooted in their understanding of and their flexibility to adapt to customer needs, their ability to function in difficult business environments, their ability to make products and services at low costs, and their ability to develop "good enough" products with the right feature-price mix for local customers to access cheap capital.[21]

What about the *how* question? From the traditional theoretical perspectives, EMNEs target the "wrong" countries by expanding to physically or economically distant countries before entering closer and more similar countries.[22] Additionally, they internationalize in the "wrong" way and at the "wrong" speed because they make high-risk and high-commitment choices—such as mergers and acquisitions—to enter new markets, rather than beginning with low-risk, low-commitment options such as using sales agents or subsidiaries.[23] However, these supposedly "wrong" methods of internationalization merely reflect Chinese MNEs' reactions to a changing environment, rather than any innate organizational trait.[24]

Firm- and Country-Specific Advantages and Disadvantages. It is insufficient to analyze only firm-specific economic reasons for Chinese entities' international competitiveness and globalization strategy. In general, a firm's success does not depend solely on firm-specific advantages. Country-specific advantages and disadvantages also have an effect on international success. China has strong country-specific advantages, particu-

field investments due to a preference for Washington Consensus policies. This set of policies, which prefers free markets and an important role for the private sector, contrasts with the

China has strong **country-specific advantages,** particularly government support, political stability, and economic growth.

larly government support, political stability, and economic growth.[25] In addition, China has advantages in terms of factor-endowment (people, natural resources, money) and in terms of governmental incentives to internationalize.[26] Whether a country-specific factor can be considered an advantage or a disadvantage, however, depends on the host-market environment. Institutional support can compensate for the ownership and locational disadvantages of Chinese firms, which may face firm-specific disadvantages when investing overseas.[27] For example, Chinese companies often have to overcome the liability of foreignness and the negative country-of-origin effect derived from the "made in China" brand. Chinese products are still perceived by many Western consumers as low-tech and low-cost, even if famous Chinese products—such as Lenovo computers, Haier refrigerators, or Volvo-Geely autos—have proven to be the opposite. One strategy for Chinese companies to overcome this burden and to catch up with world markets is to buy reputation by acquiring Western companies.

Some Western business leaders and politicians resist Chinese cross-border mergers and acquisitions and green-

Chinese Beijing Consensus (sometimes called the China model), which prefers an important role for government in the economy.[28] Because of these competing positions, home-country advantages in China (such as government support) can become disadvantages in a host country. In 2004, for example, China National Offshore Oil Corporation (CNOOC), a Chinese SOE, bid for the California-based oil firm Unocal. Although CNOOC was the highest bidder, the U.S. House of Representatives blocked the deal for political reasons.

Thus, both firm-level and country-level effects must be examined when analyzing the international competitiveness of Chinese firms.[29] Furthermore, the set of advantages and disadvantages can evolve over time due to firms' activities, competitive environmental pressures, and the impact of institutional change.[30]

Conclusion: Towards a More Open Investment Regime. It is a general psychological phenomenon that people fear what they cannot explain. As the globalization of Chinese firms can hardly be explained by traditional Western concepts, it is no wonder that

Western managers and politicians perceive the expansion of Chinese internationalization as a threat and then try to explain the development in geopolitical terms. Many ask whether the Chinese government is behind the private acquisitions, whether there are political agendas or military intentions behind these investments, and whether China will ultimately undermine the economic position of United States and other Western powers. Many of these questions have no factual basis but still generate potential political conflict. We should accept the fact that firms from the largest economy in the world will naturally behave according to economic incentives, and we must come to terms with China's rise in the global economy.

There are new internationalization theories that can explain the "why" and "how" of Chinese globalization.[31] Such modifications of existing theories have great potential to explain the competitiveness and modalities of the international business expansion of Chinese multinationals, and in doing so can show the phenomenon in a new light. An analysis of country-specific factors, both at home and in the host market, will help explain the internationalization of Chinese companies and their successes abroad.

Chinese multinationals expect equal treatment in markets around the world. Western governments should be receptive to Chinese investments, drawing China into their sphere of influence and friendship. The CNOOC-Unocal case demonstrates that Chinese companies want to invest in the United States, but the United States does not always want Chinese investment. Western governments should lower their arms and their shields. They should consider developing supporting institutions that include a combination of sinologists and business experts in order to foster diplomatic relations, joint educational programs, and bi-national business associations. They should open their arms to Chinese firms (albeit with some caution) and anticipate a better, more collaborative, and sustainable future.

NOTES

1 A. M. Rugman and C.H. Oh, "The International Competitiveness of Asian Firms," *Journal of Strategy and Management*, vol. 1 (2008): 57–71. *Also* S. T. Marinova, J. Child, and M. Marinov, "Evolution of Firm- and Country-Specific Advantages and Disadvantages in the Process of Chinese Firm Internationalization," *Advances in International Management*, vol. 24 (2011): 235–269.

2 International Monetary Fund "World Economic and Financial Surveys - World Economic Outlook Database," Internet, www.imf.org/external/pubs/ft/weo/2014/02/weodata/index.aspx (date accessed: 1 December 2014).

3 "World Investment Report Overview 2014 – Investing in the SDGs: An Action Plan," UNCTAD, Internet, http://unctad.org/en/PublicationsLibrary/wir2014_en.pdf (date accessed: 23 September 2014).

4 Ibid.

5 "China Global Investment Tracker," The Heritage Foundation, Internet, http://www.heritage.org/research/projects/china-global-investment-tracker-interactive-map (date accessed: 23 September 2014).

6 A. M. Rugman and C. H. Oh, (2008), "The International Competitiveness of Asian Firms."

7 I. Alon, J. Shen, W.H. Wang, and W. Zhang, "Chinese State-Owned Enterprises Go Global," *Journal of Business Strategy* 35, no. 6 (2014).

8 I. Alon, "The Globalization of Chinese Capital," *East Asia Forum Quarterly* 4, no. 2 (2012): 4-6.

9 M. Boisot, and M.W. Meyer, "Which Way through the Open Door? Reflections on the Internationalization of Chinese Firms," *Management and Organization Review* 4, no. 3 (2008): 349–365.

10 I. Alon, J. Child, S. Li, and J.R. McIntyre, "Globalization of Chinese Firms: Theoretical Universalism or Particularismmore," *Management and Organization Review* 7, no. 2, (2011): 191–200. *Also* M. Boisot and M.W. Meyer, "Which Way through the Open Door? Reflections on the Internationalization of Chinese Firms," *Management and Organization Review* 4, no. 3 (2008): 349–365.

11 J. Johanson and J. Vahlne, "The Mechanism of Internationalization," *International Marketing Review* 7, no. 4, (1990): 11–24. *Also* R. Vernon, "International Investment and International Trade in the Product Cycle." *Quarterly Journal of Economics* 8, no. 2 (1966): 190–207. *Also* R. Vernon, "The Product Cycle Hypothesis in a New International Environment," *Oxford Bulletin of Economics and Statistics*, no. 41(4), (1979): 255–267.

12 J.A. Mathews, *Dragon Multinational: Toward a New Model for Global Growth* (New York: Oxford University Press, 2002). *Also* M.F. Guillén, and E. García-Canal, "The American Model of the Multinational Firm and the 'New' Multinationals from Emerging Economies," *Academy of Management Perspective* 23, no. 2 (2009): 23–35. *Also* A. Madhok and M. Keyhani, "Acquisitions as Entrepreneurship: Asymmetries, Opportunities, and the Internationalization of Multinationals from

Emerging Economies," *Global Strategy Journal* 2, no. 1 (2012): 26-40.

13 M. Boisot and M.W. Meyer, "Which Way through the Open Door? Reflections on the Internationalization of Chinese Firms" (2008).

14 B.S. Silverman, (1999), Technological Resources and the Direction of Corporate Diversification: Toward an Integration of the Resource-based View and Transaction Cost Economics," *Management Science* 45, no. 8: 1109–1124.

15 Boisot and Meyer, "Which Way through the Open Door? Reflections on the Internationalization of Chinese Firms" (2008).

16 J.H. Dunning and R. Narula, "The Investment Development Path Revisited: Some Emerg¬ing Issues," in J.H. Dunning and R. Narula, eds., *Foreign Direct Investment and Governments: Cata¬lysts for Economic Restructuring* (London: Routledge, 1997), 1-41.

17 R. Ramamurti, "What Have We Learned about Emerging-Market MNEs?," in R. Ramamurti and J.V. Singh, eds., *Emerging Multinationals in Emerging Markets* (New York: Cambridge University Press, 2009): 399–426.

18 J.H. Dunning, "The Eclectic Paradigm of International Production: A Restatement and Some Possible Extensions," *Journal of International Business Studies* 19, no. 1, (1988): 1–31. *Also* A. Rugman, "Theoretical Aspects of MNEs from Emerging Markets," in: R. Ramamurti and J.V. Singh, eds., *Emerging Multinationals in Emerging Markets* (New York: Cambridge University Press, 2009): no. 42–63.

19 J.A. Mathews, *Dragon Multinational: A New Model for Global Growth* (Oxford University Press, 2002). *Also* A. Madhok and M. Keyhani, (2012). *Also* Luo, Y. and Tung, R.L. "International Expansion of Emerging Market Enterprises: A Springboard Perspective," *Journal of International Business Studies* 38, no. 4 (2007): 481–498.

20 R. Ramamurti, "What Have We Learned about Emerging-Market MNEs?" (2009). *Also* S. Collinson and A. Rugman, "The Regional Nature of Japanese Multinational Business," *Journal of International Business Studies* 39, no. 2 (2008): 215–230.

21 R. Ramamurti, "What Have We Learned about Emerging-Market MNEs?" *Also* V. Govindarajan and R. Ramamurti, "Reverse Innovation, Emerging Markets, and Global Strategy," *Global Strategy Journal* 1, no. 3/4 (2011): 191–205. *Also* P.J. Buckley, L. Clegg, A.R. Cross, X. Liu, H. Voss, and P. Zheng, "The Determinants of Chinese Outward Foreign Investment," *Journal of International Business Studies* 38, no. 4 (2007): 499–518. *Also* A. Madhok and M. Keyhani, "Acquisitions as Entrepreneurship: Asymmetries, Opportunities, and the Internationalization of Multinationals from Emerging Economies" (2012).

22 R. Ramamurti, "Commentaries: What Is Really Different About Emerging Market Multinationals?" *Global Strategy Journal* vol. 2 (2012): 41–47.

NOTES

23 A. Madhok and M. Keyhani, "Acquisitions as Entrepreneurship: Asymmetries, Opportunities, and the Internationalization of Multinationals from Emerging Economies" (2012).

24 S.D. Reid, "Firm Internationalization, Transaction Costs and Strategic Choice," *International Marketing Review* I, no. 2 (1983): 44–56.

25 A.M. Rugman and J. Li, "Will China's Multinationals Succeed Globally or Regionally?" *European Management Journal* 25, no. 5 (2007): 333-343. *Also* A.M. Rugman and C.H. Oh, "The International Competitiveness of Asian Firms" (2008).

26 R. Ramamurti, "Commentaries: What Is Really Different About Emerging Market Multinationals?" (2012).

27 H. Voss, P.J. Buckley, and A.R. Cross, "An Assessment of the Effects of Institutional Change on Chinese Outward Direct Foreign Investment Activity," in I. Alon, et al., eds., *China Rules: Globalization and Political Transformation* (London: Palgrave Macmillan, 2009): 135–165.

28 M.P. van Dijk, *New Presence of China in Africa* (Amsterdam: Amsterdam University Press, 2009).

29 A.M. Rugman, *Inside the Multinationals: The Economics of Internal Market* (New York: Columbia University Press, 1981).

30 R. Amit and P.H.J. Shoemaker, "Strategic Assets and Organisational Rents," *Strategic Management Journal*, vol. 14 (1993): 33-46. *Also* J. Child and D.K. Tse, "China's Transition and its Implications for International Business," *Journal of International Business Studies* 32, no. 1 (2001): 5-21.

31 A.M. Rugman and J. Li, "Will China's Multinationals Succeed Globally or Regionally?" *European Management Journal* 25, no. 5 (2007): 333-43. *Also* R. Ramamurti, "Commentaries: What Is Really Different About Emerging Market Multinationals?" (2012). *Also* S.T. Marinova, J. Child, and M.A. Marinov, "Evolution of Firm- and Country-Specific Advantages and Disadvantages in the Process of Chinese Firm Internationalization" (2011).

Science&Technology

Terrorist Migration to Social Media

Gabriel Weimann

On the evening of 1 March 2011, Arid Uka, an Albanian Muslim living in Germany, was online looking at YouTube videos. Like many before him, he watched a jihadist video that resented the gruesome rape of a Muslim woman by U.S. soldiers—a clip edited and posted on YouTube for jihadi propaganda purposes. Within hours of watching the video, Arid Uka boarded a bus at Frankfurt Airport, where he killed two U.S. servicemen and wounded two others with a handgun. After he was arrested, investigators reviewed the history of Arid Uka's Internet activity. It showed—most obviously in his Facebook profile—a growing interest in jihadist content, subsequent self-radicalization, and ultimately his viewing of the aforementioned video, which led him to take action in an alleged war in defense of Muslims. Arid Uka was not a member of a terrorist organization, nor had he visited any of the infamous training camps for terrorists. His entire radicalization, from early attraction to jihadi preaching to the final deadly mission, was accomplished online. Arid Uka is just one of many cases of the new trend of terrorists being engaged through the newest online platforms, commonly known as the "new media" or "social media." As cyberterrorism expert Evan Kohlmann argues:

Gabriel Weimann is a Full Professor of Communication at the University of Haifa, Israel. Previously, he was a Senior Fellow at the Woodrow Wilson Center in Washington DC.

Today, 90 percent of terrorist activity on the Internet takes place using social networking tools… These forums act as a virtual firewall to help safeguard the identities of those who participate, and they offer subscribers a chance to make direct contact with terrorist representatives, to ask questions, and even to contribute and help out the cyberjihad.[1]

The growing attraction of social media for modern terrorists relies on the combined impact of several trends: the expansion of online social media and its advantages for terrorists, the virtual interactivity that terrorist propaganda and recruitment are using, especially with the targeting of specific audiences ("narrowcasting"), and the emergence of "lone wolf" terrorists whose virtual pack is found in terrorist social media.

Since 2004, the growth of social media has been near exponential. Back in those days, Facebook only had about 1 million users. In 2014, Facebook has more than 1.3 billion active users. Twitter saw steep growth from 2010 to 2014 (reaching 271 million active users in July 2014), and Google+ saw the biggest growth of all in 2013, most likely because of Google's integration of Google+ into all associated services. A recent Pew study indicates that 72 percent of all Internet users are also social media users. Time spent on social media in the United States increased from 88 billion minutes in July 2011 to 121 billion minutes in July 2012, a 37 percent increase in only one year. These trends were noticed also by Internet-savvy terrorists, who quickly learned how to harness new social media for their purposes.

Social Media's Appeal for Terrorists.

Terrorist use of online platforms is not new. After the events of 9/11 and the antiterrorism campaign that followed, a large number of terrorist groups moved to cyberspace, establishing thousands of websites that promoted their messages and activities.[2] Many terrorist sites were targeted by intelligence and law enforcement agencies, counterterrorism services, and activists, who monitored the sites, attacked some of them, and forced their operators to seek new online alternatives. The turn to social media followed.

Social media differs from traditional and conventional media in many aspects, such as in interactivity, reach, frequency, usability, immediacy, and permanence.[3] Unlike traditional media—characterized as "one-to-many," in which only a small cohort of established institutions disseminates information to an effectively limitless audience—social media enables anyone to publish or access information and to do so in an interactive, two-way exchange. New communication technologies, such as comparatively inexpensive and accessible mobile and web-based networks, create highly interactive platforms through which individuals and communities share, co-create, discuss, and modify content. With social media, information consumers also act as communicators, vastly expanding the number of information transmitters in the communication market. This two-way communication promotes creation of small, diffused sets of communicators and groups. Virtual communities using social media are increasingly popular all over the world, especially among younger demographics.

The main motivation to use Facebook and other social media was properly outlined by terrorists themselves in a jihadi online forum calling for "Facebook Invasion":

This [Facebook] is a great idea, and better than the forums. Instead of waiting for people to [come to you so you can] inform them, you go to them and teach them! ...[I] mean, if you have a group of 5,000 people, with the press of a button you [can] send them a standardized message. I entreat you, by God, to begin registering for Facebook as soon as you [finish] reading this post. Familiarize yourselves with it. This post is a seed and a beginning, to be followed by serious efforts to optimize our Facebook usage. Let's start distributing Islamic jihadi publications, posts, articles, and pictures. Let's anticipate a reward from the Lord of the Heavens, dedicate our purpose to God, and help our colleagues.[4]

Terrorists have good reasons to use social media. First, these channels are by far the most popular with their intended audience, which allows terrorist organizations to be part of the mainstream. Second, social media channels are user-friendly, reliable, and free. Finally, social networking allows terrorists to reach out to their target audiences and virtually "knock on their doors"—in contrast to older models of websites in which terrorists had to wait for visitors to come to them. Social networking sites allow terrorists to use a targeting strategy known as narrowcasting. Narrowcasting aims messages at specific segments of the public defined by values, preferences, demographic attributes, or subscription. An online page, video, chat name, images, appeals, and information are tailored to match the profile of a particular social group. These methods enable terrorists to target youth especially.

Finally, the new social media have technical advantages for terrorists: sharing, uploading, or downloading files and videos no longer requires fast computers, or any computers for that matter; it no longer requires sharing sites or savvy members capable of uploading such videos. Rather, smart phones and social media accounts are all that is needed to instantly share material in real time with tens of thousands of jihadists. Thus, terrorists and their supporters and followers quickly adopted these tools and are utilizing the latest internet technologies and social media outlets to maintain massive, sophisticated online media campaigns used to communicate, radicalize, recruit, and intimidate. This trend is combined with the emergence of lone wolf terrorism: attacks by individual terrorists who are not members of any terrorist organization. Lone wolf terrorism is the fastest-growing kind of terrorism, especially in the West, where all recent lone wolf attacks involved individuals who were radicalized, recruited, trained, and even launched on social media platforms.[5]

Terrorists' Uses of Social Media.

Increasingly, terrorist groups and their sympathizers are using predominantly Western online communities like Facebook, Twitter, YouTube, MySpace, and Instagram, as well as their Arabic equivalents. Counterterrorism expert Anthony Bergin says that terrorists view these youth-dominated websites as recruitment tools "in the same way a pedophile might look at those sites to potentially groom would-be victims."[6] Terrorists' most important purposes online are propaganda, radicalization, and recruitment.

ed twice in the fighting in Syria. In April 2014, he announced in a video that he had decided to quit active fighting and assume a new role in the Islamic State propaganda mechanism: "That's why I pledged allegiance [to ISIS], in

Social networking allows terrorists to reach out to their target audiences and virtually "knock on their doors."

Recently, the Sunni terrorist group Islamic State, which is on a rampage in northern Syria and Iraq, launched a Twitter campaign under the hashtag #AllEyesOnIsis. It was aimed to appeal to impressionable Muslim youth, scare the Islamic State's enemies on the ground, and intimidate the rest of the world. A campaign entitled "One Billion Muslims to Support the ISIS" was launched on 13 June 2014 by the Twitter user "a_jzra." From the six re-tweets and four favorites from the initial post, the campaign has grown to encompass content shared hundreds of times an hour. On Twitter, the hashtag has been shared over 9,500 times since it was first introduced. Having transcended Twitter, the campaign includes video contributions hosted on YouTube along with activity on Facebook. Among the Facebook activity devoted to the campaign, a Facebook "causes" page using the hashtag had gathered hundreds of "likes" since being established on 16 June 2014.[7] One of the main figures active in Islamic State online propaganda and online recruitment efforts is a German rapper-turned-jihad-fighter Abu Talha Al Almani (also known as Deso Dogg), who was wound-

order to help the brothers and sisters of ISIS... and teach them how to make da'wa [preach] to people who have long lived in humiliation and do not know the laws of Allah. We are here, and we make da'wa to the children, to the elderly, to all the people."

Online radicalization is a multistep process, which requires a gradual transition and numerous phases, termed as "The Net," "The Funnel," "The Infection," and "The Activation."[8] The first step is "The Net," which views the whole population as primed for recruitment and exposes it to a video, taped lecture, or other online message. The target audience is viewed as homogeneous enough and receptive enough to be approached with a single undifferentiated pitch, to which some members will respond positively, others negatively. For this "netting" stage, all online platforms may be used, from Facebook pages to personal mail, and from YouTube video clips to Twitter or official websites. Second is "The Funnel." The potential recruits who start at one end of the process, after some culling along the way, are transformed into dedicated members when they emerge at the other end. This stage relies on a social bonding (though a virtual one), based on the target's alienation, social frustration, solitude, and personal pessimism. It involves online exchanges and further exposure to religious, political, or ideological material. Next is "The Infection," in which selected target members who are dissatisfied with their social status or have a grudge against their political or religious system are directed to self-radicalization. This stage involes advanced radicalization by continuous exposure to online radical material and by virtual online guidance. The final stage, "The Activation," launches the newly radicalized terrorist, often done by online commands and directions.

The Islamic State is using social media also to seduce, radicalize, and recruit. In 2014, the Islamic State has opened numerous social media accounts for distributing its videos,

and French, as well as other languages. For instance, it recently posted a speech by Islamic State spokesman Abu Muhammad Al-'Adnani translated into seven languages (English, Turkish, Dutch, French, German, Indonesian, and Russian). Following the aggressive Islamic State offensive in Iraq in June 2014, Twitter closed down many official Islamic State and pro-Islamic State accounts, including the main accounts of Al-Hayat Media, in German, English and French, but these were soon replaced by new Twitter accounts. The recruitment of hundreds of fighters from European and North American countries, as revealed recently in their active presence in Syria and Iraq, indicates the success of the Islamic State online campaign.

Online platforms, and especially social media, are ideal for terrorist radicalization, recruitment, and training.

Jihadists show strategic sophistication in exploiting the advantages and avoiding the disadvantages of new media.

audio, and images via various channels and in many languages, thereby avoiding online censorship. As part of these intensive propaganda efforts, it has launched Al-Hayat Media, a new media branch specifically targeting Western and non-Arabic speaking audiences. Launched in May 2014, this new media branch follows the Islamic State's general media strategy of distributing online videos, "news" reports, articles, and translated jihadi materials. Its main Twitter account is in German, but it also publishes materials in English

Terrorists can develop lists of potential recruits or sympathizers through online groups. Just as marketing companies can view members' information to find potential customers and select products to promote to them, terrorist groups can view people's profiles to decide whom to target and how to approach each individual. In closed forums, jihadists show strategic sophistication in exploiting the advantages and avoiding the disadvantages of new media. The online platforms used to promote extremism and terrorism are also used for operational warfare. In the 2008 terrorist attack on numerous locations in Mumbai, India, the Lashkar e-Toiba attackers used advanced communication technologies, including handheld GPS devices to plan and execute their attack, Google Earth satellite imagery, and mobile phones providing live updates from their handlers about the location of hostages, especially foreigners. Moreover, YouTube videos as well as Facebook postings are being used to teach the use of explosives, direct followers to websites with instructional material, promote hacking techniques, and share encryption programs. These postmodern terrorists are trained in virtual online camps, using the rich variety of new social media.

Counterterrorism on Social Media.

The terrorist migration to new online resources challenges the counterterrorism agencies, as well as the academics who research terrorism. The meteoric rise of social media has let radical groups and terrorists free-

for Naval Analysis asserted during his December 2011 testimony before the United States House of Representatives Homeland Security Subcommittee on Counterterrorism and Intelligence:

> There is little research to go on, which is striking given how data-rich the Internet is. In hard numbers, how widely distributed was Zawahiri's last message? Did it resonate more in one U.S. city than another? Who were its main distributors on Facebook and YouTube? How are they connected with one another? This sort of baseline quantitative research barely exists at the moment.[9]

The security community has to adjust counterterrorism strategies to the new arenas, applying new types of online warfare, intelligence gathering, and training for cyber warriors. The National Security Agency, the Department of Defense, the CIA, the FBI, the Defense Intelligence Agency, other U.S. and foreign intelligence agencies, and some private contractors are already fighting back. They are monitoring

Counterterrorism is certainly lingering behind terrorists' manipulative use of the new channels.

ly disseminate ideas through multiple modalities, including websites, blogs, social networking websites, forums, and video-sharing services. Counterterrorism is certainly lingering behind terrorists' manipulative use of the new channels. Despite the growth of Internet research in recent years, it has not yet provided efficient strategies or fruitful countermeasure devices or tactics. As William McCants of the Center

suspicious websites and social media, cyberattacking others, and planting bogus information. The migration of terrorists to online platforms—and especially social media—also presents new opportunities, as this migration exposes new vulnerabilities of radical groups, such as less anonymity and less security.[10]

The virtual war between terrorists and counterterrorism forces and agencies is vital, dynamic, and ferocious. Researchers around the world from disciplines such as psychology, security, communications, and computer sciences are coming together to develop tools and techniques to respond to terrorism's online activity. Recognizing the online threat, the White House's counter-radicalization strategy, published in August 2011, acknowledged "the important role the Internet and social networking sites play in advancing violent extremist narratives." In April 2013, the Bipartisan Policy Center's Homeland Security Project released the "Countering Online Radicalization in America" report, which identifies shortcomings in U.S online counter-radicalization strategy and recommends improvements.[11]

The challenge has spawned an interdisciplinary research topic—intelligence and security informatics, also known as cognitive security—for studying the development and use of advanced information technologies and systems for national, international, and societal security-related applications. In her February 2014 *Los Angeles Times* op-ed article on "Future Terrorists," Wilson Center president Jane Harman argued that "we need to employ the best tools we know of to counter radicalizing messages and to build bridges to the vulnerable...Narratives can inspire people to do terrible things, or to push back against those extremist voices." In fact, there are several attempts to launch counter-narrative campaigns online. For example, the "Think Again Turn Away" Twitter campaign is a $5 million effort by the United States Department of State to directly challenge the mes-

sages that al-Qaeda promotes as justification for its radical causes.[12]

To implement such a strategy, a political Internet campaign against terrorism must use tactics which have proven successful and that can be applied to the counterterrorism arena. The new media represents "an increasing continuation of war by other means," to adapt von Clausewitz's famous phrase. Cyberspace, with its numerous and emerging online platforms, presents new challenges and requires dramatic shifts in strategic thinking regarding national security and countering terrorism. Strategic thinkers should look beyond current challenges to future developments and emerging social media resources and the problems of anticipating and preempting terrorist abuse of these tools.

Responding to the challenge presented by terrorism on the Internet is an extremely complicated and sensitive issue, since most of the rhetoric disseminated on the Internet is considered protected speech under the United States constitution's First Amendment and under similar provisions in other societies. A realistic way to protect the Internet, to prevent its abuse by terrorists while at the same time protecting civil liberties, is to look for the "golden path," that is, the best compromise. Finding such a path means that we will have to accept both some vulnerabilities of the Internet to terrorism and some constraints on civil liberties, but the underlying guidelines should be to minimize both sorts of ills by looking at the trade-offs between securing our safety and securing our liberties.

NOTES

1 Yuki Noguchi, "Tracking Terrorists Online," *Washington Post*, 19 April 2006, Internet, http://www.washingtonpost.com/wp-dyn/content/ discussion/2006/04/11/DI2006041100626.html (date accessed: 1 December 2014).

2 Gabriel Weimann, "WWW.Terror.Net: How Modern Terrorism Uses the Internet," Special report (Washington, D.C.: United States Institute of Peace, 2004). *Also* Gabriel Weimann, *Terror on the Internet: The New Arena, the New Challenges* (Washington, D.C.: United States Institute of Peace Press, 2006).

3 Nigel Morgan, Graham Jones, and Anthony Hodges, *Social Media: The Complete Guide to Social Media from The Social Media Guys*, 2012, Internet, http://www.yumpu.com/en/document/view/5539277/the-complete-guide-to-social-media-the-social-media-guys (date accessed: 1 December 2014).

4 Department of Homeland Security, "Terrorist Use of Social Networking Facebook Case Study," *Public Intelligence*, 5 December 2010, Internet, http://pub-licintelligence.net/ufouoles-dhs-terrorist-use-of-so¬cial-networking-facebook-case-study (date accessed: 1 December 2014).

5 See Gabriel Weimann, "Virtual Packs of Lone Wolves" (Wilson Center Report, 2014), Internet, http://www.wilsoncenter.org/article/virtual-packs-lone-wolves (date accessed: 1 December 2014).

6 "Facebook terrorism investigation," *The Australian*, 4 April 2008, Internet, http://www.adelaidenow.com.au/news/facebook-ter¬rorism-investigation/story-e6freo8c1111115981529?nk=0103bb-730d8164e02806eeaa33a811ce (date accessed: 1 December 2014).

7 Site Intelligence Report, "Social Media Campaign To Promote ISIS Goes Viral: Information and Analysis," 2014, Internet, https://news.siteintelgroup.com/Jihadist-News/social-media-campaign-to-promote-isis-goes-viral-information-and-analysis.html (date accessed: 1 December 2014).

8 On the stages of online radicalization, see Gabriel Weimann, "Recruiting terrorists online" (Wilson Center Report, 2014), Internet, http://www.wilson-center.org/sites/default/files/new_terrorism_F.pdf (date accessed: 1 December 2014).

9 William McCants, "Testimony: Jihadist Use of Social Media - How to Prevent Terrorism and Pre¬serve Innovation" (U.S. House of Representatives: Subcommittee on Counterterrorism and Intelligence, 6 December 2011), Internet, http://homeland.house. gov/hearing/subcommittee-hearing-jihadist-use-so¬cial-media-how-prevent-terrorism-and-preserve-in¬novation (date accessed: 1 December 2014).

10 Torres Soriano, "The Vulnerabilities of Online Terrorism," *Studies in Conflict and Terrorism* 35, no. 4 (2012): 263-277.

11 Homeland Security Project, "Countering Online Radicalization in America" (Bipartisan Policy Center, December 2012), Internet, http://bipartisan-policy.org/sites/default/files/BPC%20_Online%20 Radicalization%20Report.pdf (date accessed: 1 December 2014).

12 Eric Schmitt, "A U.S. Reply, in English, to Terrorists' Online Lure," *The New York Times*, 4 December 2013, Internet, http://www.nytimes.com/2013/12/05/world/middleeast/us-aims-to-blunt-terrorist-re¬cruiting-of-english-speakers.html?_r=0 (date accessed: 1 December 2014).

The International Seabed Authority Turns Twenty

Caitlyn Antrim

The largest mineral province in the world is found on the deep ocean floor between Mexico and Hawaii. The seabed of this region, an area of about three million square kilometers, is covered with nodules of manganese and iron oxides enriched with metals critical to the world economy. Advances in technology and rising demand in both industrial and developing economies make this resource attractive as a means to meet future raw materials requirements and to protect supplies from disruption through diversification of sources.

The International Seabed Authority, which marked its twentieth anniversary on 16 November 2014, has a central role in the development of these resources. The Authority is a small and relatively unknown organization, but it has a global reach on an issue that impacts the availability of critical minerals consumed by every country in the world.

It took the world community more than a quarter-century to reach agreement on the structure, powers, and responsibilities of the Authority. Like the industry it oversees, the Authority is still a work in progress, but it has far exceeded the expectations of its creators. This success is worthy of assessment on its own, but it may also provide insights into

Caitlyn Antrim is the Executive Director of the Rule of Law Committee for the Oceans. She has previously served as a diplomat at the Law of the Sea Conference and the UN Conference on Environment and Development.

a new model of international organizations that can guide the development of other international regimes.

Critical Minerals from the Sea.

Nodules of iron and manganese oxides are found on the ocean floor around the world. They were mere curiosities until data gathered during the 1957-1958 International Geophysical Year were evaluated. Researchers discovered that nodules in the depths of the Pacific Ocean were enriched with nickel, copper, cobalt, and rare earth elements (REEs).[1] These metals are critical to both developing and industrial economies. Copper is used in electrical wiring, and in brass and bronze for light manufacturing. Manganese is needed for the production of steel and as an alloying element in specialized steel and aluminum alloys. Nickel is essential in the production of stainless steel, steel alloys, and superalloys that are used in jet engines. Cobalt is used in high temperature superalloys, carbide tools, and tool steels for manufacturing. Demand for cobalt is rapidly increasing for use in lithium-ion batteries for electronics and electric vehicles and in the high-strength magnets used in advanced electric generators. Demand for REEs has been surging in a range of advanced applications in optics, magnets, and electronics.

Demand in all of these uses is on the rise, but the cost of developing new land-based sources of the minerals is rising as well. New nickel and copper production is tapping deposits with lower metal content and higher infrastructure costs than past sources, while cobalt production is becoming increasingly concentrated in the Democratic

Republic of Congo (the bulk of cobalt ore from which is shipped to China for processing). Over 90 percent of rare earth production is concentrated in China. The vulnerability of national economies to supply disruption was demonstrated in 1979 when a rebellion in Zaire (now the Democratic Republic of the Congo) disrupted cobalt supplies and raised prices eightfold. More recently, China's unilateral reduction in exports of rare earth elements in 2011 threatened Japanese industries dependent upon their availability.

Production of critical minerals from the sea holds promise not just to meet growing demand, but also to shield industry and defense consumers from disruption by diversifying sources of supply. This view was first expressed by ocean industry visionaries in the 1960s and 1970s when technology from the offshore oil industry and a thirty-year trend in rising metal prices first drew major corporations, including International Nickel, Tenneco, Kennecott Copper, and Lockheed Missiles and Space, into the race to develop deep seabed minerals.

Creating a New Legal Regime.

Harvesting minerals from the seabed at depths of three miles or more is an expensive endeavor. Investors and lenders in large mineral developments require developers to have international recognition of exclusive access to mineral deposits and title to recovered minerals. These rights were not recognized in the centuries-old regime of freedom of the high seas. In order for seabed mining to proceed, a new legal regime had to be created.

After Law of the Sea conferences in

1958 and 1960 failed to reach agreement on expansions of coastal state authority over the ocean and its resources, the United States pushed for a comprehensive approach in which a package deal could draw universal acceptance. In 1970 the Nixon Administration introduced its Draft Convention on the International Seabed Area.[2] It proposed that a new, autonomous international organization, the International Seabed Resources Authority, be established to authorize, monitor, and regulate deep seabed mineral exploration and exploitation activities. Following several years of preparation, the third United Nations Conference on the Law of the Sea held its first substantive session in 1974. One of the Conference's three main negotiating committees was charged with developing the legal regime for the development of deep seabed minerals.

Interest in a new regime was not limited to governments. The American mining industry supported a multilateral approach to develop an international regime for seabed minerals based on pragmatic interests. The comments of Donald Donahue—president of the mining giant AMAX, Inc.—in 1974 remain valid today:

But let me make one point clear. The U.S. mining industry supports the creation of an intergovernmental regime to issue exclusive non-discriminatory exploration and production licenses for seabed minerals which would be available to private companies, and supports the concept that there should be reasonable sharing with developing countries of the ultimate benefits of such mining.[3]

The path to a widely accepted seabed mineral regime was not an easy one. The post-colonial era presented difficult political challenges to negotiators that resulted in compromises that the U.S. would not accept in the final Convention. These issues were identified by President Reagan as the United States prepared to return to the final negotiating session of the Conference in 1982. Objecting only to the seabed mineral provisions, he said that he would sign a Law of the Sea Convention that met specific criteria to ensure the fair and competitive regime required by commercial developers while respecting American constitutional and political interests regarding international organizations and agreements.[4]

Reagan's criteria were not met in 1982, so he declined to sign the Convention when it was opened for signature. However, his criteria served as the template for changes made by a second agreement adopted in 1994 after years of negotiation by presidents Bush and Clinton.[5] The 1994 Agreement laid out how the seabed mineral provisions of the 1982 Convention would be interpreted, implemented, or even set aside. As a package, the 1982 Convention and the 1994 Agreement met Reagan's criteria in full.[6] Once the 1994 Agreement was signed, the United States and other industrialized nations began the process of ratification of the Convention and Agreement as an integrated package.

Today, twenty years after it came into force, the Convention has 166 parties. Only 14 coastal states have yet to join and the United States is the only major maritime power still outside the Convention. Approval of the Convention has been supported by four presidents, the Joint Chiefs of Staff, the U.S. Chamber of Commerce, energy, shipping, telecommunications, and technology companies, and major environmental organizations.

Opposition to the Convention has been justified through several arguments, but it generally reflects a belief

revision, it bears a striking resemblance to the International Seabed Resource Authority proposed by President Nixon in 1970.[8] The Authority, just as Nixon had proposed, is an autonomous intergovernmental organization that is responsible to its member states. It has an Assembly of all member states that

The United States is the only **major maritime power** still outside the Convention.

that the United States cannot effectively protect its interests within multilateral organizations, along with the view that treaties negotiated under UN auspices threaten American sovereignty. Using the Senate rules of procedure and an effective grass roots campaign, opponents have stymied efforts by a majority of the Senate to bring the Convention to a vote. Another argument—that domestic legislation adopted prior to the completion of the Convention would be sufficient to allow U.S. firms to mine the deep seabed—was countered in 2012 by the chairman of the Lockheed Martin Corporation, the sole remaining U.S. licensee under that legislation, who stated that U.S. membership in the Convention and the International Seabed Authority (ISA) is essential if U.S. firms are to make multi-billion dollar investments in seabed mineral development.[7] In spite of wide support, the Convention has not yet been raised for a vote on the floor of the Senate.

The International Seabed Authority Today.
The International Seabed Authority was established in 1994. In spite of the decades of negotiation and

is responsible for policy guidance and a Council of thirty-six states that oversees the operations of the Authority with the assistance of commissions of experts. It is given exclusive authority to manage the mineral resources of the seabed beyond national jurisdiction. The Authority is also responsible for implementing the environmental provisions specified in the Convention and for collecting and sharing of benefits of seabed mineral development with developing countries.

Promoting Development.
The Authority's central effort to encourage development of the minerals of the deep seabed has been the development of its "Mining Code." To date, the Authority has adopted sections of the code that address exploration for three categories of seabed minerals: polymetallic nodules, polymetallic sulfides, and cobalt-bearing crusts.[9] Based on this code, the Authority has approved twenty-six operations sponsored by twenty states for the three types of minerals. The states that have sponsored exploration operations are evenly represented by industrialized, advanced

developing, Pacific small island, and eastern European and socialist states (see table below).

Private firms first engaged in the ISA process in 2012 when an application by U.K. Seabed Resources Ltd (UKSRL), sponsored by the United Kingdom, was approved.[10] A second application by UKSRL was approved in 2014 and a third includes an operating agreement with Singapore. The application of Belgian firm Global Sea Mineral Resources NV (GSR) was approved in 2012 and the Cook Islands have announced a collaboration with GSR to develop an area associated with the original GSR site. Nautilus Minerals, a Canadian firm, is conducting exploration of a site held by the Kingdom of Tonga.

The Authority encourages new participation in seabed mineral development through "sensitization seminars"

cies based at the UN complex. Prospective developers, sponsoring states, and other stakeholders may access the Authority's growing knowledge base of technical studies, workshop reports, and geophysical data on its website.

Protecting the Marine Environment.
The Law of the Sea Convention explicitly requires the Authority to protect the marine environment from harm resulting from seabed mineral development activities.[11] While exploration activities are considered minimally invasive in the marine environment, the Authority must address the protection of the marine environment as operations move to prototype testing, construction, and commercial operation. The Authority has adopted the "precautionary approach" of the Rio Declaration on Environment and

State Sponsors of Exploration Contracts

Industrialized States	Advanced Developing States	Pacific Small Island States	Eastern European & Socialist States
Belgium	Brazil	Cook Islands	Bulgaria
France	China	Kiribati	Czech Republic
Germany	India	Nauru	Cuba
Japan	Russia	Singapore	Poland
United Kingdom	South Korea	Tonga	Slovakia

that inform states and other stakeholders about deep seabed minerals and the regime governing their development. Since beginning the program in 2007, the Authority has held seminars in Indonesia, Brazil, Nigeria, Jamaica, and Mexico and has held two seminars in New York City for offices and agen-

Development and requires the preparation of environmental impact assessments prior to consideration of applications for contacts for exploration. In 2012, the Authority adopted an environmental management plan for the nodule province in the eastern Pacific Ocean that set aside nine large areas of particular environmental interest.[12] It supports the development of taxonomies for categorization of marine life in the region to assist in the preparation of environmental assessment studies and gathers information from research activities by contractors and academic researchers. The Authority also included environmental issues in the 2013 Stakeholder Survey that it sent to both developers and observers from environmental organizations.

Sharing the Benefits.

As did the original Nixon proposal, the Convention provides for sharing of financial benefits of exploitation. The technically complex revenue sharing system in the 1982 Convention was deleted by the 1994 Agreement, so new provisions will need to be adopted by the Authority as part of the exploitation code for nodules.

The Convention encourages developing-state participation in exploration activities through a system in which applicants prospect an area large enough to accommodate two mining claims. The applicant divides the site into two parts of equal value and the Council decides which to reserve for use by developing states. This provision has allowed several developing states, particularly small island states, to obtain sites for exploration programs that could eventually lead to exploitation.

The Convention also provides for the establishment of an operation, known as the "Enterprise," to conduct exploration and exploitations on behalf of all developing states. In its original conception in 1982 this was controversial because the Enterprise was given privileges not provided to other applicants. The 1994 Agreement on Implementation revised the status of Enterprise so that it would operate under the same conditions that apply to other contractors, and provisions that would have funded the Enterprise were eliminated.

The Authority also treats knowledge as a benefit. Applicants must incorporate training programs for developing country scientists within their exploration programs. It also promotes the sharing of knowledge through workshops and it encourages technology holders to reach commercial agreements on access to technology with interested developing countries.

Assessing the Authority's Progress.

The International Seabed Authority has been successful far beyond the cautious expectations of its creators. The approval of twenty-six applications for exploration rights from twenty countries, an exploration code addressing three categories of minerals, a growing knowledge base, predictable processes of operation, and a twenty-year history of making all substantive decisions by consensus lay a firm foundation for the organization to build upon for the future. If it is to be equally as successful as it move forward toward exploitation, it will need to build on the lessons of its past.

Factors contributing to the success of the Authority are:

Clear Priorities. The mission of the Authority is focused on three objectives: development of the resources of the deep seabed, protection of the marine environment, and sharing of benefits of development with member states.

Autonomy. The Authority is an autonomous organization that is responsible to its members under the provisions of the 1982 Convention on the Law of the Sea and the 1994 Agreement on Implementation.

Primacy of the Nation State. The member states of the Authority are the principals of the organization while the secretariat acts to execute the decisions and guidance of the members.

Outreach to Stakeholders. The Authority recognizes international and non-governmental organizations with interests in deep seabed minerals as observers and invites their advice and contributions.

Effective Application of the Consensus Process. In spite of extensive rules governing decision making by the Assembly and the Council, all decisions on substantive matters have been made by consensus.

Knowledge Support for Decision Making. The Secretariat has taken on the function of

Looking Ahead: The Future of the International Seabed Authority.

Over its first two decades, the International Seabed Authority has developed into the sole mechanism for managing the development of the minerals of the seabed beyond national jurisdiction. The Authority is recognized by all investors in deep seabed mining as the only body that can provide international recognition of exclusive access and title to recovered minerals.

The next task facing the Authority is to draft the exploitation section of the mining code, beginning with the section for polymetallic nodules. Three areas will provide challenges in three areas of regulation: protecting the marine environment, sharing of financial benefits, and effective oversight of exploitation operations.

Environmental issues to be addressed include the degree of disturbance introduced by nodule harvesting activities, the rate of recovery of the marine environment, the effects of disturbance

The International Seabed Authority has been successful far beyond the cautious expectations of its creators.

a "knowledge organization" in support of its responsibilities, providing member states, contractors, and observers access to an extensive store of knowledge related to deep seabed minerals as well as the history of the seabed regime.

Tight Budget. In accordance with the directive that the Authority be "cost effective," the Secretariat has fewer than forty members and the annual budget is approximately $7 million.

of the fine sediments that cover the ocean floor, and the monitoring and reporting requirements to be imposed on contractors. Environmental baseline studies conducted by contractors during their development activities will promote public debate and engagement during the rule-making processes in the Council. Environmental non-governmental organizations, including Conservation International, Greenpeace, World Wildlife Fund International, and the Deep Sea Conservation Coalition, are recognized observers at the ISA and will continue to contribute to the discussions of the Authority.

The revenue-sharing provisions of the code will focus on the structure and details of the revenue-sharing provisions that will apply to exploitation contracts. These provisions will be based on improved understanding of seabed mining economics and on current practices of governments related to land-based mineral production.

The transition to exploitation will require the Authority to establish rules and procedures for monitoring contractor activities at sea, ensure that sponsoring states manage operations in accordance with the exploitation code, and, if necessary to prevent harm to the marine environment, issue emergency orders pertaining to exploitation operations. Establishing a balance between the rights and duties of contractors, sponsoring states, and the Authority will be a new challenge in the development of the exploitation code. Continued success will require continued collaboration among all stakeholders and commitment to the consensus decision process that has been followed for the

Authority's first twenty years.

The most notable shortfall in the development of the Authority has been the failure of the United States to join the Law of the Sea Convention and take its guaranteed seat in the Council. As the Authority has gained stature as the "indispensable organization" for managing deep seabed mineral development, the aura of the United States as the "indispensable nation" in international affairs has diminished by its absence. More broadly, the failure to ratify an agreement modified expressly to meet criteria established by President Reagan reduces U.S. influence in the negotiation of other ocean-related agreements and undermines the universal applicability of the navigation provisions of the Convention.

With or without the United States, the International Seabed Authority will be the sole organization that promotes seabed mineral development, protects the deep seabed environment, and helps share the benefits of seabed mineral exploitation. It falls to the Senate of the United States to decide whether the U.S. will share in this success or sit on the sidelines watching the other nations reap the benefits of deep seabed minerals.

NOTES

1 Charles Morgan, "A Geological Model of Poly-metallic Nodule Deposits in the Clarion-Clipperton Fracture Zone," Briefing Paper 01/12, *International Seabed Authority*, March 2012, Internet, http://www.isa.org.jm/files/documents/EN/Pubs/BP1.pdf (date accessed: 1 December 2014).

2 "United Nations Convention on the International Seabed Area, Draft Submitted by the United States Government," *Journal of Maritime Law and Commerce* 2 (1970): 451-480.

3 Donald J. Donahue, "The Future of the World's Minerals Industry," Pre-print Number 74-AK-361, presented at the Fall Meeting of the Society of Mining Engineers, Acapulco, Mexico, 22-25 September 1974, 23.

4 Ronald Reagan, "United States Law of the Sea Policy," National Security Decision Directive Number 20, 29 January 1982, Internet, http://www.reagan.utexas.edu/archives/reference/Scanned%20NSDDS/NSDD20.pdf (date accessed: 1 December 2014).

5 "Agreement Relating to the Implementation of Part XI of the United Nations Convention on the Law of the Sea of 10 December 1982," New York, 28 July 1994, Internet, https://treaties.un.org/pages/ViewDetails.aspx?src=TREATY&mtdsg_no=XXI-6-a&chapter=21&lang=en (date accessed: 1 December 2014).

6 Bernard Oxman, "The 1994 Agreement and the Convention," *American Journal of International Law* 88 (1994): 687-695.

7 Letter from Robert J. Stevens, Chairman and CEO of Lockheed Martin Corporation to Senator John F. Kerry, Chairman, Senate Committee on Foreign Relations on 17 May 2012.

8 op. cit. Richard Nixon, Draft Convention on the International Seabed.

9 Polymetallic sulfides and cobalt bearing crusts are seabed mineral forms that came to public attention years after polymetallic nodules. The Authority has followed the same process for developing exploration regulations for these minerals as it did for nodules.

10 UK Seabed Resources Ltd. is a subsidiary of Lockheed Martin UK, which, in turn, is a wholly owned subsidiary of the Lockheed Martin Corporation in the United States.

11 United Nations Convention on the Law of the Sea, Articles 209 and 215, and Article 17 of Annex III.

12 "Decision of the Council relating to an Environmental Management Plan for the Clarion-Clipperton Zone," Document ISBA/18/C/22, 26 July 2012, Internet, http://www.isa.org.jm/files/documents/EN/18Sess/ Council/ISBA-18C-22.pdf (date accessed: 1 December 2014).

Not As Dire As It Seems

Review by Christopher Yung

Robert Kaplan. Asia's Cauldron: The South China Sea and the End of a Stable Pacific. New York: Random House, 2014. 256 pp. $26.00.

Robert Kaplan's latest book—ominously titled *Asia's Cauldron: The South China Sea and the End of a Stable Pacific*—is meant to do three things: give the reader an understanding of the Asian countries involved in the South China Sea disputes; describe the nature of these disputes and provide a sense of whether these disputes can be resolved peacefully; and address the question of whether tensions in the South China Sea portend a larger likelihood of conflict, a breakdown of political order in the Asia-Pacific, or some other dark future for the region. An appropriate review, therefore, must explore the work from three different angles: from the viewpoint of an Asia-Pacific regional expert, from the perspective of an authority on the specific territorial claims themselves, and from the vantage point of a military analyst.

Given Kaplan's many years of experience as a journalist and commentator on the ground across the globe, it is no surprise that he does a superb job in investigating what makes each of the claimant countries of the South China Sea operate. Having spoken with top experts and government officials directly involved in managing their respective countries' maritime territorial disputes, Kaplan gives the reader a vivid picture of events and perspectives.[1] Additionally, he con-

Christopher Yung is a Senior Research Fellow at the Institute for National Strategic Studies, National Defense University. He is also Deputy Director at the Center for Study of Chinese Military Affairs.

ducts a sociological deep dive and hones in on the core cultural attributes of many of these countries. In the traditions of V.S. Naipaul and Edward Said, Kaplan walks the reader through the cultural and political traditions of each of the claimant countries.[2] This tour of the region provides the backstory to these states' complex relations and gives the reader unique insights into their propensities to either negotiate or clash with one another.

In spite of the difficulties in explaining the positions of all of the South China Sea claimants, their peculiar historical fixations, and the international legal merits of each of the cases without thoroughly boring readers, Kaplan succeeds in doing just that. He explains to the lay reader the implications of the United Nations Convention on Law of the Sea (UNCLOS) for the various legal arguments, as well as the arbitration and international court options for the disputants given the provisions of UNCLOS.[3] He explains in meticulous detail the economic implications of the disputants' territorial claims, such as by illustrating what an Exclusive Economic Zone (EEZ) specifically provides for the claimants, as opposed to a territorial sea.[4]

Shortcomings.
Asia's Cauldron is at its weakest in its examination of the likelihood of real conflict in the region. Kaplan's central thesis is that the South China Sea is a bubbling cauldron ready to erupt at any moment. The historic animosities and cultural proclivities of the claimant states—in addition to economic incentives (namely oil and fishing resources)—provide important context, but not the whole picture.

There are four main components of his argument that the Asia-Pacific may be entering a period of great strife, which will be examined in turn. First, he points to a regional arms race, led by China.[5] Second, he argues that other military developments currently taking place in the region are qualitatively destabilizing.[6] Third, he contends that China's relentless rise will lead it to seek domination in the Asia-Pacific region, much as the United States sought to dominate the Western hemisphere in the nineteenth century.[7] Finally, Kaplan notes that the already-apparent decline of the United States will create a power vacuum in the Asia-Pacific, leaving it structurally unstable and heightening the potential for conflict.[8] Kaplan correctly notes that the Asia-Pacific has some elements of conflict. However, this is distinct from having a fundamentally destabilized security structure.

First, although Kaplan argues that the Asia-Pacific is in the midst of an arms race, other Asia analysts have more accurately described it as an arms crawl. David Kang observes that when measured against GDP, defense expenditures in Asia have declined over the last twenty-five years.[9] In 1988, eleven of the most developed Asian economies devoted on average 3.35 percent of GDP for defense; today, that percentage has dropped to 1.86 percent of GDP. While this region has experienced robust GDP growth over the past few decades—thus reducing defense spending as a proportion of GDP—real defense spending has still experienced healthy growth rates in the last decade.[10] Chinese defense spending has steadily increased, Japan recently announced planned changes to the interpretation of its constitution to allow an increase in defense expenditures, and all of the countries of Southeast Asia have nominally increased defense spending.[11] It is true that the countries of the Asia-Pacific are procuring weapon systems and platforms, but hardly at a rate that can be characterized as an arms race. As examples, Indonesia and Malaysia are illustrative. Indonesia is acquiring three Type-209 conventional submarines from South Korea, and acquired two Russian Su-27SK and two Su-30MK fighter jets in 2003 and 2007, respectively. It also recently received twenty-four U.S. F-16s.[12] Malaysia has recently acquired over 250 armored personnel carriers, 6 modern frigates, 4 multirole air transport aircraft, and 12 super cougar helicopters from a variety of suppliers.[13] While certainly a marked improvement in conventional capabilities, these systems hardly tip the balance and cannot be claimed to represent an arms race. Kaplan notes that from the 1980s to the 1990s, the Asia-Pacific share of all global arms sales almost doubled from 11 percent to 20 percent. As Kang notes, this may be a reflection of the fact that the rest of world has drastically reduced its defense spending, not that Asian defense spending has rocketed upward.

Second, Kaplan seems to contend that other military developments in Asia are necessarily destabilizing. He describes an Asian fixation on submarines, for instance, that he calls inherently offensive, and lists a number of developments related to naval modernization in China (including the procurement of its first aircraft carrier, the Liaoning), Japan, and South Korea.[14]

He expresses alarm at the large numbers of ballistic missiles procured by China's People's Liberation Army (PLA), China's development of anti-satellite and network attack capabilities, and its "anti-access/area denial" capabilities, all designed to erode U.S. capabilities and ultimately U.S. credibility.[15] Finally, he notes that other Asian nation-states are procuring advanced aircraft and naval platforms. According to Kaplan, Asia is becoming an "armed camp." But it is unclear why the countries of the region purchasing submarines, surface combatants, and modern aircraft is destabilizing, especially since most Southeast Asian countries have historically not possessed robust and modern air forces, navies, and other weapon systems. Why does Kaplan not consider this to be defense modernization? China has steadily improved its military capabilities for decades without being matched by other countries in the Asia-Pacific region—why do other states' military modernizations not amount to a movement toward a greater balance of naval and air power?

Additionally, Kaplan cites certain skirmishes surrounding maritime territorial disputes to demonstrate rising military tensions, but many of the cases he cites were not truly military in nature. To date, conventional militaries have had only a marginal role to play in the competitive dynamics of the South China Sea dispute. The recent China-Vietnam oil rig standoff involved dozens of Chinese vessels, but those were primarily law enforcement boats.[16] Likewise, Vietnam sent its coast guard to the area. The 2012 Scarborough Shoal incident exclusively involved the China Maritime Surveillance force, some Philippines coast guard vessels, and the Philippines's only navy frigate. The 2013 confrontation between the Philippines and Taiwan involved the Philippines Coast Guard using lethal force against a Taiwanese fisherman. Not a single submarine has been used in any of the standoffs associated with territorial disputes, and no state has escalated tensions with the use of offensive mining, blockades, or any of the advanced offensive weaponry that Kaplan argues are at the heart of growing regional instability. In fact, most claimants rely largely on lightly armed law enforcement vessels, and the skir-

in some ways. South Korea, although more inclined to maintain a neutral relationship with China, will not easily bend to Beijing's wishes. Compounding this is the shadow of close U.S. alliances with many of China's neighbors.

How the Asia-Pacific geostrategic reality described above could serve as a natural brake against rapidly escalating tensions is apparent even now. Despite China's continued rise, the Chinese still recognize that they lack the power to simply dictate Chinese dominance. Thus, the government has reasons to not act too aggressively. It faces incentives to press its claims just short of the

Despite China's continued rise, the Chinese still recognize that they lack the power to simply dictate Chinese dominance.

mishes are media-oriented and legal in nature—not conventional military in nature.

Third, Kaplan assumes that conflict is inevitable given China's rise. In accordance with John Mearsheimer's view on this subject, he asserts that China will unceasingly seek to maximize its power to the detriment of the other states in Asia. The implication is that China's rise is itself disruptive and will lead to an unstable Asia-Pacific.[17] Although China is clearly the dominant regional power—which, like the United States in the nineteenth century, is seeking to consolidate its regional hegemony and prevent foreign interference in the region—it is surrounded by prosperous and powerful nation states.[18] Japan, in particular, is equipped to counterbalance China

threshold that would otherwise trigger a regional counter-coalition and U.S. involvement. The Chinese have, therefore, simultaneously used overt displays of force while also engaging in diplomacy. Finally, they have deliberately used lightly armed law enforcement vessels in confronting their rivals in order to limit the possibility of military escalation with the United States. Chinese strategists have themselves declared that their country is currently in a period of "strategic opportunity" and counsel taking advantage of a stable international system to focus on continued economic growth. For domestic political purposes, territorial claims are to be vigorously defended and asserted, but only through means that do not disrupt the region or the international system.[19] China's annual defense white paper directly reflects this school of thought in declaring:

> [P]eace and development remain the underlying trends of our time... China has seized and made the most

no mention of India—another rising power with similarly striking projected growth rate figures—as a natural counterweight to China, if the United States either lacks the capability or the will to

Has American credibility so eroded over time that the United States is unable to sustain a successful alliance network in the region?

of this important period of strategic opportunity for its development and its modernization..[H]owever, China still faces multiple and complicated security threats and challenges... therefore China has an arduous task to safeguard its national unification, territorial integrity, and development interests.[20]

Finally, Kaplan's argument ultimately rests on the observation that the United States is in relative decline and that, when combined with China's rapid rise, China will most likely supplant the United States as the dominant power in the region. He notes the economic difficulties facing the United States and the effects these difficulties have on its ability to serve as a counterweight to China.[21] Making a straight line projection out to 2050 (which he admits should be accepted with caution), Kaplan observes that China is likely to have approximately nine carriers concentrated in the Asia-Pacific, with the United States projected to have that same number for operations covering the entire globe.[22] Kaplan concludes that the possible replacement of the American order in the Asia-Pacific with a Chinese one is bound to lead to instability. Curiously, Kaplan makes

continue to play this role.

Although Kaplan is right to observe some troubling long-term trends for U.S. and Chinese military capabilities in the Far East, he goes too far in downplaying the role of political actions on the region's security future. He correctly notes that Chinese preeminence is one possible trajectory for the region, and that an economic downturn in China is another; however, he largely ignores the possibility that policy actions can impact the strategic stability of the region. He does not thoroughly consider the effects of a U.S. economic recovery or of effective alliance management with regional partners in order to check Chinese coercive behavior. Has American credibility so eroded over time that the United States is unable to sustain a successful alliance network in the region? Moreover, he could explore whether future U.S. administrations can still levy "cost imposing" actions on China so as to alter Beijing's calculus for coercion, as well as whether China will assume the role of dominant regional power smoothly. These issues, which Kaplan does not fully address, lay at the heart of whether the Asia-Pacific regional order remains a stable one.

In *Asia's Cauldron*, Robert Kaplan successfully elucidates a difficult and complex subject, and the book is worth reading. He does an outstanding job explaining the cultural and historical roots of the claimant states of the South China Sea and clearly outlines all of the maritime territorial claims in the region, including their legal merits and their potential for resolution. *Asia's Cauldron* falls short, however, in advancing Kaplan's larger argument that the tensions and possible conflicts associated with the South China Sea portend the end of stability in the Asia-Pacific region. Despite this shortcoming, the book will help advance serious discussions amongst defense and foreign policy circles on both sides of the Pacific.

NOTES

1 Robert D. Kaplan, *Asia's Cauldron: The South China Sea and the End of a Stable Pacific* (New York: Random House, 2014), 51-183.

2 Ibid.

3 Ibid.

4 Ibid.

5 Ibid., 18-19.

6 Ibid., 34-35.

7 Ibid., 180-181.

8 Ibid., 176-178.

9 David C. Kang, "A Looming Arms Race in East Asia?" *The National Interest* (May 2014): 3, Internet, http://www. nationalinterest.org/feature/looming-arms-race-east-asia-10461 (date accessed: 1 December 2014).

10 *The Military Balance 2014*, The International Institute for Strategic Studies (IISS), (Routledge Press: London, 2014), 204.

11 Ibid., 201-2, 204, 209-12.

12 Wenell Minnick, "Tighter Budgets Limit Southeast Asian Plans," *Defense News* (13 April 2014). *Also* "Indonesia's Air Force Adds More Flankers," *Defense Industry Daily* (7 January 2014).

13 *The Military Balance 2014*, 295.

14 Kaplan, 34.

15 Ibid., 34-40.

16 While it is true that many coast guards in the region are formally part of the navies of their associated countries, their characteristics are nonetheless distinctly non-military in nature (e.g., lightly armed, small, and not specifically designed to survive a strike from a missile). Whether as part of their nation's navy or as a separate law enforcement oriented service, these types of lightly armed vessels have been at the heart of the Southeast Asian maritime territorial disputes.

17 Ibid., 43-44.

18 Ibid., 43-50.

19 Christopher Yung, interviews with researchers from the PLA Academy of Military Sciences (AMS), March 2011 and September 2013. For a published account of this perspective, see "Changing Global Order," *Crux of Asia: China, India, and the Emerging Global Order* (Carnegie Endowment for International Peace, 2013), 46.

20 *The Diversified Employment of China's Armed Forces*, Information Office of the State Council, the People's Republic of China, April 2013, Beijing, China.

21 Kaplan, 36.

22 Ibid., 36.

The Costs of the Knife

Review by David H. Schanzer & LtCol Timothy Nichols, USMC (Ret.)

Mark Mazzetti. The Way of the Knife: The CIA, a Secret Army and a War at the Ends of the Earth. New York: Penguin Press, 2013. 400 pp. $29.95.

When CIA contractor Raymond Davis shot and killed two Pakistani nationals in the streets of Lahore, Pakistan denied Davis diplomatic immunity and charged him with double murder, all the complexities and tensions of the U.S. shadow war against global terrorist networks were laid bare for the world to see. In theory, the shadow war can work cleanly: with smooth coordination and collaboration between the United States and its international partners, clear definition of roles and responsibilities between the CIA and the Department of Defense (DoD), and surgical action against identified terrorist targets. But, as Mark Mazzetti ably demonstrates in his book *The Way of the Knife*, in practice, the shadow war is often messy, complex, and fraught with moral and strategic tension. Generally, Mazzetti provides a great deal of insight as to how this shadow war developed and has been conducted over the past decade; however, he does little to evaluate its effectiveness or explore alternatives. As tensions boil over in the Middle East and extremist organizations proliferate across the globe, the United States needs to focus less on the tactical aspects of counterterrorism, and instead to engage in a broader national discussion on the direction and execution of its counterterrorism strategy.

David H. Schanzer is the Director of the Triangle Center on Terrorism and Homeland Security and an Associate Professor of the Practice at the Sanford School of Public Policy at Duke University. He is also the Co-Director of the Institute for Homeland Security Solutions.

LtCol Timothy Nichols is a Visiting Associate Professor of the Practice at the Sanford School of Public Policy at Duke University and the Executive Director of the Counterterrorism and Public Policy Fellowship Program. He is a retired LtCol and served in the USMC for twenty-two years.

The "way of the knife" is Mazzeti's euphemism for the U.S. approach to counterterrorism after 9/11—practices and policies steeped in invasive intelligence collection, lethal preemption of terrorist threats, and minimal transparency. This "shadow war" was the U.S. response to the unprecedented strategic challenge 9/11 presented to a national security apparatus that was ill-equipped to confront an enemy that hides in densely populated cities and ungoverned sanctuaries. America's lumbering, hierarchical security agencies were trained and equipped to defeat any conventional military force. But to confront al-Qaeda, the United States needed to find a way to collect intelligence and conduct lethal operations inside sovereign nations with which it was not at war.

Mazzetti reveals the "muddled" state of this shadow war after a decade of its development and execution. Through his use of detailed vignettes, Mazzetti describes how after 9/11 neither the military nor the CIA demonstrated a refined understanding of the terrorist threat or how to collect useful intelligence about it. With minimal DoD assets in embassies and few military intelligence collectors in threat areas, Secretary of Defense Donald Rumsfeld found that his agency was unable to direct the powerful U.S. military towards enemy personnel in this new context. Responding to Rumsfeld's inquiry two weeks after 9/11 about what special operations were being planned, General Charles Holland replied: "Well, it would be difficult, because we don't have any actionable intelligence."[1] Likewise, the CIA lacked human sources within terrorist organizations and

was overly dependent on liaison activities with unreliable host nation intelligence services (such as Pakistan's Inter-Services Intelligence) for tactical information. Because of this, the CIA was also incapable of providing Rumsfeld's military forces the specific information they needed to strike.

Mazzetti next discusses the mismatch in the legal authority and capabilities possessed by the military and the CIA. While the military enjoyed a robust capability to conduct strikes and collect intelligence on rival military forces in specified war zones, it had little ability or legal authority to find and contend with non-state actors operating outside of those designated war zones. Rumsfeld mused: "Given the nature of our world, isn't it conceivable that the Department ought not to be in a position of near total dependence on the CIA in situations such as this?"[2] Presidential directives provided the CIA greater operational latitude than the DoD in areas such as Pakistan and Yemen, but the intelligence agency did not possess offensive capabilities that could be deployed against emergent targets. Rather than developing a coordinated whole-of-government approach to address these gaps, both the military and the CIA scrambled to construct the capabilities they lacked. Rumsfeld created a new intelligence under-secretariat and charged his confidant Stephen Cambone with overseeing new and deeply resourced "Pentagon spying efforts."[3] The CIA responded by creating its own lethal drone capabilities. The Bush administration permitted this duplication to occur, casting off the 9/11 Commission's recommendation that paramilitary activities should be consolidated in the Department of Defense.

Despite these efforts, the thirst for actionable intelligence was virtually unquenchable. Mazzetti catalogues the government's effort to meet this demand by turning to commercial profiteers to construct and operate their own independent spy networks. Efforts to set up these private networks by businesswoman Michele Ballarin, former CIA operative Dewey Clarridge, and shadowy Defense Department civilian Michael Furlong, initially gained traction and funding, but withered upon legal review. These efforts were finally terminated when senior intelligence officials doubted the reliability of the private intelligence sources and opposed diverting resources to them.

Finally, Mazzetti explores the hot disputes between diplomats and the CIA regarding the effectiveness of preemptive drone strikes. While they undoubtedly took enemies off the battlefield, the strikes simultaneously undermined international relationships, heightened global anti-American sentiment, and stoked the flames of radicalization. Mazzetti refers to an incident when Cameron Munter, then the U.S. Ambassador to Pakistan, requested to be notified in advance of planned drone strikes and be provided the authority to veto them. Munter believed that he was better equipped than the CIA to weigh the value of targeted killings against their negative impact on diplomatic relations. The CIA, with President Obama's support, refused to make such a concession. Subsequently, even some CIA officers, like Ross Newland, began to question whether the CIA should be conducting such strikes. Referring to the drone program, he observed that "the predator ends up hurting the CIA. This is just not an intelligence mission."[4]

Mazzetti's description of the contours and tensions of the shadow war

Mazzetti's reporting on drone strikes demonstrates how **excessive secrecy** has damaged U.S. counterterrorism interests.

encourages the reader to consider normative judgments on the strategic and moral issues his book brings to light. Do all of our counterterrorism activities need to be secret? Is the shadow war an effective antidote to terrorism, or is it treating the symptoms rather than the cause of violent extremism? If not the shadow war, what are the alternatives?

Mazzetti's reporting on drone strikes demonstrates how excessive secrecy has damaged U.S. counterterrorism interests. For years, our government remained silent as drone strikes proliferated in Pakistan, Yemen, and elsewhere. Instead of explaining exactly whom we killed and why we killed them, the entire program was shrouded in secrecy. Had we been more transparent, the global debate would have been about the heinous actions of the militants that were killed and the damage inflicted on al-Qaeda by removing its militants from the battlefield. Instead, the world expressed outrage at the United States' use of unilateral force, violation of other countries' sovereignty, and disregard for civilian casualties. Despite the fact that drones are weakening groups that pose a threat to many countries around the world, a recent Pew Research Center poll showed that the U.S. drone program was opposed by majorities in 37 of the 44 countries surveyed.[5] The level of opposition is stunning. Large majorities of the public in NATO allies Spain (86 percent), Turkey (83 percent), France (72 percent), Germany (67 percent), and even the UK (59 percent) oppose U.S. drone strikes, even though these countries have experienced terrorist attacks on their soil.[6] It appears that our preoccupation with excessive secrecy about drones and other aspects of our counterterrorism program has been akin to unilateral disarmament in the battle for hearts and minds around the world.

War in the shadows has also precluded a comprehensive public assessment of U.S. counterterrorism policy. America's stated goals are to deny safe havens to al-Qaeda and its affiliates and associates, dismantle al-Qaeda cells through targeted use of force and financial pressure, build the capacity of partner governments to counteract these movements themselves, and address the underlying political and social grievances that give rise to extremist movements. But, with a dearth of public information, it is virtually impossible to assess progress on these goals or evaluate the validity of public officials' statements, such as President Obama's proclamation that "al-Qaeda has been decimated."[7]

For example, denying safe havens

for terrorist organizations anywhere in the world is a lofty goal, oft repeated by politicians, but it does not appear to be achievable at an acceptable cost. The United States spent about $25 billion to train and equip Iraq's army, but the Islamic State of Iraq and Syria (ISIS) routed it in a matter of weeks and now enjoys a safe haven spanning large swaths of the Levant.[8] Extremist organizations like Boko Haram already have safe havens; it and other groups will continue to do so in pockets of North Africa, the Sahel, the Middle East, and South Asia. Unless we are willing to send ground troops and then deal with the hazards of occupation and reconstruction, there is very little we can do to address the safe haven problem other than support governments willing to take up the fight against the extremists themselves.

Yet, our effort to develop a network of governmental counterterrorism partners has borne little fruit to date. The large-scale capacity building exercise in Iraq failed, and most are predicting that Afghanistan will follow course. Elsewhere, many countries are happy to accept American financial assistance, and perhaps some advisors, but these are transactional encounters, not strategic ones. The global unpopularity of the shadow war makes it difficult, if not impossible, for many governments to work with the United States overtly. And the detritus of the shadow war—Guantanamo, black sites and extraordinary rendition, drone strikes that hit civilians—continues to loom over us like a dark cloud, diminishing our soft power. Now, well into the second decade of this conflict, it is worth asking whether national security policymakers are grappling with the dire state of U.S. counterterrorism strategy, or remain mired in the mindset of the shadow war that Mazzetti has described.

It goes without saying that clandestine activity must be, by definition, secret. Yet there are ways to talk about how we pursue our counterterrorism goals that would not breach the operational secrecy of the missions themselves. We can also be far more transparent—and frankly, honest—about the mixed results that our efforts have produced without increasing the risk to the people who are bravely executing dangerous counterterrorism missions ordered by the government.

Are there alternatives to the shadow war? Sure. Perhaps the Obama administration is slowly gravitating in that direction. There were only 6 drone strikes in Pakistan in the first half of 2014, down from a high of 122 in 2010.[9] Drone and air strikes in Yemen have also become less frequent, with 11 in the first six months of 2014, down from a high of 56 in 2012.[10] After unleashing military force in Libya only to end up with chaos, Obama resisted pressure to become deeply involved in Syria for two years before deciding to lead a coalition military effort against ISIS in September 2014. Finding the sweet spot between sweeping interventionism and excessive caution, however, has proven to be a challenge.

Some claim that our failure to intervene militarily wherever conflicts pop up around the globe is a sign of American withdrawal and weakness. But, it could also be seen as a message to perpetual free-riders on the American security enterprise that it is time to step up their game, take up the fight, and start addressing core governance problems that are undermining their (not U.S.) security and prosperity. This tension is precisely what we are seeing in the effort against ISIS. Now that the United States has intervened, other countries appear to be content to allow the United States to take care of the ISIS problem for them. Of course there is no substitute for American leadership, and leaving large-scale problems—such as ISIS—to fester is unacceptable. But the shadow war assumes that America can be in all places, at all times, and effectively address counterterrorism threats through clandestine means. Recent experience suggests that this is a cross the shadow war cannot bear. As the shadow war suffers through the law of diminishing returns, the effectiveness of American counterterrorism policy will depend on the ability to rediscover the virtue of patient, persistent diplomacy, the efficacy of soft power, and the benefit of truly reciprocal alliances, rather than transactional relationships.

Looking back, the way of the knife that Mazzetti has explored was an irresistible path for leaders seeking a quick solution to the dangers presented in their daily threat briefing in the post-9/11 era. And undoubtedly they will resort to this path again at times of insecurity and fear. But when they consider the promised benefits of the shadow war, they should also recall the repulsive scene at the Pakistani court room where Raymond Davis was whisked away by U.S. consular authorities after the embassy indemnified the families with "blood money," leaving many with the impression that the United States believes it can send armed killers into any country it wants and then buy its way out of accountability. *The way of the knife* is replete with unspoken pitfalls and challenges; it is rarely as clean, simple, and cost-free as its purveyors claim.

NOTES

1 Mark Mazzetti, *The Way of the Knife* (New York: Penguin Books, 2014), 67.

2 Ibid., 63.

3 Ibid., 79.

4 Ibid., 318.

5 Pew Research Global Attitudes Project, "Global Opposition to U.S. Surveillance and Drones but Limited Harm to America's Image," Internet, http://www.pewglobal.org/2014/07/14/global-opposition-to-u-s-surveillance-and-drones-but-limited-harm-to-americas-image./ (date accessed: 4 August 2014).

6 Ibid.

7 Barack Obama, "Remarks by the President at a Campaign Event" (Green Bay, WI, 1 November 2012).

8 Eric Schmitt and Michael R. Gordon, "U.S. Sees Risks in Assisting a Compromised Iraqi Force," *The New York Times*, 13 July 2014.

9 "Drone Wars Pakistan: Analysis," *The New American Foundation*, Internet, http://securitydata.newamerica.net/drones/pakistan/analysis (date accessed: 4 August 2014).

10 "Drone Wars Yemen: Analysis," *The New America Foundation*, Internet, http://securitydata.newamerica.net/drones/yemen/analysis (date accessed: 4 August 2014).

Experimental Transnational Relations
A New Paradigm for Combating Global Challenges?

Review by Angelic Young

Michael G. Findley, Daniel L. Nielson, and J.C. Sharman. Global Shell Games: Experiments in Transnational Relations, Crime, and Terrorism. Cambridge: Cambridge University Press, 2014. 271 pp. $32.99.

Sergei Magnitsky was a Russian lawyer who discovered a $230 million tax fraud perpetrated by corrupt Russian officials. After sharing this information with the Russian government, he was promptly arrested for his efforts. The tax fraud was perpetrated through the use of an ultimately untraceable shell company.[1] This story, told by authors Michael G. Findley, Daniel L. Nielson, and J.C. Sharman in *Global Shell Games: Experiments in Transnational Relations, Crime, and Terrorism*, is but one of a myriad of examples illustrated in this thoroughly rich read.

The book examines the use of shell companies to disguise the transfer of dirty money. While some shell companies are legitimate businesses, anonymous shell companies enable people to shield their identities and move massive sums of money around the world without being traced. For example, a drug trafficker might set up a shell company disguised as a plumbing service. He deposits his "earnings" with the shell company, which provides an invoice for plumbing services rendered and a receipt to account for the deposit (quite frequently in cash). The shell company then either makes a withdrawal, returning the money to the drug trafficker, or passes it to another shell company (to further shield

Angelic Young is Senior Coordinator of The Institute for Inclusive Security's Resolution to Act, a multi-tier campaign that seeks to utilize and promote women's ability to aid and sustain peace. Young is also a core faculty member of the Peace Operations graduate studies program at George Mason University. She previously worked at the U.S. Department of State.

the activity). The anonymity facilitated through the potentially endless transactions provides a convenient way for the trafficker to both earn and spend his "dirty" money.

The authors use data obtained through a massive field experiment in which researchers posed as customers soliciting access to prohibited, untraceable, or anonymous shell corporations. More traditional methods for collecting data include case studies, public opinion surveys (which measure perception of the extent of the corruption), and observational data analysis, broadly. However, these methods are prone to bias and error—because you cannot control the variables, it is more difficult to establish causality. Instead, the design of the experiment enabled researchers to apply a variety of conditions to their email solicitations suggesting a range of suspect motives, including money laundering, corruption, and terrorist financing. The object of the exercise was twofold: first, to test whether international rules mandating the collection of identity documents are effective, and second, to gain insight into the causes of compliance (or non-compliance). For example, researchers discovered that rigid enforcement appears to be the only clear measure leading to better compliance of private-sector actors, a crucial finding.

The authors highlight a critically important and alarming reality: shell companies are both an effective and a relatively easily-obtained tool for people seeking to launder money, engage in corrupt practices, and finance terrorism. In bringing this issue to light, the authors hope to induce governments to take steps to better enforce

corporate transparency.[2] The purpose of the experiment they conducted, however, was not solely to demonstrate the gaps in systems to combat the illicit use of shell companies—it was also to highlight the utility of what they refer to as the "experimental science of transnational relations" or "Experimental TR."[3] In short, Experimental TR focuses on non-state actors (for example, examining the behavior of firms rather than governments) and relies on field experimental methods (allowing for greater control and ability to demonstrate causality).

Given their desire to establish Experimental TR as an advantageous approach to international relations, the authors devote a significant amount of time to a painstakingly thorough explanation of their methodology. They cover an enormous amount of material in the book, making a truly comprehensive review infeasible. Instead, this review will focus on the broad applicability of Experimental TR, a particularly interesting aspect of their analysis and one that may prove most useful to practitioners working to combat transnational crime and corruption and to promote human rights and the rule of law.

In the experiment, they sent 7,456 emails to 3,771 firms in 181 countries. Each email requested confidential information. They assigned different conditions, or "treatments," to emails at random to see whether the various treatments would increase or decrease the rate at which those selling shell companies would require the identity documents mandated by international rules. They called this the "compliance rate." They also assessed the extent to which the identity of the requester impacted compliance rates (for example, whether the alias used was for that of a U.S. citizen, a citizen of a

in scientific jargon. Though necessary to give credence to their argument, a simpler way to describe it would be to

Shell companies are both an effective and a relatively easily-obtained tool for **people seeking to launder money.**

corruption-prone country working in government procurement, or a citizen of a country associated with terrorism claiming to work for Islamic charities).

In short, they found that firms in wealthy countries (compared to those in poor countries) were less likely to comply with international standards; that prompting firms with information about internal law had no significant effect on the compliance rate (with a marginal increase in compliance where rules were attributed to a private standards body); that promising premium payments decreased compliance; and that the only condition that significantly decreased non-compliance was to associate the rules with the Internal Revenue Service (IRS) in the United States. Additionally, while imposing the corruption condition decreased the response rate, it also decreased the compliance rate—a truly concerning finding given the damage that corruption causes on a global scale (such as weakened development prospects and reduced confidence in governments).[4] All of these results help to underscore their argument for the Experimental TR approach, given its attention to non-state actors—the key locus of this kind of criminal activity.

The researchers cloak their explanation of the Experimental TR approach

call it a shift in perspective. Rather than viewing states as the primary source of rules, enforcement, and behavior (and thus the primary target of advocacy for those engaged in combating transnational crime and corruption or in protecting and promoting human rights), we should focus our efforts on non-state actors. As the authors note, states do not perform the majority of actions central to compliance with international standards—individuals, firms, and non-governmental organizations do.

Why is this so groundbreaking? For many practitioners, it is not. If one asked if international rules, regulations, and norms calling for greater participation of women in peace processes have had a significant impact on the behavior of non-state actors, the answer would be either "no" or "not significant enough." If one were to ask whether the international rules, regulations, and norms designed to combat trafficking of narcotics have significantly altered the behavior of non-state actors, the answer would likely be similar.

While we "know" this to be true, most practitioners continue to focus their resources on traditional state actors. The creation of new laws criminalizing sexual and gender-based violence or creating harsher penalties for drug trafficking does little in communities where people are not inclined to report offenders—or where the likelihood of prosecution by a weak state is next to nil. Absent complementary efforts to educate the population as to what constitutes a violation of the law, why the populace should report such behaviors, and how punishment of offenders will improve the safety of the community, such laws tend to be under-utilized, if not completely ignored. It is far easier to convince a state to create a new law than it is to ensure the state can enforce it.

Despite the shortcomings of additional international agreements, the authors ultimately conclude that rules, regulations, and norms can and often do have an impact on the behavior of states. They point to the example of the Financial Action Task Force's

to non-state actors, however, the mere existence of rules does little on a global scale to change behavior. The only condition they found in their research that seemed to make any difference at all was rigid, reliable enforcement. In other words, when private actors perceive that commission of a prohibited act is likely to result in severe punishment, they are more likely to be compliant.

The authors conclude that on the whole, compliant providers are relatively difficult to find, even where it should have been apparent that the solicitors were attempting to engage in corrupt practices. Perhaps, they suggest, providers are not aware of the damaging (and potentially destabilizing) effects of corruption and the international policy measures designed to respond to it. So, they added a condition to their experiment to determine whether

It is far easier to convince a state to create a new law than it is to ensure the state can enforce it.

(FATF) blacklist of "Non-Cooperative Countries and Territories" (NCCT). When countries like Russia, the Philippines, Israel, Hungary, Nigeria, and Ukraine were added, they quickly reformed their domestic laws and policies to ensure their removal from the NCCT.[5] Few countries enjoy being on any sort of "bad" list, whether related to corruption, drugs, or human trafficking (for example, the annual U.S. Department of State's Trafficking in Persons Report, the International Narcotics Control Strategy Report, and Transparency International's Corruption Perception Index). With regard

knowledge of the international rules (and the implied threat of enforcement) or reference to norms (e.g., we are both reputable businessmen, and I am sure we want to do right by the rules) made a difference in the level of compliance.[6] Their results tell us that the threat of international enforcement—in this case, the FATF—does not make a statistically significant dent in the non-state actors' levels of non-compliance. However, bringing a domestic agency well known for its zealous enforcement, such as the IRS, drastically changed the picture.[7] The difference here could be relatively well explained by simple, rational behavior: the IRS is known for its willingness to pursue enforcement, so the motivation to comply is based on the strong likelihood that failure to comply will produce negative results for latter."[9]

So what does this mean for practitioners? Traditional approaches to combating global scourges like crime, corruption, and abuse of human rights

There is a strong correlation between inadequate enforcement and increased levels of non-compliance.

either state or non-state actors. Where the likelihood of enforcement is less sure due to the capacity or willingness of authorities to do so (such as with international enforcement), non-state actors are not compelled to comply. State actors, on the other hand, may be motivated by the potential for negative press resulting from bad behavior.

The authors use the results of the research to conclude that providers rarely comply with international law, despite theories that would suggest such behavior is unusual. For example, the authors note that one school of thought in international law, referred to as the managerial approach, presumes that significant non-compliance is unusual. When such non-compliance happens, it most likely stems from ambiguity, incapacity, or built-in expectations that compliance will increase incrementally over time.[8] What the authors demonstrate is that the rules do not matter—only enforcement makes a difference. They conclude that "commitments to international rules may say nothing about what actually occurs on the ground, and even where commitments to rules and compliance with those rules do match up, we've not been able to tell whether the former causes the

tend to rely on and call for increasingly strong international rules and regulation. Much attention (not to mention significant resources) is devoted to the negotiation of new international agreements that seek to curb bad behavior. But according to the authors, international rules do not matter—so what does? As the authors note, strict enforcement does impact behavior (as with aggressive IRS enforcement versus weak international enforcement). Accordingly, one could argue that there is a strong correlation between inadequate enforcement and increased levels of non-compliance. Outside of strengthening international enforcement mechanisms, then, how do we compel actors to adhere to global standards? Unfortunately, the authors do not proffer any practical suggestions as to where to go from here. There are no proposed fixes and no recommendations, which is a disappointing conclusion to an otherwise fascinating work.

The results of this study are important and should be shared with a broader audience. Making the language more accessible and developing a set of recommendations for next steps (a difficult task given the complexity of the topic) could elevate this from an academic endeavor to a general audience best seller. Ultimately, one could take the results of their study to be an endorsement of activities aimed at changing the behavior of non-state actors (such as education, advocacy, and strengthening those institutions responsible for enforcing rules and regulations). But, for those working in fields impacted by their results, that is really nothing new. Most have "known" for quite some time that the promulgation of rules cannot change the behavior of private actors. So what should the reader do with this evidence?

One of their central goals was to establish the value of similar TR experiments for scholars of international relations well beyond the particular focus of the book. In that, they succeeded brilliantly. But in fact, their findings are relevant far beyond the academic world—perhaps even more relevant for government actors. The last three pages provide several exam-

ples of similar experiments on topics ranging from developing a scorecard on accountability and transparency for non-governmental organizations in Uganda to municipal incentives for foreign direct investment in the United States. Truthfully, their recommendation is to simply do more experiments. Despite the "knowledge" referenced above, there is yet to be any significant movement among practitioners to stray from more traditional approaches and explore (potentially) more effective approaches. More experiments equal more evidence. Since traditional methods often fail to establish causality, they also fail to offer practicable solutions. The benefits of exploring Experimental TR, therefore, are in in identifying stronger links between actions, motivations, and thus potential solutions to the challenge of combating corruption, terrorism and transnational crime. Perhaps as we dig deeper, we will learn what does compel compliance.

NOTES

1 Michael G. Finley, Daniel L. Nielson, and J.C. Sharman, *Global Shell Games: Experiments in Transnational Relations, Crime, and Terrorism* (Cambridge: Cambridge University Press, 2014), 36-37.

2 Ibid., 4-18.

3 Ibid., 4.

4 For further information on the impact of corruption on global scale, see Transparency International at www.transparency.org.

5 Ibid., 124.

6 Ibid., 148-160.

7 Ibid., 121-144.

8 Ibid.,121.

9 Ibid., 173.

Lessons from the Irish Peace Process

An Interview with Gerry Adams

GJIA: In April 2012, former U.S. Senator George J. Mitchell stated before the Joint Oireachtas (Irish Parliament) Committee on the Implementation of the Good Friday Agreement that "the implementation of agreements is as important as reaching them," adding: "Getting it done is more difficult than getting an agreement to do it." Many agree with this sentiment and describe the situation in Northern Ireland as a "fragile peace," particularly in light of recent events such as the failure of the Haass-O'Sullivan talks and your arrest following disclosures from Boston College's Belfast Project. What, in your view, are the main obstacles to the successful implementation of the Good Friday Agreement and what steps would you recommend for consolidating the peace process in Northern Ireland?

Adams: George Mitchell said famously after signing the Good Friday Agreement that agreeing on the deal was the easy bit and the hard part was going to be implementing it. The Agreement is essentially an accord, not a settlement. It represents an agreement to a journey without an agreement of the destination. It is less than what many people would want and it is more than what others would want. Therein lie

Gerard "Gerry" Adams is the president of the Irish Sinn Féin political party and is a member of the lower house of the Parliament of the Republic of Ireland.

the obstacles and the difficulties.

While some say that the unionists do not have a strategy, in my view they do—to maintain the union with Britain. They see any movement towards equality in the north of Ireland, or the building of cross-border relationships in Ireland, as a threat to the union. Their strategy, therefore, is to dilute and to delay the process of change.

The chemistry of how the Agreement has worked is that without encouragement from the British and Irish governments there has been no incentive for political unionism to move the peace process forward. I think unionist political leaders are out of step with broader unionist opinion, the business community, and civic society, who, whatever reservations they might have about the Agreement, support the peace process and know that it is better to have respect and tolerance than it is to have what we once had.

Because the Agreement is an agreement of international standing, both the Irish and British governments are obliged to honor their commitments.

Charter of Rights.

So how do we move the peace process forward? We need a pro-Agreement axis to present an alternative to the anti-Agreement axis that has now clearly emerged within political unionism, and for the Irish and British governments to champion change and the peace process. There also exists a very important role for the United States, which has invested heavily in the peace process under different presidential administrations.

GJIA: You alluded to the legacy of the past, which many consider as one of the major unresolved issues of the Northern Ireland peace process. What do you consider an effective mechanism for dealing with the past, particularly Troubles-related atrocities, and what can Ireland learn from other societies that have dealt with similar phenomena, most notably South Africa's Truth and Reconciliation Commission? Truth and justice are important parts of the reconciliation process in Ireland, but is it possible to have both?

We need a pro-Agreement axis to present an alternative to the anti-Agreement axis...and for the Irish and British governments to champion change.

This has not been the case on a range of matters, particularly in dealing with the past, and on major issues such as the killing of human rights lawyer Pat Finucane and the Dublin and Monaghan bombings. In the north of Ireland there is no *Acht na Gaeilge* (Irish Language Act) and no Bill of Rights. For the island of Ireland there is no Civic Forum and no

Adams: Sinn Féin's policy is to have an independent truth recovery process that is victim-centered and facilitated by a reputable international agency, such as the United Nations. It would be a voluntary process and would allow people the right to challenge allegations. It would grant anonymity, which would give immunity from prosecution with respect to the information brought forward.

We think that the Haass-O'Sullivan proposals on dealing with the past and on the truth recovery process—although a compromise for us—provide the way forward. It was a mistake for the British government not to sign up for these proposals.

GJIA: You mentioned the influence of the United States and Britain, but there is no consensus concerning the importance of external mediators in the Northern Ireland peace process. Can you shed light on the significance of third-party interventions in the negotiation and implementation of the Good Friday Agreement and its lessons for areas of the world embroiled in seemingly intractable conflicts?

Adams: Sinn Féin developed a peace strategy beginning with the publication of *A Scenario for Peace* (1987) and *Towards a Lasting Peace in Ireland* (1992). I also wrote a short pamphlet while in the Long Kesh internment camp in the mid-1970s entitled *Peace in Ireland*. This shows that Sinn Féin, although in the middle of a conflict, was trying to find a way to head toward peace.

Republicanism is a way of life, a political philosophy, and a way of organizing society. It has to be done peacefully and democratically, so our goal was to find a peaceful and democratic way of pursuing these objectives at a time when Sinn Féin was banned and open democratic politics were very difficult to sustain against shoot to kill, internment without trial, and censorship.

Accordingly, we observed the need to internationalize the peace process and to win international support for broad principles and concepts. The Irish diaspora is very strong in the United States and we looked to them as we sought to develop an alternative to armed struggle. A number of Irish-Americans hosted events inviting presidential hopefuls to support a number of peace initiatives. This included Bill Clinton, who made a commitment to grant me an American visa. When President Clinton was elected, he kept those commitments.

During this time, the British always closed down involvement from outside bodies by stating that all of the issues related to the north of Ireland were an internal matter for the government of the United Kingdom. The British resisted the decision to grant me an American visa. Then-British Prime Minister John Major refused to talk to President Clinton for a considerable time and it was described as the greatest crisis in Anglo-American relations since the Suez crisis in 1956.

Now the peace process as a whole is seen as a great success and one of the finer things Tony Blair, Bill Clinton, George Bush and any of the other people that were involved had accomplished during their respective careers. This shows how quickly things can change. The mediation of George Mitchell, who was an outsider and an international figure—and the various commissions that were set up to deal with a range of issues ranging from decommissioning to policing—all involved the international community.

Obviously the remit, or terms of reference, on which these outsiders were acting had to be satisfactory to the people in the north of Ireland, because the only people who are going to make peace are the people who are actually in the conflict zone. Nobody

Sinn Féin is appreciative of the support that the U.S. government has given to the Irish peace process, but we have been opposed to aspects of U.S. foreign

Although it is the people that make peace, the international community can set and develop conditions.

can come in and make peace on their behalf. Although it is the people that make peace, the international community can set and develop conditions where it is possible for people who are locked into a cycle of violence to be taken out of that cycle. This applies to the Middle East or any other conflict area. So, I think that the Irish peace process is a good example of where the international community played a very positive role.

GJIA: Do you believe that using an independent mediator, similar to the role that George Mitchell played in helping broker the Good Friday Agreement, is the best means of solving the Israeli-Palestinian conflict? Or is the United States part of the problem in terms of forging a lasting peace settlement?

Adams: The first thing that we have to do is uphold international law. Under international law, the people of the Palestinian territories have rights and we have to uphold those rights. The building of a separation wall in the West Bank, the ongoing blockade of Gaza, and the 2014 onslaught and dreadful casualties in the Gaza Strip and Gaza City are in breach of international law.

policy for some time, particularly in Afghanistan, Iraq, Iran, and other parts of the Middle East.

While Washington quite rightly condemns the attacks on civilians in Gaza, the U.S. government is giving the Israeli government the ammunition to carry out these attacks. This is clearly a contradiction. The first thing for the U.S. government to do is to uphold international law. The second thing it should do is use its influence. I know that George Mitchell has tried and John Kerry is now trying to resolve the conflict, but we must go back to first principles. When we uphold international law, we create conditions allowing peace to be brokered in what seems to be an intractable situation.

I have travelled to the Middle East— including the Gaza Strip—on a number of occasions, and it is my firm belief that peace can be brokered in that region based upon the rights of both the people of Israel and the people of Palestine. The security of the people of Israel lies in upholding the rights of the people of Palestine.

GJIA: Are there any other lessons from the Northern Ireland peace process that can be critically applied to the Israeli-Palestinian conflict based on your experiences of travelling to the region and as someone who was a key player in helping broker the Good Friday Agreement?

Adams: I am always loath to say or believe that the north of Ireland has lessons to teach anyone or that it is a template for conflict resolution in other parts of the world. I do believe, however, that the starting point of any peace process and the necessary ingredient of any peace process is direct dialogue. There needs to be direct dialogue with every issue that people want to place on the agenda. People have a right to choose their own leaders. People have the right to put their own issues on the table. There needs to be political will; without it, progress is very difficult. The situation in the north of Ireland is imperfect but it is better than war.

related. When the proposition was put forth to the IRA—and one can think what they want of the IRA—that there was an alternative, peaceful way forward, they embraced it. All of the other steps, difficult as they may have been, were in consequence of the IRA decommissioning or putting its arms beyond use, and the IRA then taking itself off the stage. The IRA cessation, which facilitated peacemaking, is a logical consequence of a decision by that organization to embrace another way forward and to go out of business as a result.

Those who attribute this to the IRA being on their last legs, or defeated as a consequence of 9/11, or the policies of the Bush administration are, quite frankly, totally and absolutely misinformed. In terms of peacemaking, the events of 9/11 vindicated the position of

The starting point of any peace process and the necessary ingredient of any peace process is direct dialogue.

GJIA: In what ways did the broader international environment fundamentally facilitate or undermine the peace process in Northern Ireland? For example, the decision by the Irish Republican Army (IRA) to begin decommissioning its weapons in October 2001 was a key development in the Northern Ireland peace-building process. To what extent was this decision a product of broader international events such as 9/11 and the Bush administration's "Global War on Terror"?

Adams: Well, the two events are not

those of us who had fought for a peace process in Ireland—that the way forward was as we have tried to chart it.

GJIA: You state that the peace process is viewed as a "great success"—but how would you respond to critics of the consociational power sharing arrangement in Northern Ireland who argue that consociationalism reinforces or institutionalizes divisions and conflicts between the nationalist and unionist communities and that it is an unsuitable framework for conflict resolution in Northern Ireland and other parts of the world?

Adams: Well, it might be an unsuitable framework—and that is why I am saying we do not have a template that can be transplanted elsewhere. It is an involuntary coalition, and one could think of better ways of governing. The fact is that the power sharing arrangements are the alternative to war. The major political blocs in the Legislative Assembly at Stormont can exercise a veto over decisions. When those who do not want to see change assert vetoes, they complicate the business of making decisions and forging progress.

The Good Friday Agreement is not an internal six-county settlement, it is an all-Ireland settlement, and all of us have to work on the ground with our neighbors, political institutions, and every sector possible to eradicate sectarianism. The process of power sharing will probably need to continue in some form similar to the current one until we succeed in doing that. I said earlier that the Good Friday Agreement is an agreement to a journey without an agreement of the destination. As an Irish Republican, I want the destination to be a united Irish people. I want to unite the people of Ireland, to get rid of partition, and work out our own society. Although I want to stop British involvement in Irish affairs, I am not anti-British and would like to have good relations with the British based upon mutual respect and equality.

There is a potential for all this to happen now because of the Good Friday Agreement and because the vast majority of people on the island of Ireland support equality, justice, fairness, tolerance for all, and a peaceful and democratic way forward. Sinn Féin is committed to bringing about these ideals. Challenging as it may be, this is a good challenge to have.

Interviewed by Barry McCarron, 31 July 2014

Assessing Diplomatic Tools for Advancing Human Dignity and Democracy

An Interview with Tom Malinowski

GJIA: As the needs of the Syrian people become increasingly overwhelming, there is much debate in policy and academic communities about how to prioritize the U.S. and international response. As the lead American diplomat for human rights and democracy, what do you see as being the most urgent priorities for U.S. and international action in Syria?

Tom Malinowski is the Assistant Secretary of State for the Bureau of Democracy, Human Rights, and Labor (DRL). He was previously Washington Director for Human Rights Watch.

Malinowski: Syria is a classic example of a human rights catastrophe that ended up yielding serious national security consequences for the United States. There is no question that we have a vital interest in dealing with the threat posed by ISIL [the Islamic State in Iraq and the Levant] and are doing so. There is also little question that ISIL came into being in part because of the apocalyptic situation that arose in Syria as a result of the conflict between an authoritarian regime and its own people, and the way in which that regime has sought to crush a popular democratic uprising.

The problem then spread to Iraq and manifested itself in a particularly grave way there. Our response has focused initially on the immediate threat that ISIL posed in Iraq. We understand that we cannot degrade and destroy ISIL—as the President has committed we will do—and protect the American people from the threat if we do not deal with the underlying problem in Syria. It is that crisis that has inspired so many misguided people from other parts of the world to go and join what some

sanctions can be, the more effective they generally are. When you can target sanctions on those most clearly responsible for significant human rights abuses or corruption, you can both avoid the kinds of broader sanctions regimes that hurt populations and divide the

There is little question that ISIL came into being in part because of the apocalyptic situation that arose in Syria.

of them mistakenly think is a morally decent fight against the atrocities that Assad has committed against his people.

And it is that problem that has led some people inside Syria, out of desperation, to turn for deliverance to this awful organization that is in fact only adding to their suffering. So, I think there is just a general recognition that we need to redouble our efforts to achieve an end to the killing and atrocities in Syria for humanitarian reasons, and also because it now affects us in a very profound way.

GJIA: You also have many years of experience working on Russia, and you have been a vocal supporter of the Magnitsky Act. Do you think that sanctions such as these, which target individual human rights abusers, should be a model for other cases? Could you comment on the advantages or disadvantages of this type of sanction?

Malinowski: Sanctions are not always an appropriate response to problems like this [in Iraq and Syria], but when they are, I think we have found over the years that the more targeted the

people who you are targeting from the broader populations that you are ultimately trying to support.

It becomes harder for those you target to turn to their own people and say, "these sanctions hurt us as a country, they hurt us as a people." It is harder for them to rally their own people in opposition to U.S. or Western-imposed sanctions if the sanctions are clearly and meticulously targeted. Because of our place in the global economy and the international system, targeted financial sanctions by the United States can have a great impact on individuals, even on those who do not necessarily own bank accounts in the United States.

GJIA: During your confirmation hearing, you stressed the need for the U.S. government, specifically the Bureau of Democracy, Human Rights, and Labor (DRL), to counter the global crackdown on civil society. We have seen recent assaults on civil society in Egypt, China, Russia, and Azerbaijan. Recognizing that these cases are all quite different, what overarching strategies do you think DRL should adopt? For example, do you think civil society assistance should be implemented in coordination with the host government, outside of its purview, or some combination thereof?

Malinowski: The president actually addressed this question recently at an event at the UN General Assembly where he announced, among other things, a Presidential Memorandum that instructs all of us in the agencies of his administration to step up our efforts to stand with beleaguered civil society groups around the world. And there is definitely a crackdown. Just as we try to spread best practices, governments that have pioneered creative ways of restricting the ability of nongovernmental organizations to do their jobs have spread worst practices. We have seen many countries adopt laws

keep them safe. So, that is what we will continue to do.

GJIA: You were declared a *persona non grata* by the Bahraini regime. Having worked on Bahrain both as the Washington Director of Human Rights Watch and now at DRL, can you explain why Bahrain is such an important country for the United States? In addition, what does your expulsion expose about prospects for reform there?

Malinowski: Bahrain is an important country because, despite its very small size, it exists on the fault line between the Sunni and Shia worlds at a time when that fault line drives a lot of the problems that we are seeing in the Middle East. It is important because there is and always has been a potential

Foreign policy is 90 percent words.

that are modeled on what has happened in Russia and Egypt and Ethiopia, to name just three emblematic examples of the problem.

We are determined to continue to support civil society groups in these societies. The President has said that we are not going to accede to the insistence of some governments that we channel assistance through them. Civil society is something that is independent of government control and we do not want to do anything that undermines that principle. We found that we can continue to support organizations, even in very challenging circumstances, where they want to continue to have that kind of relationship with us in ways that still

to show that that divide can be overcome through dialogue and through democratic politics. We very much need this little country to serve as an example to others that that can be done. So, the United States has invested a lot of diplomatic effort in recent years in an effort to promote that kind of solution inside Bahrain.

There are forces in Bahrain that resist a reconciliation of that sort. This is always the case; there is always inertia in status quo and there are certain individuals who benefit from it. This inertia explains why it has been hard recently, and why awkward things [such as my expulsion] do occasionally happen. What remains important to us is not those awkward moments, but reaching a point of reconciliation between the two sides there. Bahrain is a member of our coalition against ISIL, and it has made contributions that we very much appreciate. But the most important contribution that country can make is to serve as an example of how these two communities can cooperate and come together through a democratic process.

GJIA: You have also worked as a speechwriter for numerous foreign policy leaders. Can you share any insights on the importance of careful public rhetoric, or of the challenges of designing official messaging?

Malinowski: Foreign policy is 90 percent words. Choosing the right words is a very important part of what we do. I have always thought that the public part of that challenge is as important as the challenge of what to say in a private meeting with a diplomat. Our public messaging is an indispensable way of reinforcing the private diplomacy. It is something that foreign governments read very, very carefully and closely.

Part of the challenge is that you always have multiple audiences when you speak publicly about foreign policy. You are talking to the American people, you are talking to foreign publics, you are talking to foreign governments, and you are talking to our Congress. And your words are mediated by the press in multiple countries, so you do have to be careful. At the same time, you have to be clear, and sometimes the tendency to be careful trumps the need to be clear. A good purveyor of words in our world understands that you need to be able to do both.

Interviewed by Anna Newby, 30 October 2014

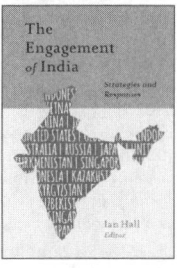

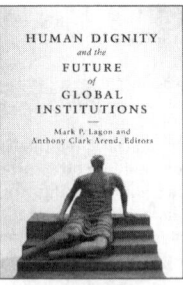